The Gospel Truth:

A LECTIONARY-BASED CATECHISM FOR ADULTS

Cross-referenced to the U.S. Catholic Catechism for Adults

KENNETH OGOREK

Foreword by Archbishop Donald W. Wuerl, S.T.D.

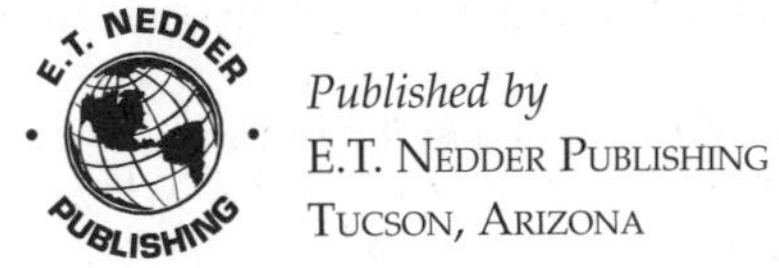

Published by
E.T. NEDDER PUBLISHING
TUCSON, ARIZONA

Nihil Obstat: Reverend Kris D. Stubna, S.T.D., Censor Librorum

Imprimatur: Most Rev. Paul J. Bradley, D.D., M.S.W., Auxiliary Bishop of Pittsburgh

The Nihil Obstat and the Imprimatur are declarations that work is considered to be free from doctrinal or moral error. It is not implied that those who have granted the same agree with the contents, opinions or statements expressed.

E.T. Nedder Publishing
Tucson, Arizona 85749
Cover design and layout by Types
Cover photograph by Anthony Ricci

Printed in the United States of America
11 10 09 08 07 1 2 3 4

Library of Congress Control Number: 1-893757-53-6

ISBN: 978-1-893757-53-0

Additional copies of this publication may be purchased by calling toll free 1-888-247-3023. Fax: 1-317-733-8799 or email files@tofg.com. To order by mail: 7313 Mayflower Park Dr., Zionsville, IN 46077. Be sure to check our Website for a list of other products: www.nedderpublishing. com.

Order no.: 757-530 Individual copies: $20.00 plus shipping and handling

To my parents, to my bride of several years, and to all adults who remain in the race—fighting the good fight of Faith.

—2 Timothy 4:7

To my parents, to my bride of several years, and to all adults who remain in the race—fighting the good fight of Faith.

—2 Timothy 4:7

Contents

Foreword

The Most Reverend Donald W. Wuerl, S.T.D.
Archbishop of Washington

The Sunday liturgy offers us an opportunity to bring the Gospel truth to our Catholic faithful. All of the data continues to affirm that there is no other setting comparable to the liturgy to put a priest in contact, in a consistent and regular manner, with a very large number of the faithful. At every Sunday liturgy, we have an occasion both to proclaim the word of God and to respond to the challenges of the Gospel reflected in the living teaching tradition of the Church. Our task, as Saint Paul expressed it in the Second Letter to Timothy, is to: "Proclaim the word; be persistent whether it is convenient or inconvenient; convince, reprimand, encourage through all patience and teaching" (2 Timothy 4:2).

We recognize that before us are many, especially some young adults, who do not have a profound grounding in the teaching of the Church rooted in the revelation of Christ. In the context of the Sunday Eucharistic Liturgy, they receive what for some is their only information and teaching about the faith. Thus, the pedagogical aspect of the liturgy, and especially the homily, becomes increasingly important. In a sense, each bishop, priest or deacon who preaches today finds himself in the role of one of the early Church Fathers, such as Saint Augustine, who recognized the homily as an ideal time to open the word of God for his hearers in a way that would encompass what the deposit of faith contains and how the Sunday readings were meant to respond to the circumstances of the day.

Basing our homily on the Lectionary presents us with an enormous opportunity. The early Church, in its desire to capture in written form the story of Jesus and the impact of his death and resurrection in our lives, wrote and compiled what we now know as the New Testament. The Church also recognized those writings that we refer to as the Old Testament.

The challenge in preaching to a congregation in the twenty-first century is that two millennia of Spirit-filled teaching reflecting on the human experience needs to be imparted. The Body of Christ is a living reality, and the teaching of the Church reflects a living, deepening understanding of the word of God and its application to our lives today.

Together with the Lectionary and its three-year Sunday cycle of readings covering most of the Bible, we also have as resources the Catechism of the Catholic Church, an authoritative and complete compendium of our Catholic faith, and the new United States Catholic Catechism for Adults, which applies the Catechism of the Catholic Church to our time and cultural experience in the United States.

Kenneth Ogorek's latest book, *The Gospel Truth*, provides an opportunity to experience the Lectionary as the basis for a comprehensive overview of the faith by tying together the regular Sunday readings and the content of the teaching of the Church that grows out of the revelation so carefully passed on in sacred Scripture and Tradition. What results is a resource especially useful for every homilist who is conscious of both the demands of our age and the need for solid teaching rooted in the Lectionary readings.

It is a pleasure for me to recommend *The Gospel Truth* as a helpful tool at the service of content-rich and faith-inspiring homilies. My hope is that this resource will help all of us to enrich our faith and the faith of those who come to us Sunday-after-Sunday open to hearing, some for the first time, the breadth and width, depth, beauty and astounding coherence of the teaching of Christ and his Church.

August 31, 2006

Note Regarding the Lectionary Cycle

The Lectionary is our Church's way of helping us work through Sacred Scripture over the course of time in the context of worship. A three-year cycle of Bible readings allows us to hear most of God's Word proclaimed at Sunday Mass.

How do I know what year and week it is in the lectionary cycle?

Two ways to keep track of what pages to read in *The Gospel Truth* are:

- † Check your missallette at Mass, which will tell you what week it is as well as what readings you will hear when you celebrate Mass the following week; and
- † Many Church bulletins list the readings for the upcoming week, including those for the next Sunday.

If you have access to the internet, a great site to find the week in our lectionary cycle is the United States Conference of Catholic Bishops website *www.usccb.org*.

A final note about the choice of Gospels

The Gospel readings in this book are almost exclusively Sunday Gospels. This means holy days that can or always do occur during the week do not appear here. The only exception is the Solemnity of the Most Sacred Heart of Jesus; my hope is that including this special day will introduce and encourage the practice of celebrating Mass—at least occasionally—on days in addition to Sunday.

Introduction

This book is intended as a good step in a good direction. The step is a blending of lectionary-oriented catechesis with the doctrinal thoroughness needed to be found in conformity with the Catechism of the Catholic Church (CCC) by the United States Conference of Catholic Bishops. Both seem to be intimated by the National Directory for Catechesis.

The Gospel Truth, then, is written to be in conformity with the Catechism. It was submitted to the USCCB for the conformity review.

The approach of *The Gospel Truth* is intentionally simple. It is meant to help facilitate a basic reflection on the Sunday gospel readings and various points of Catholic doctrine that they call to mind. Depth and detail can certainly be added by skillful RCIA ministers and others involved in adult faith formation.

Parents as Primary Educators

Parents play a crucial role in the formation of their children, and hence the shaping of entire societies and cultures. While not exclusively for parents, this book is written with them in mind.

Most adults have significant children in their lives, even if they are not parents per se. Each weekly installment of *The Gospel Truth* encourages adults to appropriate their faith at deeper and deeper levels, and to share that faith with at least one child.

How to Use "The Gospel Truth"

This resource can be used individually, within a family, in small faith-sharing and prayer groups, or in many types of larger group settings.

1. One key to using this book is to set aside a quiet moment or two at some point during the week.

2. Offer a brief prayer for enlightenment, ongoing conversion and a deeper faith.
3. Read the gospel passage at the beginning of each installment. Read it twice if you would like.
4. Then look at the two brief catechetical reflections following each gospel reading, pausing between them to meditate on their truth.
5. Consider the three questions that follow—the first for yourself, the last regarding your relationship to your various communities. The middle question, For a Child in My Life, can be posed to a young person on the way to or from Mass or at another opportune moment.
6. Additional readings are suggested for further life application and deeper understanding. Group discussion of the questions above can also be most fruitful.
7. Finally, the Alleluia verse for the week draws your time to a prayerful close. An additional prayer of your own may be added.

Eventually, the basic pattern of *The Gospel Truth* could be adapted in catechetical resources for all age levels. Also, enhanced content or an alternate arrangement of the doctrinal points may be worth considering in the future. For now, again, this book is meant to be a good step in a good direction. May our Good Shepherd, Jesus, guide your use of this resource so that your relationship with Him and participation in His Church will be deepened to your benefit and that of all the communities blessed by your presence.

A First Sunday of Advent

The Gospel

Jesus said to his disciples:
"As it was in the days of Noah,
so it will be at the coming of the Son of Man.
In those days before the flood,
they were eating and drinking,
marrying and giving in marriage,
up to the day that Noah entered the ark.
They did not know until the flood came and carried them all away.
So will it be also at the coming of the Son of Man.
Two men will be out in the field;
one will be taken, and one will be left.
Two women will be grinding at the mill;
one will be taken, and one will be left.
Therefore, stay awake!
For you do not know on which day your Lord will come.
Be sure of this: if the master of the house
had known the hour of night when the thief was coming,
he would have stayed awake
and not let his house be broken into.
So too, you also must be prepared,
for at an hour you do not expect, the Son of Man will come."

—Matthew 24:37–44

Truths of Our Catholic Faith

It is significant that Jesus mentions Noah. It tells us that Noah is a real person, a person to whom—after the flood—God made a promise. God promised never again to wreak such havoc directly on the entire human race. Not until the world as we know it ends will the life of every person be abruptly, profoundly, permanently affected.

God made an everlasting covenant with Noah and with all living beings (cf. Gen 9:16). It will remain in force as long as the world lasts. (CCC 71)

Life as we know it will in fact end at some point unknown to us. Every person simultaneously will stand before Jesus, our loving and fair Judge, when this world passes away and eternity proceeds in earnest for every person whoever lived. And although God's mercy alone ultimately makes heaven a possibility for each person, we must also be mindful of our deeds, of our actions, of how we spend our time. We should, in a sense, live each day as if it were our last—being prepared, staying awake.

> *The holy Roman Church firmly believes and confesses that on the Day of Judgment all men will appear in their own bodies before Christ's tribunal to render an account of their own deeds (Council of Lyons II [1274]: DS 859; cf. DS 1549). (CCC 1059)*

A Question for Me

Without obsessing over it, am I mindful of the fact that one day I will stand before the judgment seat of Jesus?

For a Child in My Life

What did God promise Noah after the Flood?

My Role in the Community

What kind of example do I set for those with whom I work in the field or grind at the mill? If the Lord comes soon, will my example have helped so that my companions as well as I enter eternal life?

For Depth and Further Life Application

Isaiah 2:1–5
Psalm 122
Romans 13:11–14

📖 United States Catholic Catechism for Adults, preface, pages ix–xii

REFLECTION

Show us, Lord, your love; and grant us your salvation.

—cf. Psalm 85:8

A Second Sunday of Advent

The Gospel

John the Baptist appeared, preaching in the desert of Judea
and saying, "Repent, for the kingdom of heaven is at hand!"
It was of him that the prophet Isaiah had spoken when he said:
A voice of one crying out in the desert,
Prepare the way of the Lord,
make straight his paths.
John wore clothing made of camel's hair
and had a leather belt around his waist.
His food was locusts and wild honey.
At that time Jerusalem, all Judea,
and the whole region around the Jordan
were going out to him
and were being baptized by him in the Jordan River
as they acknowledged their sins.

When he saw many of the Pharisees and Sadducees
coming to his baptism, he said to them, "You brood of vipers!
Who warned you to flee from the coming wrath?
Produce good fruit as evidence of your repentance.
And do not presume to say to yourselves,
'We have Abraham as our father.'
For I tell you,
God can raise up children to Abraham from these stones.
Even now the ax lies at the root of the trees.
Therefore every tree that does not bear good fruit
will be cut down and thrown into the fire.
I am baptizing you with water, for repentance,
but the one who is coming after me is mightier than I.
I am not worthy to carry his sandals.
He will baptize you with the Holy Spirit and fire.
His winnowing fan is in his hand.
He will clear his threshing floor
and gather his wheat into his barn,
but the chaff he will burn with unquenchable fire."

—Matthew 3:1–12

Truths of Our Catholic Faith

Saint John the Baptist called people to repent and told their leaders to show evidence of repentance. What is repentance exactly? It is returning to God. It is also known as conversion. You feel sorry about sins you have committed—detesting them. You resolve to cooperate better with God's grace to avoid sin.

The Baptizer points out our need to constantly turn away from sinful thoughts, words, deeds and omissions. His call was, and is, urgent.

> *The movement of return to God, called conversion and repentance, entails sorrow for and abhorrence of sins committed, and the firm purpose of sinning no more in the future. Conversion touches the past and the future and is nourished by hope in God's mercy. (CCC 1490)*

Baptism in the Name of the Father and of the Son and of the Holy Spirit admits us to the family of faith, to the People of God. Jesus wants all people to be united with Him and with each other in His Church. Unity doesn't have to mean uniformity in all things. But the call to be a united family is unmistakable, and baptism joins us with all God's new people.

> *One enters into the People of God by faith and Baptism. "All men are called to belong to the new People of God"* (LG 13)*, so that, in Christ, "men may form one family and one People of God"* (AG 1). *(CCC 804)*

A Question for Me

Do I think of conversion as a once-and-for-all change, or do I acknowledge it as a process needing persistent attention on my part?

For a Child in My Life

When did you become a member of God's family?

My Role in the Community

Does my treatment of all fellow Christians show that I consider them as family members? Do I treat all members of my family as I would treat Jesus Himself?

For Depth and Further Life Application

Isaiah 11:1–10
Psalm 72
Romans 15:4–9

📖 United States Catholic Catechism for Adults, introduction, pages xv–xxiv

REFLECTION

Prepare the way of the Lord, make straight his paths: all flesh shall see the salvation of God.

—Luke 3:4, 6

Third Sunday of Advent

The Gospel

When John the Baptist heard in prison of the works of the Christ,
he sent his disciples to Jesus with this question,
"Are you the one who is to come,
or should we look for another?"
Jesus said to them in reply,
"Go and tell John what you hear and see:
the blind regain their sight,
the lame walk,
lepers are cleansed,
the deaf hear,
the dead are raised,
and the poor have the good news proclaimed to them.
And blessed is the one who takes no offense at me."

As they were going off,
Jesus began to speak to the crowds about John,
"What did you go out to the desert to see?
A reed swayed by the wind?
Then what did you go out to see?
Someone dressed in fine clothing?
Those who wear fine clothing are in royal palaces.
Then why did you go out? To see a prophet?
Yes, I tell you, and more than a prophet.
This is the one about whom it is written:
Behold, I am sending my messenger ahead of you;
he will prepare your way before you.
Amen, I say to you,
among those born of women
there has been none greater than John the Baptist;
yet the least in the kingdom of heaven is greater than he."

—Matthew 11:2–11

Truths of Our Catholic Faith

The one who is to come. How do we know that Jesus is the one who is to come? Jesus had a reply for his cousin John in the Gospel above; plus we know what many, many others have seen and heard about Jesus of Nazareth—the Son of God. God sent His only Son to reveal what is needed for our salvation from sin and death.

> *God has revealed himself fully by sending his own Son, in whom he has established his covenant for ever. The Son is his Father's definitive Word; so there will be no further Revelation after him. (CCC 73)*

Jesus' reply pointed out signs of God's reign. God's Son went on to teach the crowds a bit about the Kingdom of Heaven. God's Kingdom burst onto the scene when Jesus began His public life and ministry. Like yeast in a loaf of bread the Kingdom of God has been affecting reality ever since.

We know that the Reign of God will not be fully realized until the end times. Though, as sure as the loaf will rise when everything is in place, His Kingdom will indeed come.

> *At the end of time, the Kingdom of God will come in its fullness. Then the just will reign with Christ for ever, glorified in body and soul, and the material universe itself will be transformed. God will then be "all in all" (1 Cor 15:28), in eternal life. (CCC 1060)*

A Question for Me

Although knowing about someone isn't exactly the same as knowing the person, it certainly helps. How extensively do I try to learn about Jesus?

For a Child in My Life

Who did Saint John the Baptist prepare the people to receive?

My Role in the Community

What role do I play in helping the blind, the lame, the deaf, the poor? In addition to what I might do directly, do I financially support effective efforts to help people with various legitimate needs?

For Depth and Further Life Application

Isaiah 35:1–6a, 10
Psalm 146
James 5:7–10

United States Catholic Catechism for Adults, pages 151–152

REFLECTION

The Spirit of the Lord is upon me, because he has anointed me to bring glad tidings to the poor.

—Isaiah 61:1 (cited in Luke 4:18)

A Fourth Sunday of Advent

The Gospel

This is how the birth of Jesus Christ came about.
When his mother Mary was betrothed to Joseph,
but before they lived together,
she was found with child through the Holy Spirit.
Joseph her husband, since he was a righteous man,
yet unwilling to expose her to shame,
decided to divorce her quietly.
Such was his intention when, behold,
the angel of the Lord appeared to him in a dream and said,
"Joseph, son of David,
do not be afraid to take Mary your wife into your home.
For it is through the Holy Spirit
that this child has been conceived in her.
She will bear a son and you are to name him Jesus,
because he will save his people from their sins."
All this took place to fulfill what the Lord had said through the prophet:
Behold, the virgin shall conceive and bear a son,
and they shall name him Emmanuel,
which means "God is with us."
When Joseph awoke,
he did as the angel of the Lord had commanded him
and took his wife into his home.

—Matthew 1:18–24

Truths of Our Catholic Faith

Have you ever wondered where Jesus gets His name? What does the word *Jesus* mean? In this Gospel reading is the answer.

Incidentally, to a person who doesn't believe that she or he needs to be saved from anything—especially sin—neither Jesus nor His name probably mean all that much. To those who know that salvation is a most basic human need, though, Jesus literally means everything.

The name Jesus means "God saves." The child born of the Virgin Mary is called Jesus, "for he will save his

> *people from their sins"* (Mt *1:21): "there is no other name under heaven given among men by which we must be saved"* (Acts *4:12). (CCC 452)*

Jesus, Mary and Joseph are prominent in this Gospel reading. Notice, though, that the Holy Spirit is also a major presence. The uniquely Christian perception of God as the Holy Trinity is held out for us to grasp often throughout the Gospels, as Jesus and the Spirit often are mentioned in the same breath.

> *From the beginning to the end of time, whenever God sends his Son, he always sends his Spirit: their mission is conjoined and inseparable. (CCC 743)*

A Question for Me

How do I treat the Most Holy Name of Jesus? Could my use of Jesus' name use a bit of extra attention?

For a Child in My Life

What does the name Jesus mean? Why do you think the Son of God's name is Jesus?

My Role in the Community

Mary could have been exposed to shame. Am I prone to gossip about people or jump to negative conclusions about them? Can I be a person who puts a stop to others' attempts to spread information they consider shameful?

For Depth and Further Life Application

Isaiah 7:10–14
Psalm 24
Romans 1:1–7

United States Catholic Catechism for Adults, pages 101–102

REFLECTION

The virgin shall be with child and bear a son, and they shall name him Emmanuel.

—Matthew 1:23

A The Holy Family

The Gospel

When the magi had departed, behold,
the angel of the Lord appeared to Joseph in a dream and said,
"Rise, take the child and his mother, flee to Egypt,
and stay there until I tell you.
Herod is going to search for the child to destroy him."
Joseph rose and took the child and his mother by night
and departed for Egypt.
He stayed there until the death of Herod,
that what the Lord had said through the prophet might be fulfilled,
Out of Egypt I called my son.

When Herod had died, behold,
the angel of the Lord appeared in a dream
to Joseph in Egypt and said,
"Rise, take the child and his mother and go to the land of Israel,
for those who sought the child's life are dead."
He rose, took the child and his mother,
and went to the land of Israel.
But when he heard that Archelaus was ruling over Judea
in place of his father Herod,
he was afraid to go back there.
And because he had been warned in a dream,
he departed for the region of Galilee.
He went and dwelt in a town called Nazareth,
so that what had been spoken through the prophets
might be fulfilled,
He shall be called a Nazorean.

—Matthew 2:13–15, 19–23

Truths of Our Catholic Faith

Herod possessed both freedom and authority. He demonstrates that all women and men are susceptible to using freedom in inappropriate ways.

Since our first parents, part of human nature seems to have a tendency toward poor behavior. Because Herod possessed great power, his evil was dramatic and far-reaching. Our evil should be no less a concern, because sin is always immediate, serious and damaging.

> *Man, having been wounded in his nature by original sin, is subject to error and inclined to evil in exercising his freedom. (CCC 1714)*

Herod abused his authority. The vast majority of us have authority of some sort. Not only must we use our authority well, but we also should hold those with public authority accountable to the extent that we can.

When original sin is acknowledged, it may be easier to escape the pitfalls that go with possessing authority. When our innate inclination toward poor behavior is denied, the potentially corrupting power of authority is staggering and has all too often led to tragic results.

> *Public authority is obliged to respect the fundamental rights of the human person and the conditions for the exercise of his freedom. (CCC 2254)*

A Question for Me

How comfortable am I with original sin's effect on me? Can I acknowledge it without giving in to despair or, perhaps worse, apathy?

For a Child in My Life

What do we know for sure about angels? How are the angels portrayed in the Gospel different from the way angels are sometimes shown on TV and other places?

My Role in the Community

When public authority is used well, do I respect and obey it? If I have authority of any sort, how well do I carry it out in light of the Gospel?

For Depth and Further Life Application

Sirach 3:2–7, 12–14
Psalm 128
Colossians 3:12–21

📖 United States Catholic Catechism for Adults, pages 373–375

REFLECTION

Let the peace of Christ control your hearts; let the word of Christ dwell in you richly.

—Colossians 3:15a, 16a

A,B&C Epiphany

The Gospel

When Jesus was born in Bethlehem of Judea,
in the days of King Herod,
behold, magi from the east arrived in Jerusalem saying,
"Where is the newborn king of the Jews?
We saw his star at its rising
and have come to do him homage."
When King Herod heard this,
he was greatly troubled,
and all Jerusalem with him.
Assembling all the chief priests and the scribes of the people,
He inquired of them where the Christ was to be born.
They said to him, "In Bethlehem of Judea,
for thus it has been written through the prophet:
And you, Bethlehem, land of Judah,
are by no means least among the rulers of Judah;
since from you shall come a ruler,
who is to shepherd my people Israel."
Then Herod called the magi secretly
and ascertained from them the time of the star's appearance.
He sent them to Bethlehem and said,
"Go and search diligently for the child.
When you have found him, bring me word,
that I too may go and do him homage."
After their audience with the king they set out.
And behold, the star that they had seen at its rising preceded them,
until it came and stopped over the place where the child was.
They were overjoyed at seeing the star,
and on entering the house
they saw the child with Mary his mother.
They prostrated themselves and did him homage.
Then they opened their treasures
and offered him gifts of gold, frankincense, and myrrh.
And having been warned in a dream not to return to Herod,
they departed for their country by another way.

—Matthew 2:1–12

Truths of Our Catholic Faith

It would be bad enough if Herod had a good intention and felt he had to lie in order to achieve it. In this case both his goal (harming a Child) and his method (lying) are wrong. No matter what the goal, lying is simply always wrong.

> *Lying consists in saying what is false with the intention of deceiving one's neighbor. (CCC 2508)*

Mary witnessed the magi prostrating themselves and doing Jesus homage. Not only was she the mother of a beautiful baby boy, she is indeed the Mother of God. Knowing Mary, she would never make a fuss about the latter. But seeing what they did, Mary must have sensed the awesome gift that God had bestowed upon her—and us.

> *Mary is truly "Mother of God" since she is the mother of the eternal Son of God made man, who is God himself. (CCC 509)*

Our Gospel reading today is read each of the three years in our liturgical cycle on this feast of the Epiphany. Each Sunday at each Mass, whether we're hearing a Gospel the only time in the three-year cycle or whether it's being repeated, we always recite the Our Father together during the Liturgy of the Eucharist. The Lord's Prayer and the Good News are intimately related.

> *The Lord's Prayer is the quintessential prayer of the Church. It is an integral part of the major hours of the Divine Office and of the sacraments of Christian initiation: Baptism, Confirmation, and Eucharist. Integrated into the Eucharist it reveals the eschatological character of its petitions, hoping for the Lord, "until he comes" (1 Cor 11:26). (CCC 2776)*

A Question for Me

Am I willing to prostrate myself and do Jesus homage?

For a Child in My Life

Why do we call Mary the Mother of God?

My Role in the Community

A community depends in large part on truthfulness. Have I accepted the illusion that there is such a thing as a little white lie? Do I conscientiously avoid saying what is false with the intention of deceiving my neighbor?

For Depth and Further Life Application

Isaiah 60:1–6
Psalm 72
Ephesians 3:2-3a, 5–6

United States Catholic Catechism for Adults, pages 481–483

REFLECTION

We saw his star at its rising and have come to do him homage.

—Matthew 2:2

A The Baptism of the Lord

The Gospel

Jesus came from Galilee to John at the Jordan
to be baptized by him.
John tried to prevent him, saying,
"I need to be baptized by you,
and yet you are coming to me?"
Jesus said to him in reply,
"Allow it now, for thus it is fitting for us
to fulfill all righteousness."
Then he allowed him.
After Jesus was baptized,
he came up from the water and behold,
the heavens were opened for him,
and he saw the Spirit of God descending like a dove
and coming upon him.
And a voice came from the heavens, saying,
"This is my beloved Son, with whom I am well pleased."

—Matthew 3:13-17

Truths of Our Catholic Faith

"This is my beloved Son." While Jesus is one of us, we must also remember how He is entirely unique. He is both human and divine. Jesus is God almighty.

> *The title "Son of God" signifies the unique and eternal relationship of Jesus Christ to God his Father: he is the only Son of the Father (cf.* Jn *1:14,18; 3:16,18); he is God himself (cf.* Jn *1:1). To be a Christian, one must believe that Jesus Christ is the Son of God (cf.* Acts *8:37;* 1 Jn *2:23). (CCC 454)*

Jesus sets a good example for us in many ways. He is concerned about how we live. He gives us grace to live as we should.

Because he wants us to have life and have it in abundance, Jesus sends the Holy Spirit among us. We hope one day to bask in the light of our triune God—Father, Son and Spirit—joyful for all eternity.

He who believes in Christ has new life in the Holy Spirit. The moral life, increased and brought to maturity in grace, is to reach its fulfillment in the glory of heaven. (CCC 1715)

A Question for Me

A voice coming from the heavens; that is pretty convincing. What would it take to deepen my belief that Jesus is God's Son?

For a Child in My Life

What did the voice from heaven say when Jesus was baptized?

My Role in the Community

If I'm a godparent, how do I fulfill this responsibility? If not, what might I do to carry out this honor in the event that I am asked?

For Depth and Further Life Application

Isaiah 42:1–4, 6–7
Psalm 29
Acts 10:34–38

📖 United States Catholic Catechism for Adults, pages 553–560

REFLECTION

The heavens were opened and the voice of the Father thundered: This is my beloved Son, listen to him.

—cf. Mark 9:7

A First Sunday of Lent

The Gospel

At that time Jesus was led by the Spirit into the desert
to be tempted by the devil.
He fasted for forty days and forty nights,
and afterwards he was hungry.
The tempter approached and said to him,
"If you are the Son of God,
command that these stones become loaves of bread."
He said in reply,
"It is written:
One does not live on bread alone,
but on every word that comes forth
from the mouth of God."

Then the devil took him to the holy city,
and made him stand on the parapet of the temple,
and said to him, "If you are the Son of God, throw yourself down.
For it is written:
He will command his angels concerning you
and with their hands they will support you,
lest you dash your foot against a stone."
Jesus answered him,
"Again it is written,
You shall not put the Lord, your God, to the test."
Then the devil took him up to a very high mountain,
and showed him all the kingdoms of the world in their magnificence,
and he said to him, "All these I shall give to you,
if you will prostrate yourself and worship me."
At this, Jesus said to him,
"Get away, Satan!
It is written:
The Lord, your God, shall you worship
and him alone shall you serve.
Then the devil left him and, behold,
angels came and ministered to him.

—Matthew 4:1–11

Truths of Our Catholic Faith

Angels came and ministered to him. It seems that angels are very popular lately. Clarity on who angels are, and who they are not, is a good Christian goal.

These heavenly beings are more than just cute little cherubic creatures. They are more than characters on television shows that sometimes portray angels accurately, and sometimes do not. Angels are servants and messengers of almighty God, who loves us enough to save us from sin and death.

Sin and death are real. God is real. True angels are real, too.

> *Angels are spiritual creatures who glorify God without ceasing and who serve his saving plans for other creatures: "The angels work together for the benefit of us all" (St. Thomas Aquinas,* STh *I, 114, 3,* ad *3). (CCC 350)*

Satan tempted Jesus to break the First Commandment as well as several other laws of God. Putting God to the test, prostrating ourselves before any other person or thing, abusing any sacred name or object all show profound disrespect and lack of understanding about who God is.

Aside from legitimate stipends, thinking that we could actually buy or sell God's love or grace shows a disordered notion of God, one that can be changed in part by acts of penance. Lent is an excellent time to examine our basic notions about God, sin, death, love and salvation.

> *Tempting God in words or deeds, sacrilege, and simony are sins of irreligion forbidden by the first commandment. (CCC 2139)*

A Question for Me

Do I intentionally place myself in situations dangerously close to sin? If so, I am a willing participant in temptation, and this behavior should be altered.

For a Child in My Life
Will you join me in the prayer to our Guardian Angels?

My Role in the Community
Do I place demands on others that make it difficult for them to serve and worship the Lord, our God, particularly on Sundays?

For Depth and Further Life Application

Genesis 2:7–9; 3:1–7
Psalm 51
Romans 5:12–19

📖 United States Catholic Catechism for Adults, pages 339–341

REFLECTION

One does not live on bread alone, but on every word that comes forth from the mouth of God.

—Matthew 4:4b

A Second Sunday of Lent

The Gospel

Jesus took Peter, James, and John his brother,
and led them up a high mountain by themselves.
And he was transfigured before them;
his face shone like the sun
and his clothes became white as light.
And behold, Moses and Elijah appeared to them,
conversing with him.
Then Peter said to Jesus in reply,
"Lord, it is good that we are here.
If you wish, I will make three tents here,
one for you, one for Moses, and one for Elijah."
While he was still speaking, behold,
a bright cloud cast a shadow over them,
then from the cloud came a voice that said,
"This is my beloved Son, with whom I am well pleased;
listen to him."
When the disciples heard this, they fell prostrate
and were very much afraid.
But Jesus came and touched them, saying,
"Rise, and do not be afraid."
And when the disciples raised their eyes,
they saw no one else but Jesus alone.

As they were coming down from the mountain,
Jesus charged them,
"Do not tell the vision to anyone
until the Son of Man has been raised from the dead."

—Matthew 17:1–9

Truths of Our Catholic Faith

In the Transfiguration, Jesus reveals Himself as God as clearly as He can. Peter's response was to babble something barely coherent—something about making tents.

The Transfiguration says something about the ultimate mysteriousness of God. Peter, James and John didn't seem to understand what had occurred, nor would they until after the Holy Spirit arrived and helped them grasp this mystery.

> *Even when he reveals himself, God remains a mystery beyond words: "If you understood him, it would not be God" (St. Augustine,* Sermo *52, 6, 16: PL 38:360 and* Sermo *117, 3, 5: PL 38, 663). (CCC 230)*

Peter, in all his human frailty, was blessed with a unique gift: the responsibility of leading the disciples, keeping them free from error. The Holy Spirit powerfully transformed Peter at Pentecost, and his teaching authority (Magisterium) was born along with the Church that day.

Properly understood, the concept of infallibility is a necessary outgrowth of believing that Jesus founded a Church and fulfills His promise of guiding Her teaching. The Holy Spirit is a spirit of truth, and when it comes to basic matters of faith, He keeps our Church unerring or, in a word, infallible.

> *The infallibility of the Magisterium of the Pastors extends to all the elements of doctrine, including moral doctrine, without which the saving truths of the faith cannot be preserved, expounded, or observed. (CCC 2051)*

A Question for Me

If I am to listen to Jesus well, how will this occur? How does Jesus speak to me? What will I do when I hear Him?

For a Child in My Life

What are a few ways that Jesus communicates with you?

My Role in the Community

Infallibility is not always a popular concept. How might I help others understand and appreciate this important, actually indispensable, truth of our Catholic faith?

For Depth and Further Life Application

Genesis 12:1–4a
Psalm 33
Timothy 1:8b–10

United States Catholic Catechism for Adults, pages 307–309

REFLECTION

From the shining cloud the Father's voice is heard: This is my beloved Son, hear him.

—cf. Matthew 17:5

A Third Sunday of Lent

The Gospel

Jesus came to a town of Samaria called Sychar,
near the plot of land that Jacob had given to his son Joseph.
Jacob's well was there.
Jesus, tired from his journey, sat down there at the well.
It was about noon.

A woman of Samaria came to draw water.
Jesus said to her,
"Give me a drink."
His disciples had gone into the town to buy food.
The Samaritan woman said to him,
"How can you, a Jew, ask me, a Samaritan woman, for a drink?"
—For Jews use nothing in common with Samaritans.—
Jesus answered and said to her,
"If you knew the gift of God
and who is saying to you, 'Give me a drink, '
you would have asked him
and he would have given you living water."
The woman said to him,
"Sir, you do not even have a bucket and the cistern is deep;
where then can you get this living water?
Are you greater than our father Jacob,
who gave us this cistern and drank from it himself
with his children and his flocks?"
Jesus answered and said to her,
"Everyone who drinks this water will be thirsty again;
but whoever drinks the water I shall give will never thirst;
the water I shall give will become in him
a spring of water welling up to eternal life."
The woman said to him,
"Sir, give me this water, so that I may not be thirsty
or have to keep coming here to draw water.

"I can see that you are a prophet.
Our ancestors worshiped on this mountain;
but you people say that the place to worship is in Jerusalem."
Jesus said to her,
"Believe me, woman, the hour is coming

when you will worship the Father
neither on this mountain nor in Jerusalem.
You people worship what you do not understand;
we worship what we understand,
because salvation is from the Jews.
But the hour is coming, and is now here,
when true worshipers will worship the Father in Spirit and truth;
and indeed the Father seeks such people to worship him.
God is Spirit, and those who worship him
must worship in Spirit and truth."
The woman said to him,
"I know that the Messiah is coming, the one called the Christ;
when he comes, he will tell us everything."
Jesus said to her,
"I am he, the one who is speaking with you."

Many of the Samaritans of that town began to believe in him.
When the Samaritans came to him,
they invited him to stay with them;
and he stayed there two days.
Many more began to believe in him because of his word,
and they said to the woman,
"We no longer believe because of your word;
for we have heard for ourselves,
and we know that this is truly the savior of the world."

—John 4:5–15, 19b–26, 40–42

Truths of Our Catholic Faith

Jesus and the Samaritan woman bring up differences in worship styles and practices. Most Catholics in America worship according to the Roman rite; these Roman Catholics are sometimes unaware that other Catholic rites or liturgical traditions exist.

It is good to know at least a little bit about the variety of rites that currently thrive within that enormous group of Christians who acknowledge the Bishop of Rome as their Supreme Pontif. The legitimate diversity in our Catholic Church reminds us that while unity is supremely important, it need not always mean complete uniformity.

> *The diverse liturgical traditions or rites, legitimately recognized, manifest the catholicity of the Church, because they signify and communicate the same mystery of Christ. (CCC 1208)*

The Samaritan woman came to have faith in Jesus as the Messiah, the Christ, the Savior. Her words apparently lead several others toward belief in Jesus' saving power. Faith, both having it and sharing it, is profoundly important for ourselves and others.

> *Faith is necessary for salvation. The Lord himself affirms: "He who believes and is baptized will be saved; but he who does not believe will be condemned"* (Mk *16:16). (CCC 183)*

A Question for Me
Do I pray for faith regularly? Could I learn an Act of Faith and pray it at least once a week?

For a Child in My Life
The Samaritan woman helped others believe that Jesus is our Savior. What could you do or say to help others have faith in Jesus?

My Role in the Community
Have I taken advantage of opportunities to celebrate Mass according to Catholic rites other than my own?

For Depth and Further Life Application

Exodus 17:3–7
Psalm 95
Romans 5:1–2, 5–8

United States Catholic Catechism for Adults, pages 35–36

REFLECTION

Lord, you are truly the Savior of the world; give me living water, that I may never thirst again.

—cf. John 4:42, 15

A Fourth Sunday of Lent

The Gospel

As Jesus passed by he saw a man blind from birth.
He spat on the ground and made clay with the saliva,
and smeared the clay on his eyes,
and said to him,
"Go wash in the Pool of Siloam"—which means Sent—.
So he went and washed, and came back able to see.

His neighbors and those who had seen him earlier as a beggar said,
"Isn't this the one who used to sit and beg?"
Some said, "It is, "
but others said, "No, he just looks like him."
He said, "I am."

They brought the one who was once blind to the Pharisees.
Now Jesus had made clay and opened his eyes on a sabbath.
So then the Pharisees also asked him how he was able to see.
He said to them,
"He put clay on my eyes, and I washed, and now I can see."
So some of the Pharisees said,
"This man is not from God,
because he does not keep the sabbath."
But others said,
"How can a sinful man do such signs?"
And there was a division among them.
So they said to the blind man again,
"What do you have to say about him,
since he opened your eyes?"
He said, "He is a prophet."

They answered and said to him,
"You were born totally in sin,
and are you trying to teach us?"
Then they threw him out.

When Jesus heard that they had thrown him out,
he found him and said, "Do you believe in the Son of Man?"
He answered and said,
"Who is he, sir, that I may believe in him?"
Jesus said to him,

"You have seen him, and
the one speaking with you is he."
He said,
"I do believe, Lord," and he worshiped him.
—John 9:1, 6–9, 13–17, 34–38

Truths of Our Catholic Faith

Why on earth did Jesus use earth—clay—to heal the man blind from birth?! Jesus had a habit of using elements perceivable to our senses, such as bread and wine, in opportunities to experience His powerful presence in unique and special ways.

This helps explain why sacraments hold such a special place in the life of a Catholic. Sacraments are much more than merely man-made ceremonies; they are real opportunities to experience the grace of God.

> *The sacraments are efficacious signs of grace, instituted by Christ and entrusted to the Church, by which divine life is dispensed to us. The visible rites by which the sacraments are celebrated signify and make present the graces proper to each sacrament. They bear fruit in those who receive them with the required dispositions. (CCC 1131)*

Those Pharisees were upset that Jesus was working with clay and curing the blind on the Sabbath day. As Christians, we too have our Lord's Day. And although unnecessary labor is to be avoided then, reasonable efforts toward charity are—as most people of Jewish faith then and now might agree—perfectly acceptable and appropriate.

> *The sabbath, which represented the completion of the first creation, has been replaced by Sunday which recalls the new creation inaugurated by the Resurrection of Christ. (CCC 2190)*

A Question for Me
How do I think of sacraments? Do I see them as essentially man-made ceremonies, or as truly God-given opportunities to experience His presence in a special, grace-filled, way?

For a Child in My Life
Why is Sunday a special day?

My Role in the Community
The Pharisees were disdainful toward the man blind from birth. Is there anyone in my life toward whom I would feel indignant were she or he to try teaching me something?

For Depth and Further Life Application

Samuel 16:1b, 6–7, 10–13a
Psalm 23
Ephesians 5:8–14

📖 United States Catholic Catechism for Adults, pages 361–363

REFLECTION

I am the light of the world, says the Lord; whoever follows me will have the light of life.

—John 8:12

A Fifth Sunday of Lent

The Gospel

The sisters of Lazarus sent word to Jesus, saying,
"Master, the one you love is ill."
When Jesus heard this he said,
"This illness is not to end in death,
but is for the glory of God,
that the Son of God may be glorified through it."
Now Jesus loved Martha and her sister and Lazarus.
So when he heard that he was ill,
he remained for two days in the place where he was.
Then after this he said to his disciples,
"Let us go back to Judea."

When Jesus arrived, he found that Lazarus
had already been in the tomb for four days.
When Martha heard that Jesus was coming,
she went to meet him;
but Mary sat at home.
Martha said to Jesus,
"Lord, if you had been here,
my brother would not have died.
But even now I know that whatever you ask of God,
God will give you."
Jesus said to her,
"Your brother will rise."
Martha said,
"I know he will rise,
in the resurrection on the last day."
Jesus told her,
"I am the resurrection and the life;
whoever believes in me, even if he dies, will live,
and everyone who lives and believes in me will never die.
Do you believe this?"
She said to him, "Yes, Lord.
I have come to believe that you are the Christ, the Son of God,
the one who is coming into the world."

He became perturbed and deeply troubled, and said,
"Where have you laid him?"
They said to him, "Sir, come and see."
And Jesus wept.
So the Jews said, "See how he loved him."
But some of them said,
"Could not the one who opened the eyes of the blind man
have done something so that this man would not have died?"

So Jesus, perturbed again, came to the tomb.
It was a cave, and a stone lay across it.
Jesus said, "Take away the stone."
Martha, the dead man's sister, said to him,
"Lord, by now there will be a stench;
he has been dead for four days."
Jesus said to her,
"Did I not tell you that if you believe
you will see the glory of God?"
So they took away the stone.
And Jesus raised his eyes and said,
"Father, I thank you for hearing me.
I know that you always hear me;
but because of the crowd here I have said this,
that they may believe that you sent me."
And when he had said this,
He cried out in a loud voice,
"Lazarus, come out!"
The dead man came out,
tied hand and foot with burial bands,
and his face was wrapped in a cloth.
So Jesus said to them,
"Untie him and let him go."

Now many of the Jews who had come to Mary
and seen what he had done began to believe in him.

—John 11:3–7, 17, 20–27, 33b–45

Truths of Our Catholic Faith

"This illness is not to end in death." The same could be said for all illness, really. As Catholics we believe that while on the one hand sickness certainly isn't something we should pursue as a good, on the other it can be a mystery through which Jesus reveals something of His suffering to us.

When a Catholic is seriously unhealthy for any reason, we should see to it that she or he has access to one of our seven sacraments, the Anointing of the Sick. This sacrament offers special grace to those suffering from severe illness.

> *The special grace of the sacrament of the Anointing of the Sick has as its effects:*
>
> † *the uniting of the sick person to the passion of Christ, for his own good and that of the whole Church;*
>
> † *the strengthening, peace, and courage to endure in a Christian manner the sufferings of illness or old age;*
>
> † *the forgiveness of sins, if the sick person was not able to obtain it through the Sacrament of Penance;*
>
> † *the restoration of health, if it is conducive to the salvation of his soul;*
>
> † *the preparation for passing over to eternal life. (CCC 1532)*

And Jesus wept. Jesus cries because He loves Lazarus. He loves Martha and Mary. He is filled with love for every human person who has ever lived and who has yet to be conceived and born.

It is mind-boggling and heart-stirring to ponder the depth of Jesus' love for all humanity—including you. God the Father, God the Son and God the Holy Spirit are a Trinity of love; individually and as a Trinity they love you equally to their divine love for every human person, a love that is infinite, immeasurable, limitless.

"See how He loved him." See how He loves us. See how He loves you.

> *Our salvation flows from God's initiative of love for us, because "he loved us and sent his Son to be the expiation for our sins"* (1 Jn *4:10). "God was in Christ reconciling the world to himself"* (2 Cor *5:19).*

Jesus freely offered himself for our salvation. Beforehand, during the Last Supper, he both symbolized this offering and made it really present: "This is my body which is given for you" (Lk 22:19). *(CCC 620–21)*

A Question for Me

What does it mean to unite my suffering to the passion of Christ, for my good and that of the whole Church? How well do I do it? How frequently do I engage in the corporal work of mercy of visiting the sick?

For a Child in My Life

Jesus says, "whoever believes in me, even if he dies, will live." What does He mean?

My Role in the Community

What might I do to ensure that the terminally ill are not seen by society as a burden, and certainly are not pressured directly or even indirectly to commit assisted suicide?

For Depth and Further Life Application

Ezekiel 37:12–14
Psalm 130
Romans 8:8–11

📖 United States Catholic Catechism for Adults, pages 89–90

REFLECTION

I am the resurrection and the life, says the Lord; whoever believes in me, even if he dies, will never die.

—John 11:25a, 26

A Palm Sunday

The Gospel

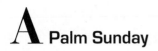

Jesus stood before the governor, Pontius Pilate, who questioned him,
"Are you the king of the Jews?"
Jesus said, "You say so."
And when he was accused by the chief priests and elders,
he made no answer.
Then Pilate said to him,
"Do you not hear how many things they are testifying against you?"
But he did not answer him one word,
so that the governor was greatly amazed.

Now on the occasion of the feast
the governor was accustomed to release to the crowd
one prisoner whom they wished.
And at that time they had a notorious prisoner called Barabbas.
So when they had assembled, Pilate said to them,
"Which one do you want me to release to you,
Barabbas, or Jesus called Christ?"
For he knew that it was out of envy
that they had handed him over.
While he was still seated on the bench,
his wife sent him a message,
"Have nothing to do with that righteous man.
I suffered much in a dream today because of him."
The chief priests and the elders persuaded the crowds
to ask for Barabbas but to destroy Jesus.
The governor said to them in reply,
"Which of the two do you want me to release to you?"
They answered, Barabbas!"
Pilate said to them,
"Then what shall I do with Jesus called Christ?"
They all said,
"Let him be crucified!"
But he said,
"Why? What evil has he done?"
They only shouted the louder,
"Let him be crucified!"
When Pilate saw that he was not succeeding at all,

but that a riot was breaking out instead,
he took water and washed his hands in the sight of the crowd,
saying, "I am innocent of this man's blood.
Look to it yourselves."
And the whole people said in reply,
"His blood be upon us and upon our children."
Then he released Barabbas to them,
but after he had Jesus scourged,
he handed him over to be crucified.

Then the soldiers of the governor took Jesus inside the praetorium
and gathered the whole cohort around him.
They stripped off his clothes
and threw a scarlet military cloak about him.
Weaving a crown out of thorns, they placed it on his head,
and a reed in his right hand.
And kneeling before him, they mocked him, saying,
"Hail, King of the Jews!"
They spat upon him and took the reed
and kept striking him on the head.
And when they had mocked him,
they stripped him of the cloak,
dressed him in his own clothes,
and led him off to crucify him.

As they were going out, they met a Cyrenian named Simon;
this man they pressed into service
to carry his cross.

And when they came to a place called Golgotha
—which means Place of the Skull—,
they gave Jesus wine to drink mixed with gall.
But when he had tasted it, he refused to drink.
After they had crucified him,
they divided his garments by casting lots;
then they sat down and kept watch over him there.
And they placed over his head the written charge against him:
This is Jesus, the King of the Jews.
Two revolutionaries were crucified with him,
one on his right and the other on his left.

Those passing by reviled him, shaking their heads and saying,
"You who would destroy the temple and rebuild it in three days,
save yourself, if you are the Son of God,
and come down from the cross!"
Likewise the chief priests with the scribes and elders
mocked him and said,
"He saved others; he cannot save himself.
So he is the king of Israel!
Let him come down from the cross now,
and we will believe in him.
He trusted in God;
let him deliver him now if he wants him.
For he said, 'I am the Son of God.'"
The revolutionaries who were crucified with him
also kept abusing him in the same way.

From noon onward, darkness came over the whole land
until three in the afternoon.
And about three o'clock Jesus cried out in a loud voice,
"Eli, Eli, lema sabachthani?"
which means, "My God, my God, why have you forsaken me?"
Some of the bystanders who heard it said,
"This one is calling for Elijah."
Immediately one of them ran to get a sponge;
he soaked it in wine, and putting it on a reed,
gave it to him to drink.
But the rest said,
"Wait, let us see if Elijah comes to save him."
But Jesus cried out again in a loud voice,
and gave up his spirit.

Here all kneel and pause for a short time.

And behold, the veil of the sanctuary
was torn in two from top to bottom.
The earth quaked, rocks were split, tombs were opened,
and the bodies of many saints who had fallen asleep were raised.
And coming forth from their tombs after his resurrection,
they entered the holy city and appeared to many.

> The centurion and the men with him who were
> keeping watch over Jesus
> feared greatly when they saw the earthquake
> and all that was happening, and they said,
> "Truly, this was the Son of God!"
>
> —Matthew 27:11–54

Truths of Our Catholic Faith

Some of the dead were raised. Some of the living acknowledged the divinity of Jesus. All had sinned. All were in need of salvation. All had temporal as well as spiritual needs.

Among other things, the Eucharist is a sacrifice—a very real sacrifice. We offer the Eucharistic sacrifice, making Jesus' once-for-all offering on the cross present for all throughout human history, in part because we desire blessings for ourselves and others.

> *As sacrifice, the Eucharist is also offered in reparation for the sins of the living and the dead and to obtain spiritual or temporal benefits from God. (CCC 1414)*

Judgments were made by this society of Jesus'. Authorities and citizens conducted themselves in ways showing their view of the human person.

Jesus' society desperately needed to hear His Good News, as does ours. Instead, elements in society rejected and continue rejecting the saving message of God's Son. The results for Jesus were tragic—or so it seemed for three days…

> *Every society's judgments and conduct reflect a vision of man and his destiny. Without the light the Gospel sheds on God and man, societies easily become totalitarian. (CCC 2257)*

A Question for Me

What is the closest I have come to feeling forsaken by God? How did I respond? (Consider reading Psalm 22 as suggested below.)

For a Child in My Life

Why is the Eucharist called a sacrifice? Whose sacrifice becomes present every time we celebrate the Holy Eucharist?

My Role in the Community

If others were to judge my vision of man and his destiny based on my judgments and conduct in society, what might their conclusions be?

For Depth and Further Life Application

Isaiah 50:4–7
Psalm 22
Philippians 2:6–11

📖 United States Catholic Catechism for Adults, pages 375–380

REFLECTION

Christ became obedient to the point of death, even death on a cross. Because of this, God greatly exalted him and bestowed upon him the name which is above every name.

—Philippians 2:8–9

A,B&C Easter Sunday

The Gospel

On the first day of the week,
 Mary of Magdala came to the tomb early in the morning,
 while it was still dark,
 and saw the stone removed from the tomb.
So she ran and went to Simon Peter
 and to the other disciple whom Jesus loved, and told them,
 "They have taken the Lord from the tomb,
 and we don't know where they put him."
So Peter and the other disciple went out and came to the tomb.
They both ran, but the other disciple ran faster than Peter
 and arrived at the tomb first;
 he bent down and saw the burial cloths there, but did not go in.
When Simon Peter arrived after him,
 he went into the tomb and saw the burial cloths there,
 and the cloth that had covered his head,
 not with the burial cloths but rolled up in a separate place.
Then the other disciple also went in,
 the one who had arrived at the tomb first,
 and he saw and believed.
For they did not yet understand the Scripture
that he had to rise from the dead.

—John 20:1–9

Truths of Our Catholic Faith

None of us has seen the Risen Lord. Yet we know that many disciples did spend time with Him. They told other followers, who told others, and so on down through the generations.

None of us has heard the voice of Jesus teaching. Yet when we hear the teaching of His Church, we know what our Lord wants us to understand, He makes it available to us and all believers; He will continue to do so until He comes again.

> *What Christ entrusted to the apostles, they in turn handed on by their preaching and writing, under the inspiration of the Holy Spirit, to all generations, until Christ returns in glory. (CCC 96)*

The Resurrection is not merely a myth meant to symbolize something for our benefit. Jesus *did* rise from being dead. And so shall we all.

> *Faith in the Resurrection has as its object an event which is historically attested to by the disciples, who really encountered the Risen One. At the same time, this event is mysteriously transcendent insofar as it is the entry of Christ's humanity into the glory of God. (CCC 656)*

Our initiation into the death and resurrection of Jesus occurs sacramentally through baptism, confirmation and Eucharist. For most Roman Catholics, baptism occurs during infancy, followed by First Eucharist at the age of reason (about age seven) and confirmation a few years later.

A growing number of Catholics are celebrating confirmation immediately before First Holy Communion; this has always been the practice among Eastern (or Byzantine) Catholics as well as Eastern Orthodox Christians. Within this legitimate diversity we see various expressions of these three sacraments' interrelatedness.

> *In the East this sacrament is administered immediately after Baptism and is followed by participation in the Eucharist; this tradition highlights the unity of the three sacraments of Christian initiation. In the Latin Church this sacrament is administered when the age of reason has been reached, and its celebration is ordinarily reserved to the bishop, thus signifying that this sacrament strengthens the ecclesial bond. (CCC 1318)*

A Question for Me

How would I describe the relationship between the three sacraments of initiation?

For a Child in My Life

Who saw Jesus after He rose from the dead?

My Role in the Community
Knowing that Easter is a season, not just a day, what are some ways I could extend the observance and celebration of Jesus' resurrection in my family, my parish and other communities to whom I belong?

For Depth and Further Life Application

Acts of the Apostles 10:34a, 37–43
Psalm 118
Colossians 3:1–4

United States Catholic Catechism for Adults, pages 201–202

REFLECTION

Christ, our paschal lamb, has been sacrificed; let us then feast with joy in the Lord.

—cf. 1 Corinthians 5:7b–8a

Second Sunday of Easter

The Gospel

On the evening of that first day of the week,
when the doors were locked, where the disciples were,
for fear of the Jews,
Jesus came and stood in their midst
and said to them, "Peace be with you."
When he had said this, he showed them his hands and his side.
The disciples rejoiced when they saw the Lord.
Jesus said to them again, "Peace be with you.
As the Father has sent me, so I send you."
And when he had said this, he breathed on them and said to them,
"Receive the Holy Spirit.
Whose sins you forgive are forgiven them,
and whose sins you retain are retained."

Thomas, called Didymus, one of the Twelve,
was not with them when Jesus came.
So the other disciples said to him, "We have seen the Lord."
But he said to them,
"Unless I see the mark of the nails in his hands
and put my finger into the nailmarks
and put my hand into his side, I will not believe."

Now a week later his disciples were again inside
and Thomas was with them.
Jesus came, although the doors were locked,
and stood in their midst and said, "Peace be with you."
Then he said to Thomas, "Put your finger here and see my hands,
and bring your hand and put it into my side,
and do not be unbelieving, but believe."
Thomas answered and said to him, "My Lord and my God!"
Jesus said to him, "Have you come to believe because
you have seen me?
Blessed are those who have not seen and have believed."

Now, Jesus did many other signs in the presence of his disciples
that are not written in this book.

> But these are written that you may come to believe
> that Jesus is the Christ, the Son of God,
> and that through this belief you may have life in his name.
>
> —John 20:19–31

Truths of Our Catholic Faith

The Risen Jesus could have said a lot of things to His friends when He came and stood among them. But what He said was "Whose sins you forgive are forgiven them, and whose sins you retain are retained."

Forgiveness should be relatively commonplace. Sacramentally, we have a way of celebrating God's forgiveness through Jesus. In the Sacrament of Penance, those entrusted with authority to forgive sins today help bring us God's mercy and grace.

> *Only priests who have received the faculty of absolving from the authority of the Church can forgive sins in the name of Christ. (CCC 1495)*

"Peace be with you," says our Lord. Jesus' fondest desire apparently has to do with the absence of war and the peaceful resolution of conflicts.

> *Because of the evils and injustices that all war brings with it, we must do everything reasonably possible to avoid it. The Church prays: "From famine, pestilence, and war, O Lord, deliver us." (CCC 2327)*

A Question for Me

Who do I need to forgive today? What will I do to show this forgiveness?

For a Child in My Life

What did the Risen Jesus say to His friends after He said, "Receive the Holy Spirit"?

My Role in the Community

How might I bring reconciliation to where it is needed in my various communities?

For Depth and Further Life Application

Acts of the Apostles 2:42–47
Psalm 118
1 Peter 1:3–9

📖 United States Catholic Catechism for Adults, pages 6–7

REFLECTION

You believe in me, Thomas, because you have seen me, says the Lord; blessed are they who have not seen me, but still believe!

—John 20:29

A Third Sunday of Easter

The Gospel

That very day, the first day of the week,
two of Jesus' disciples were going
to a village seven miles from Jerusalem called Emmaus,
and they were conversing about all the things that had occurred.
And it happened that while they were conversing and debating,
Jesus himself drew near and walked with them,
but their eyes were prevented from recognizing him.
He asked them,
"What are you discussing as you walk along?"
They stopped, looking downcast.
One of them, named Cleopas, said to him in reply,
"Are you the only visitor to Jerusalem
who does not know of the things
that have taken place there in these days?"
And he replied to them, "What sort of things?"
They said to him,
"The things that happened to Jesus the Nazarene,
who was a prophet mighty in deed and word
before God and all the people,
how our chief priests and rulers both handed him over
to a sentence of death and crucified him.
But we were hoping that he would be the one to redeem Israel;
and besides all this,
it is now the third day since this took place.
Some women from our group, however, have astounded us:
they were at the tomb early in the morning
and did not find his body;
they came back and reported
that they had indeed seen a vision of angels
who announced that he was alive.
Then some of those with us went to the tomb
and found things just as the women had described,
but him they did not see."
And he said to them, "Oh, how foolish you are!
How slow of heart to believe all that the prophets spoke!
Was it not necessary that the Christ should suffer these things
and enter into his glory?"

Then beginning with Moses and all the prophets,
he interpreted to them what referred to him
in all the Scriptures.
As they approached the village to which they were going,
he gave the impression that he was going on farther.
But they urged him, "Stay with us,
for it is nearly evening and the day is almost over."
So he went in to stay with them.
And it happened that, while he was with them at table,
he took bread, said the blessing,
broke it, and gave it to them.
With that their eyes were opened and they recognized him,
but he vanished from their sight.
Then they said to each other,
"Were not our hearts burning within us
while he spoke to us on the way and opened the Scriptures to us?"
So they set out at once and returned to Jerusalem
where they found gathered together
the eleven and those with them who were saying,
"The Lord has truly been raised and has appeared to Simon!"
Then the two recounted
what had taken place on the way
and how he was made known to them in the breaking of bread.

—Luke 24:13–35

Truths of Our Catholic Faith

Jesus, while in a sense clever during this Gospel passage, is remarkably truthful in His conversation with His friends. He "plays dumb" as a teaching technique. He openly calls them foolish (so much for attempts to depict Jesus as so mild He'd never risk rubbing anyone the wrong way).

He thoroughly interprets the Scriptures to help them understand. Although these friends get the impression He is going beyond Emmaus, Jesus as usual shows us the virtue of truthfulness.

Truth or truthfulness is the virtue which consists in showing oneself true in deeds and truthful in words,

> *and guarding against duplicity, dissimulation, and hypocrisy.* (CCC 2505)

Notice a pattern in this passage from the Gospel. The Word of God is proclaimed. A blessing is said—bread is blessed and broken. The bread is received by Jesus' followers and they receive new insight.

Mass follows a pattern, too—one that goes back to our Church's earliest days, days shortly after Jesus appeared on the road to Emmaus, days when Luke's Gospel and the other three were composed.

> *The Eucharistic celebration always includes: the proclamation of the Word of God; thanksgiving to God the Father for all his benefits, above all the gift of his Son; the consecration of bread and wine; and participation in the liturgical banquet by receiving the Lord's body and blood. These elements constitute one single act of worship.* (CCC 1408)

A Question for Me

How does my practice of the virtue of truth or truthfulness compare to the description offered above? (CCC 2505)

For a Child in My Life

When did Jesus' friends finally recognize Him?

My Role in the Community

Am I habitually late for Mass and/or do I usually leave early? These behaviors have an impact on the faith community as well as on you!

For Depth and Further Life Application

Acts of the Apostles 2:14, 22–33
Psalm 16
1 Peter 1:17–21

📖 United States Catholic Catechism for Adults, pages 213–214

REFLECTION

Lord Jesus, open the Scriptures to us; make our hearts burn while you speak to us.

—cf. Luke 24:32

A Fourth Sunday of Easter

The Gospel

Jesus said:
"Amen, amen, I say to you,
whoever does not enter a sheepfold through the gate
but climbs over elsewhere is a thief and a robber.
But whoever enters through the gate is the shepherd of the sheep.
The gatekeeper opens it for him, and the sheep hear his voice,
as the shepherd calls his own sheep by name and leads them out.
When he has driven out all his own,
he walks ahead of them, and the sheep follow him,
because they recognize his voice.
But they will not follow a stranger;
they will run away from him,
because they do not recognize the voice of strangers."
Although Jesus used this figure of speech,
the Pharisees did not realize what he was trying to tell them.

So Jesus said again, "Amen, amen, I say to you,
I am the gate for the sheep.
All who came before me are thieves and robbers,
but the sheep did not listen to them.
I am the gate.
Whoever enters through me will be saved,
and will come in and go out and find pasture.
A thief comes only to steal and slaughter and destroy;
I came so that they might have life and have it more abundantly."

—John 10:1–10

Truths of Our Catholic Faith

In theory there are many ways to enter a sheepfold. If the person to whom the sheep belong makes it known there is a preferred way to enter, it seems reasonable that those wanting to enter for good purposes would use it.

God has revealed that the ordinary means of entering eternal life—His most abundant life—is initiation and active membership in the Church He clearly intended to establish. Jesus the Good

Shepherd calls you by name to accept His gift of life.

> *All salvation comes from Christ the Head through the Church which is his Body.* (CCC 846)

Thieves and robbers steal, slaughter and destroy—a sharp contrast to the Good Shepherd. The voice of conscience, following natural law, tells us clearly that robbery in any form is wrong, if only we listen for and hear this trustworthy voice.

> *The seventh commandment forbids theft. Theft is the usurpation of another's goods against the reasonable will of the owner.* (CCC 2453)

A Question for Me

Among the voices I hear day in and day out via radio, television and other media, how intently do I listen for the voice of Jesus, the Good Shepherd?

For a Child in My Life

We know that our Church is the Body of Christ. Who is the Head of our Church?

My Role in the Community

There are many ways to steal, most of them not very dramatic or obvious. Do I need to compensate anyone for goods and services that I currently use without permission?

For Depth and Further Life Application

Acts of the Apostles 2:14a, 36–41
Psalm 23
1 Peter 2:20b–25

📖 United States Catholic Catechism for Adults, pages 417–418

REFLECTION

I am the good shepherd, says the Lord; I know my sheep, and mine know me.

—John 10:14

A Fifth Sunday of Easter

The Gospel

Jesus said to his disciples:
"Do not let your hearts be troubled.
You have faith in God; have faith also in me.
In my Father's house there are many dwelling places.
If there were not,
would I have told you that I am going to prepare a place for you?
And if I go and prepare a place for you,
I will come back again and take you to myself,
so that where I am you also may be.
Where I am going you know the way."
Thomas said to him,
"Master, we do not know where you are going;
how can we know the way?"
Jesus said to him, AI am the way and the truth and the life.
No one comes to the Father except through me.
If you know me, then you will also know my Father.
From now on you do know him and have seen him."
Philip said to him,
"Master, show us the Father, and that will be enough for us."
Jesus said to him, "Have I been with you for so long a time
and you still do not know me, Philip?
Whoever has seen me has seen the Father.
How can you say, 'Show us the Father'?
Do you not believe that I am in the Father and the Father is in me?
The words that I speak to you I do not speak on my own.
The Father who dwells in me is doing his works.
Believe me that I am in the Father and the Father is in me,
or else, believe because of the works themselves.
Amen, amen, I say to you,
whoever believes in me will do the works that I do,
and will do greater ones than these,
because I am going to the Father."

—John 14:1–12

Truths of Our Catholic Faith

Jesus still has work to do in a sense. His whole life is in some ways an act of worship, an offering to His Father and to our Father.

Worship is important. It matters. When we worship in Spirit and in Truth we get a preview of our Father's house, our ultimate dwelling place.

> *Christ's work in the liturgy is sacramental: because his mystery of salvation is made present there by the power of his Holy Spirit; because his Body, which is the Church, is like a sacrament (sign and instrument) in which the Holy Spirit dispenses the mystery of salvation; and because through her liturgical actions the pilgrim Church already participates, as by a foretaste, in the heavenly liturgy. (CCC 1111)*

Our works matter, too. While the salvation pledged to us is of course a gift, some of our works can help lead us closer to it; the same can not be said for others. The Father speaks words to us, words that help us do His works.

> *According to Scripture the Law is a fatherly instruction by God which prescribes for man the ways that lead to the promised beatitude, and proscribes the ways of evil. (CCC 1975)*

A Question for Me

What is my basic attitude toward God's Law as communicated in Catholic moral teaching? Do I see it as somehow being a mean-spirited burden, or do I accurately perceive the Moral Law as the loving, fatherly instruction it is?

For a Child in My Life

Why does God give us Laws?

My Role in the Community

By keeping in mind that at Mass I am participating in the heavenly liturgy, can I participate actively in ways that encourage those around me to do so as well, thereby making Mass more "heavenly"?

For Depth and Further Life Application

Acts of the Apostles 6:1–7
Psalm 33
1 Peter 2:4–9

📖 United States Catholic Catechism for Adults, pages 561–569

REFLECTION

I am the way, the truth and the life, says the Lord; no one comes to the Father, except through me.

—John 14:6

A Sixth Sunday of Easter

The Gospel

Jesus said to his disciples:
"If you love me, you will keep my commandments.
And I will ask the Father,
and he will give you another Advocate to be with you always,
the Spirit of truth, whom the world cannot accept,
because it neither sees nor knows him.
But you know him, because he remains with you,
and will be in you.
I will not leave you orphans; I will come to you.
In a little while the world will no longer see me,
but you will see me, because I live and you will live.
On that day you will realize that I am in my Father
and you are in me and I in you.
Whoever has my commandments and observes them
is the one who loves me.
And whoever loves me will be loved by my Father,
and I will love him and reveal myself to him."

—John 14:15–21

Truths of Our Catholic Faith

Jesus promises you that you will live. That life is caught up in the powerful action of the Advocate, the Spirit of truth, the Holy Spirit.

> *The grace of the Holy Spirit confers upon us the righteousness of God. Uniting us by faith and Baptism to the Passion and Resurrection of Christ, the Spirit makes us sharers in his life. (CCC 2017)*

Actions sometimes speak louder than words. When you say "I love you" sooner or later you have to show it—and keep on showing it.

When it comes to God, saying we love Him in worship is important. Irreplaceable, actually. In addition, we can and should show God our love by the way we live every aspect of life, always drawing and relying upon the grace He makes available to us, which helps us reveal our ever-deepening love ever more sincerely.

> *The moral life is a spiritual worship. Christian activity finds its nourishment in the liturgy and the celebration of the sacraments.* (CCC 2047)

A Question for Me

How would I describe my feelings about actually sharing in the life that Jesus offers me?

For a Child in My Life

In the Gospel reading, what is one way Jesus says we can show we love Him?

My Role in the Community

What additional thoughts come to mind when I think of the nourishment God offers to me in liturgy celebrated with others as well as in sacramental grace—grace usually celebrated with other members of my community?

For Depth and Further Life Application

Acts of the Apostles 8:5–8, 14–17
Psalm 66
1 Peter 3:15–18

📖 United States Catholic Catechism for Adults, pages 310–317

REFLECTION

Whoever loves me will keep my word, says the Lord, and my Father will love him and will come to him.

—John 14:23

A Seventh Sunday of Easter

The Gospel

Jesus raised his eyes to heaven and said,
"Father, the hour has come.
Give glory to your son, so that your son may glorify you,
just as you gave him authority over all people,
so that your son may give eternal life to all you gave him.
Now this is eternal life,
that they should know you, the only true God,
and the one whom you sent, Jesus Christ.
I glorified you on earth
by accomplishing the work that you gave me to do.
Now glorify me, Father, with you,
with the glory that I had with you before the world began.

"I revealed your name to those whom you gave me out of the world.
They belonged to you, and you gave them to me,
and they have kept your word.
Now they know that everything you gave me is from you,
because the words you gave to me I have given to them,
and they accepted them and truly understood that I came from you,
and they have believed that you sent me.
I pray for them.
I do not pray for the world but for the ones you have given me,
because they are yours, and everything of mine is yours
and everything of yours is mine,
and I have been glorified in them.
And now I will no longer be in the world,
but they are in the world, while I am coming to you."

—John 17:1–11a

Truths of Our Catholic Faith

Jesus sets a good example by glorifying our Father. In a sense, glory is not something entirely reserved for God. When we think, say and do things for the glory of God, we share in that glory and allow ourselves in an appropriate sense to be glorified.

God created the world to show forth and communicate his glory. That his creatures should share in his truth,

> *goodness, and beauty—this is the glory for which God created them.* (CCC 319)

Our Lord Jesus never prays to Himself, although we certainly may do so. He does not pray to the Holy Spirit—the Third Person of the Most Blessed Trinity—although again that is something we might do.

The Son of God prays to the Father and teaches us how to pray the Our Father.

> *Prayer is primarily addressed to the Father; it can also be directed toward Jesus, particularly by the invocation of his holy name: "Lord Jesus Christ, Son of God, have mercy on us sinners."* (CCC 2680)

A Question for Me

To whom among the Three Persons of the Holy Trinity do I usually find myself praying?

For a Child in My Life

Who created our world? Why is it important to keep this in mind?

My Role in the Community

How might I live within my many communities to reflect an awareness that every human person is a child of the same Father, my Father, our Father?

For Depth and Further Life Application

Acts of the Apostles 1:12–14
Psalm 27
1 Peter 4:13–16

📖 United States Catholic Catechism for Adults, pages 461–462

REFLECTION

I will not leave you orphans, says the Lord. I will come back to you, and your hearts will rejoice.

—cf. John 14:18

A Pentecost Sunday

The Gospel

On the evening of that first day of the week,
when the doors were locked, where the disciples were,
for fear of the Jews,
Jesus came and stood in their midst
and said to them, "Peace be with you."
When he had said this, he showed them his hands and his side.
The disciples rejoiced when they saw the Lord.
Jesus said to them again, "Peace be with you.
As the Father has sent me, so I send you."
And when he had said this, he breathed on them and said to them,
"Receive the Holy Spirit.
Whose sins you forgive are forgiven them,
and whose sins you retain are retained."

—John 20:19–23

Truths of Our Catholic Faith

The Holy Spirit is active in this Gospel passage as the followers of Jesus experience the presence of their Risen Lord. This same Spirit is at work every time we celebrate Holy Mass, helping us recognize Jesus and respond to His sending forth of us, His command to go in peace to love and serve Him.

> *The mission of the Holy Spirit in the liturgy of the Church is to prepare the assembly to encounter Christ; to recall and manifest Christ to the faith of the assembly; to make the saving work of Christ present and active by his transforming power; and to make the gift of communion bear fruit in the Church. (CCC 1112)*

Jesus' friends must find it hard at first to believe He really stands in their midst. Realizing that His presence is real, they rejoice.

Joy seems a fitting response to the opportunity for participation in the saving work of Jesus—a work truly made present each time Mass is celebrated by God's people.

The Eucharist is the memorial of Christ's Passover, that is, of the work of salvation accomplished by the life, death, and resurrection of Christ, a work made present by the liturgical action. (CCC 1409)

A Question for Me

What is my reaction to the truth that the life, death and resurrection of Jesus are actually made present at every Mass?

For a Child in My Life

Why does the Risen Jesus show His hands and side to His friends?

My Role in the Community

Jesus says "As the Father has sent me, so I send you." How might I best respond to this reality of being sent by God?

For Depth and Further Life Application

Acts of the Apostles 2:1–11
Psalm 104
1 Corinthians 12:3b–7, 12–13

📖 United States Catholic Catechism for Adults, pages 215–224

REFLECTION

Come, Holy Spirit, fill the hearts of your faithful and kindle in them the fire of your love.

A Trinity Sunday

The Gospel

God so loved the world that he gave his only Son,
so that everyone who believes in him might not perish
but might have eternal life.
For God did not send his Son into the world to condemn the world,
but that the world might be saved through him.
Whoever believes in him will not be condemned,
but whoever does not believe has already been condemned,
because he has not believed in the name of the only Son of God.

—John 3:16–18

Truths of Our Catholic Faith

The giving of God's only Son to us and for us is a central mystery of our faith known as the Incarnation. This "enfleshment" of the Divine without loss of Godhood is amazing, not so much because it shows how powerful God is, but more so because the Incarnation demonstrates God's boundless love for each human person.

> *At the time appointed by God, the only Son of the Father, the eternal Word, that is, the Word and substantial Image of the Father, became incarnate; without losing his divine nature he has assumed human nature. (CCC 479)*

The Good News would not be good if it did not counteract some bad news. And the bad news is this: condemnation is at least theoretically possible. It is possible for you to make decisions that could eternally separate you from God.

This is why we need a Savior. Thank God you have a Savior in the only Son of God—Jesus the Christ.

> *To choose deliberately—that is, both knowing it and willing it—something gravely contrary to the divine law and to the ultimate end of man is to commit a mortal sin. This destroys in us the charity without which eternal beatitude is impossible. Unrepented, it brings eternal death. (CCC 1874)*

A Question for Me

What affect does this truth have on me: without losing His divine nature He (Jesus of Nazareth) has assumed our human nature?

For a Child in My Life

Why are mortal sins called mortal?

My Role in the Community

At televised sporting events sometimes you will see a crowd member holding up a large sign saying John 3:16. What are some ways I can subtly remind others of God's existence and great love for each person?

For Depth and Further Life Application

Exodus 34:4b–6, 8–9
Deuteronomy 3:52–55
2 Corinthians 13:11–13

United States Catholic Catechism for Adults, pages 503–504

REVELATION

Glory to the Father, the Son, and the Holy Spirit; to God who is, who was, and who is to come.

—cf. Revelation 1:8

A Corpus Christi

The Gospel

Jesus said to the Jewish crowds:
"I am the living bread that came down from heaven;
whoever eats this bread will live forever;
and the bread that I will give
is my flesh for the life of the world."

The Jews quarreled among themselves, saying,
"How can this man give us his flesh to eat?"
Jesus said to them,
"Amen, amen, I say to you,
unless you eat the flesh of the Son of Man and drink his blood,
you do not have life within you.
Whoever eats my flesh and drinks my blood
has eternal life,
and I will raise him on the last day.
For my flesh is true food,
and my blood is true drink.
Whoever eats my flesh and drinks my blood
remains in me and I in him.
Just as the living Father sent me
and I have life because of the Father,
so also the one who feeds on me
will have life because of me.
This is the bread that came down from heaven.
Unlike your ancestors who ate and still died,
whoever eats this bread will live forever."

—John 6:51–58

Truths of Our Catholic Faith

"Unless you eat the flesh of the Son of Man . . . you do not have life within you." These are strong words that help explain why the Church places so much emphasis on the Most Holy Body and Blood of Christ—the Eucharist.

The Eucharist is the heart and the summit of the Church's life, for in it Christ associates his Church and

> *all her members with his sacrifice of praise and thanksgiving offered once for all on the cross to his Father; by this sacrifice he pours out the graces of salvation on his Body which is the Church.* (CCC 1407)

What happens to bread and wine when they are consecrated by the priest at Mass is called *transubstantiation*. The reality that transubstantiation describes is so important that Jesus takes pain not to be misunderstood. Whether or not you recall this vocabulary term, do not misunderstand or under-appreciate the gift Jesus gives to you in the Eucharist—the gift of Himself, the gift of salvation, the gift of eternal life.

> *By the consecration the transubstantiation of the bread and wine into the Body and Blood of Christ is brought about. Under the consecrated species of bread and wine Christ himself, living and glorious, is present in a true, real, and substantial manner: his Body and his Blood, with his soul and his divinity (cf. Council of Trent: DS 1640; 1651).* (CCC 1413)

A Question for Me

How might I define transubstantiation to a person curious about truths revealed concerning the Eucharist?

For a Child in My Life

Why is the Eucharist the heart and summit of the Church's life?

My Role in the Community

When community members quarrel among themselves regarding the Eucharist or any matter of faith, how might I follow the example Jesus sets in this Gospel passage?

For Depth and Further Life Application

Deuteronomy 8:2–3, 14b–16a
Psalm 147
1 Corinthians 10:16–17

📖 United States Catholic Catechism for Adults, pages 224–228

REFLECTION

I am the living bread that came down from heaven, says the Lord; whoever eats this bread will live forever.

—John 6:51

A Sacred Heart

The Gospel

At that time Jesus exclaimed:
"I give praise to you, Father, Lord of heaven and earth,
for although you have hidden these things
from the wise and the learned
you have revealed them to little ones.
Yes, Father, such has been your gracious will.
All things have been handed over to me by my Father.
No one knows the Son except the Father,
and no one knows the Father except the Son
and anyone to whom the Son wishes to reveal him.

"Come to me, all you who labor and are burdened,
and I will give you rest.
Take my yoke upon you and learn from me,
for I am meek and humble of heart;
and you will find rest for yourselves.
For my yoke is easy, and my burden light."

—Matthew 11:25–30

Truths of Our Catholic Faith

A person doesn't need extensive formal education to discern basic truths about goodness and how we ought to treat each other. A truly good education can of course help deepen our knowledge and lead to real progress. Even the most intelligent and learned person, though, cannot change natural law.

> *The natural law is a participation in God's wisdom and goodness by man formed in the image of his Creator. It expresses the dignity of the human person and forms the basis of his fundamental rights and duties.* (CCC 1978)

Labor in this Gospel passage is not necessarily linked to being burdened. One can labor or work and enjoy a justified sense of fulfillment. When we realize that our work can be a way of cooperating with God, and then act accordingly, it can be an offering to our Father who has handed all things over to Jesus our Redeemer.

> *The primordial value of labor stems from man himself, its author and beneficiary. By means of his labor man participates in the work of creation. Work united to Christ can be redemptive.* (CCC 2460)

A Question for Me

With what am I truly burdened, and in what ways can I learn from my Lord how to find rest?

For a Child in My Life

How can you get more wisdom and goodness?

My Role in the Community

What are the similarities and differences between rights and duties, both in general and as they relate to my role in the community?

For Depth and Further Life Application

Deuteronomy 7:6–11
Psalm 103
1 John 4:7–16

United States Catholic Catechism for Adults, pages 419–424

REFLECTION

Take my yoke upon you, says the Lord; and learn from me, for I am meek and humble of heart.

—Matthew 11:29ab

A Second Sunday of Ordinary Time

The Gospel

John the Baptist saw Jesus coming toward him and said,
"Behold, the Lamb of God, who takes away the sin of the world.
He is the one of whom I said,
'A man is coming after me who ranks ahead of me
because he existed before me.'
I did not know him,
but the reason why I came baptizing with water
was that he might be made known to Israel."
John testified further, saying,
"I saw the Spirit come down like a dove from heaven
and remain upon him.
I did not know him,
but the one who sent me to baptize with water told me,
'On whomever you see the Spirit come down and remain,
he is the one who will baptize with the Holy Spirit.'
Now I have seen and testified that he is the Son of God."

—John 1:29–34

Truths of Our Catholic Faith

Jesus, God (the Father) and the Holy Spirit are all mentioned in this Gospel passage. And while the Most Blessed Trinity is a mystery, it is fruitful to contemplate this triune nature of the Godhead and what it might mean for us—adopted daughters and sons of our Father—redeemed by the Son and gifted with the Spirit.

> *Inseparable in what they are, the divine persons are also inseparable in what they do. But within the single divine operation each shows forth what is proper to him in the Trinity, especially in the divine missions of the Son's Incarnation and the gift of the Holy Spirit.* (CCC 267)

Baptismal grace is perfected in confirmation. The Sacrament of Confirmation provides us with many important gifts and effects.

This sacred anointing draws us ever more deeply into the beautiful mystery that is the Trinity—Father, Son and Holy Spirit.

> *Confirmation perfects Baptismal grace; it is the sacrament which gives the Holy Spirit in order to root us more deeply in the divine filiation, incorporate us more firmly into Christ, strengthen our bond with the Church, associate us more closely with her mission, and help us bear witness to the Christian faith in words accompanied by deeds.* (CCC 1316)

A Question for Me

How might I be incorporated more firmly in Christ?

For a Child in My Life

What does Saint John the Baptist say immediately after seeing Jesus coming toward him?

My Role in the Community

What are some ways I can strengthen my bond with the Church, associate myself more closely with her mission, and bear even better witness to the Christian faith in words accompanied by deeds?

For Depth and Further Life Application

Isaiah 49:3, 5–6
Psalm 40
1 Corinthians 1:1–3

📖 United States Catholic Catechism for Adults, pages 203–207

REFLECTION

The Word became flesh and dwelt among us. To those who accepted him, he gave power to become children of God.

—John 1:14a, 12a

A Third Sunday of Ordinary Time

The Gospel

When Jesus heard that John had been arrested,
he withdrew to Galilee.
He left Nazareth and went to live in Capernaum by the sea,
in the region of Zebulun and Naphtali,
that what had been said through Isaiah the prophet
might be fulfilled:
Land of Zebulun and land of Naphtali,
the way to the sea, beyond the Jordan,
Galilee of the Gentiles,
the people who sit in darkness have seen a great light,
on those dwelling in a land overshadowed by death
light has arisen.
From that time on, Jesus began to preach and say,
"Repent, for the kingdom of heaven is at hand."

—Matthew 4:12–17

Truths of Our Catholic Faith

Sometimes a person can truly sit in darkness. It is possible for a conscience to remain uninformed in some way and therefore partially unformed. For most of us who have the benefit of access to the Good News, though, these situations are probably rare. For we have seen a great light and been called to repentance.

> *Conscience can remain in ignorance or make erroneous judgments. Such ignorance and errors are not always free of guilt. (CCC 1801)*

To repent is to turn away from the darkness of sin toward the light of God and His kingdom. Grace helps you, and so because of Jesus' saving action, you are justified.

> *Like conversion, justification has two aspects. Moved by grace, man turns toward God and away from sin, and so accepts forgiveness and righteousness from on high. (CCC 2018)*

A Question for Me

From what sin might I have a need to turn away or repent?

For a Child in My Life

What is the difference between a sin and mistake? How could a sin and a mistake be similar?

My Role in the Community

What do I know about the kingdom of heaven, and how does this kingdom compare to my various communities?

For Depth and Further Life Application

Isaiah 8:23–9:3
Psalm 27
1 Corinthians 1:10–13, 17

United States Catholic Catechism for Adults, page 532

REFLECTION

Jesus proclaimed the Gospel of the kingdom and cured every disease among the people.

—cf. Matthew 4:23

A Fourth Sunday of Ordinary Time

The Gospel

When Jesus saw the crowds, he went up the mountain,
and after he had sat down, his disciples came to him.
He began to teach them, saying:
"Blessed are the poor in spirit,
for theirs is the kingdom of heaven.
Blessed are they who mourn,
for they will be comforted.
Blessed are the meek,
for they will inherit the land.
Blessed are they who hunger and thirst for righteousness,
for they will be satisfied.
Blessed are the merciful,
for they will be shown mercy.
Blessed are the clean of heart,
for they will see God.
Blessed are the peacemakers,
for they will be called children of God.
Blessed are they who are persecuted for the sake of righteousness,
for theirs is the kingdom of heaven.
Blessed are you when they insult you and persecute you
and utter every kind of evil against you falsely because of me.
Rejoice and be glad,
for your reward will be great in heaven."

—Matthew 5:1–12a

Truths of Our Catholic Faith

The Beatitudes help us understand the kingdom of heaven. Without specifics like the Beatitudes, this kingdom remains a vague notion that also leaves unclear the difference between happiness and what all too often passes for it, leaving our hearts restless and unfulfilled.

> *The Beatitudes take up and fulfill God's promises from Abraham by ordering them to the Kingdom of heaven. They respond to the desire for happiness that God has placed in the human heart.* (CCC 1725)

To be hungry and thirsty for righteousness are desires that should not be unduly frustrated by human societies. Granted, the kingdom of heaven is called that because it is not entirely of this earth; still, the People of God can take reasonable steps toward building communities that reflect His goodness, His life, His beauty.

Genuine, essential rights (like the right to life) should be promoted openly, with related societal goods (e.g. religious freedom, access to education, reasonable hope of employment) built upon them. Societies that acknowledge virtue can help us all to be glad and rejoice.

> *Society ought to promote the exercise of virtue, not obstruct it. It should be animated by a just hierarchy of values. (CCC 1895)*

A Question for Me

God has placed the desire for happiness in my heart; what do the Beatitudes tell me about what happiness is, what happiness isn't, and how to attain authentic happiness?

For a Child in My Life

Tell me as many Beatitudes as you can. What is your understanding of what each one means?

My Role in the Community

In what ways do my communities promote the exercise of virtue. How can I build upon this or help remove any communal obstructions to practicing the virtues?

For Depth and Further Life Application

Zephaniah 2:3; 3:12–13
Psalm 146
1 Corinthians 1:26–31

📖 United States Catholic Catechism for Adults, pages 505–506

REFLECTION

Rejoice and be glad; your reward will be great in heaven.

–Matthew 5:12a

A Fifth Sunday of Ordinary Time

The Gospel

Jesus said to his disciples:
"You are the salt of the earth.
But if salt loses its taste, with what can it be seasoned?
It is no longer good for anything
but to be thrown out and trampled underfoot.
You are the light of the world.
A city set on a mountain cannot be hidden.
Nor do they light a lamp and then put it under a bushel basket;
it is set on a lampstand,
where it gives light to all in the house.
Just so, your light must shine before others,
that they may see your good deeds
and glorify your heavenly Father."

—Matthew 5:13–16

Truths of Our Catholic Faith

A good habit, simply put, is called a virtue. It is important to distinguish between values and virtues. Everyone has values; not all values, however, are healthy. For example, a bank robber values money above obeying just laws against theft.

For a Catholic, virtue is the more specific pursuit. So the next time you hear someone touting values, make sure they are the right values. Be sure the pursuit of virtue is being encouraged.

> *Virtue is a habitual and firm disposition to do good. (CCC 1833)*

The opposite of being light for the world is committing the sin of scandal. If you scandalize someone you nudge her or him toward sinning.

Jesus has some pretty harsh words for scandalous behavior—being thrown out and trampled underfoot. When you cultivate virtue and nurture it in others, you fittingly honor and glorify our Father in heaven.

Scandal is a grave offense when by deed or omission it deliberately leads others to sin gravely. (CCC 2326)

A Question for Me

What are some of my main virtues; i.e., in what specific ways do I strongly tend to do the right things?

For a Child in My Life

What did Jesus say might happen when you let others see your good deeds?

My Role in the Community

On the spectrum of hiding my good deeds and showing them off to the point of being obnoxious, where do I stand?

For Depth and Further Life Application

Isaiah 58:7–10
Psalm 112
1 Corinthians 2:1–5

📖 United States Catholic Catechism for Adults, pages 540–541

REFLECTION

I am the light of the world, says the Lord; whoever follows me will have the light of life.

—John 8:12

A Sixth Sunday of Ordinary Time

The Gospel

Jesus said to his disciples:
"I tell you, unless your righteousness surpasses
that of the scribes and Pharisees,
you will not enter the kingdom of heaven.

"You have heard that it was said to your ancestors,
You shall not kill; and whoever kills will be liable to judgment.
But I say to you,
whoever is angry with his brother
will be liable to judgment.

"You have heard that it was said, You shall not commit adultery.
But I say to you,
everyone who looks at a woman with lust
has already committed adultery with her in his heart.

"Again you have heard that it was said to your ancestors,
Do not take a false oath,
but make good to the Lord all that you vow.
But I say to you, do not swear at all.
Let your 'Yes' mean 'Yes,' and your 'No' mean 'No.'
Anything more is from the evil one."

—Matthew 5:20–22a, 27–28, 33–34a, 37

Truths of Our Catholic Faith

Jesus apparently does not think too highly of adulterous behavior. Marriage, according to the Church that Jesus founded, is to be protected, encouraged and supported. That which undermines marriage is, simply put, wrong.

> *Adultery, divorce, polygamy, and free union are grave offenses against the dignity of marriage. (CCC 2400)*

Outward behavior is not the only thing that can be beneath the dignity of a human person. Your mental state, to the extent that you can control it, is something to be monitored within reason. Being balanced, avoiding near occasions of sin, including inappropriate entertainment, will help you to remain pure of heart and, as Jesus promises, to be blessed.

> *The struggle against carnal lust involves purifying the heart and practicing temperance.* (CCC 2530)

A Question for Me

How prudent am I in my entertainment choices? Am I a consumer of media likely to give me impure thoughts—to commit adultery in my heart?

For a Child in My Life

Why does it make sense to avoid being extreme most of the time. This is called temperance.

My Role in the Community

Another grave offense against the dignity of marriage is the notion of same-sex unions. What are ways I can tell my elected officials that marriage concerns a woman and a man? How might I encourage others in my community to be assertive about this pressing issue?

For Depth and Further Life Application

Sirach 15:15–20
Psalm 119
1 Corinthians 2:6–10

📖 United States Catholic Catechism for Adults, pages 439–440

REFLECTION

Blessed are you, Father, Lord of heaven and earth; you have revealed to little ones the mysteries of the kingdom.

—cf. Matthew 11:25

A Seventh Sunday of Ordinary Time

The Gospel

Jesus said to his disciples:
"You have heard that it was said,
An eye for an eye and a tooth for a tooth.
But I say to you, offer no resistance to one who is evil.
When someone strikes you on your right cheek,
turn the other one as well.
If anyone wants to go to law with you over your tunic,
hand over your cloak as well.
Should anyone press you into service for one mile,
go for two miles.
Give to the one who asks of you,
and do not turn your back on one who wants to borrow.

"You have heard that it was said,
You shall love your neighbor and hate your enemy.
But I say to you, love your enemies
and pray for those who persecute you,
that you may be children of your heavenly Father,
for he makes his sun rise on the bad and the good,
and causes rain to fall on the just and the unjust.
For if you love those who love you, what recompense will you have?
Do not the tax collectors do the same?
And if you greet your brothers only,
what is unusual about that?
Do not the pagans do the same?
So be perfect, just as your heavenly Father is perfect."

—Matthew 5:38–48

Truths of Our Catholic Faith

Sometimes this Gospel passage is misinterpreted as a prohibition against all violence. While Jesus certainly doesn't advocate violence in general, Church teaching does not rule out somewhat dramatic action if needed to protect innocent, defenseless human persons.

The prohibition of murder does not abrogate the right to

> *render an unjust aggressor unable to inflict harm. Legitimate defense is a grave duty for whoever is responsible for the lives of others or the common good. (CCC 2321)*

Jesus calls us to be perfect. On our own, striving for perfection would be absurd. Knowing that God's grace, accessible through prayer and the sacraments, can make all things possible, we can respond to His call and make real progress in the moral life commanded by our Lord. Calling on our Father in prayer regularly is essential.

> *God tirelessly calls each person to this mysterious encounter with Himself. Prayer unfolds throughout the whole history of salvation as a reciprocal call between God and man. (CCC 2591)*

A Question for Me

When I feel the somewhat natural desire for revenge, how do I ultimately handle this emotion?

For a Child in My Life

How does Jesus say we should treat our enemies?

My Role in the Community

Retaliation is sometimes instigated by community members. How might I help reduce any tendencies toward revenge in my communities?

For Depth and Further Life Application

Leviticus 19:1–2, 17–18
Psalm 103
1 Corinthians 3:16–23

📖 United States Catholic Catechism for Adults, pages 463–475

REFLECTION

Whoever keeps the word of Christ, the love of God is truly perfected in him.

—1 John 2:5

A Eighth Sunday of Ordinary Time

The Gospel

Jesus said to his disciples:
"No one can serve two masters.
He will either hate one and love the other,
or be devoted to one and despise the other.
You cannot serve God and mammon.

"Therefore I tell you, do not worry about your life,
what you will eat or drink,
or about your body, what you will wear.
Is not life more than food and the body more than clothing?
Look at the birds in the sky;
they do not sow or reap, they gather nothing into barns,
yet your heavenly Father feeds them.
Are not you more important than they?
Can any of you by worrying add a single moment to your life-span?
Why are you anxious about clothes?
Learn from the way the wild flowers grow.
They do not work or spin.
But I tell you that not even Solomon in all his splendor
was clothed like one of them.
If God so clothes the grass of the field,
which grows today and is thrown into the oven tomorrow,
will he not much more provide for you, O you of little faith?
So do not worry and say, 'What are we to eat?'
or 'What are we to drink?' or 'What are we to wear?'
All these things the pagans seek.
Your heavenly Father knows that you need them all.
But seek first the kingdom of God and his righteousness,
and all these things will be given you besides.
Do not worry about tomorrow; tomorrow will take care of itself.
Sufficient for a day is its own evil."

—Matthew 6:24–34

Truths of Our Catholic Faith

Jesus is touching upon the virtue of hope. Interestingly, when you hope in the Lord to provide your daily bread, you are exercising faith in Him and freeing yourself to show love for Him by being more charitable toward all fellow citizens of His kingdom. These good habits engender a whole host of additional virtues.

> *There are three theological virtues: faith, hope, and charity. They inform all the moral virtues and give life to them. (CCC 1841)*

In the end, seeking God's kingdom first is not really optional. If you are inappropriately attached to earthly riches, you will lack the only possession that ultimately matters—eternal life and happiness in the heavenly kingdom with God the Father, God the Son and God the Holy Spirit. Amen!

> *Detachment from riches is necessary for entering the Kingdom of heaven. "Blessed are the poor in spirit." (CCC 2556)*

A Question for Me

Knowing that it is normal to focus on material goods up to a point, what role does worldly riches play in my life?

For a Child in My Life

What are the three theological virtues? How do they relate to all other good habits of thought, word and deed?

My Role in the Community

What percentage of my time, treasure and talent do I devote to community needs? Up to what percentages can I reasonably increase these at this time?

For Depth and Further Life Application

Isaiah 49:14–15
Psalm 62
1 Corinthians 4:1–5

📖 United States Catholic Catechism for Adults, pages 447–448

REFLECTION

The word of God is living and effective; discerning reflections and thoughts of the heart.

—Hebrews 4:12

A Ninth Sunday of Ordinary Time

The Gospel

Jesus said to his disciples:
"Not everyone who says to me, 'Lord, Lord,'
will enter the kingdom of heaven,
but only the one who does the will of my Father in heaven.
Many will say to me on that day,
'Lord, Lord, did we not prophesy in your name?
Did we not drive out demons in your name?
Did we not do mighty deeds in your name?'
Then I will declare to them solemnly,
'I never knew you. Depart from me, you evildoers.'

"Everyone who listens to these words of mine and acts on them
will be like a wise man who built his house on rock.
The rain fell, the floods came,
and the winds blew and buffeted the house.
But it did not collapse; it had been set solidly on rock.
And everyone who listens to these words of mine
but does not act on them
will be like a fool who built his house on sand.
The rain fell, the floods came,
and the winds blew and buffeted the house.
And it collapsed and was completely ruined."

—Matthew 7:21–27

Truths of Our Catholic Faith

Building solidly on rock is apparently important to Jesus. He chooses to establish His Church on the solid rock of Saint Peter and his profession of faith in Jesus as God's Son. Peter's successor today, the pope, continues to shepherd our Church throughout the world with guidance and authority from Jesus.

> *The Lord made St. Peter the visible foundation of his Church. He entrusted the keys of the Church to him. The bishop of the Church of Rome, successor to St. Peter, is "head of the college of bishops, the Vicar of Christ and Pastor of the universal Church on earth" (CIC, can. 331). (CCC 936)*

People who say "Lord, Lord" may have good intentions at first. But unless they do the will of our heavenly Father when they have reasonable opportunities to do so, they cannot be said to be acting morally.

The moral nature of human actions, then, is determined by three aspects: the act itself, the goal in taking action, and the conditions surrounding a decision to proceed. When all three lead to appropriate activity with intentional effort to do the Father's will, you can accurately be described as proceeding morally and wisely.

> *The object, the intention, and the circumstances make up the three "sources" of the morality of human acts. (CCC 1757)*

A Question for Me

How might I pray more consistently for the pope, asking Saint Peter to intercede for his successor, the Vicar of Christ on earth?

For a Child in My Life

What does Jesus say you should do when you listen to His words?

My Role in the Community

How might I encourage a greater respect and affection for the pope among my friends, coworkers, family and other acquaintances?

For Depth and Further Life Application

Deuteronomy 11:18, 26–28, 32
Psalm 31
Romans 3:21–25, 28

United States Catholic Catechism for Adults, pages 507–508

REFLECTION

I am the vine, you are the branches, says the Lord; whoever remains in me and I in him will bear much fruit.

—John 15:5

A Tenth Sunday of Ordinary Time

The Gospel

As Jesus passed on from there,
 he saw a man named Matthew sitting at the customs post.
He said to him, "Follow me."
And he got up and followed him.
While he was at table in his house,
 many tax collectors and sinners came
 and sat with Jesus and his disciples.
The Pharisees saw this and said to his disciples,
 "Why does your teacher eat with tax collectors and sinners?"
He heard this and said,
 "Those who are well do not need a physician, but the sick do.
Go and learn the meaning of the words,
 'I desire mercy, not sacrifice.'
I did not come to call the righteous but sinners."

—Matthew 9:9–13

Truths of Our Catholic Faith

Matthew could have pursued power and riches. Yet he chose to follow Jesus in response to His call. Matthew put his faith in God's Son, focusing on Him instead of focusing on what could never bring him righteousness and well-being.

> *Faith in God leads us to turn to him alone as our first origin and our ultimate goal, and neither to prefer anything to him nor to substitute anything for him. (CCC 229)*

Power and riches can of course be used well. All too often, though, they are overvalued and become consuming goals, drawing us away from the Source of all good things. We must remain on guard against coveting more than our just share of the world's goods.

> *The tenth commandment forbids avarice arising from a passion for riches and their attendant power. (CCC 2552)*

A Question for Me

What role does power play in my life in terms of seeking it, using it, and submitting to it when used justly?

For a Child in My Life

What bad things might happen if a person loves money and power too much?

My Role in the Community

How do I use power to be a force of goodness in my communities?

For Depth and Further Life Application

Hosea 6:3–6
Psalm 50
Romans 4:18–25

United States Catholic Catechism for Adults, pages 449–454

REFLECTION

The Lord sent me to bring glad tidings to the poor, and to proclaim liberty to captives.

—cf. Luke 4:18

A Eleventh Sunday of Ordinary Time

The Gospel

At the sight of the crowds, Jesus' heart was moved with pity for them
because they were troubled and abandoned,
like sheep without a shepherd.
Then he said to his disciples,
"The harvest is abundant but the laborers are few;
so ask the master of the harvest
to send out laborers for his harvest."

Then he summoned his twelve disciples
and gave them authority over unclean spirits
to drive them out and to cure every disease and every illness.
The names of the twelve apostles are these:
first, Simon called Peter, and his brother Andrew;
James, the son of Zebedee, and his brother John;
Philip and Bartholomew, Thomas and Matthew the tax collector;
James, the son of Alphaeus, and Thaddeus;
Simon from Cana, and Judas Iscariot who betrayed him.

Jesus sent out these twelve after instructing them thus,
"Do not go into pagan territory or enter a Samaritan town.
Go rather to the lost sheep of the house of Israel.
As you go, make this proclamation: 'The kingdom of heaven
is at hand.'
Cure the sick, raise the dead, cleanse lepers, drive out demons.
Without cost you have received; without cost you are to give."

—Matthew 9:36–10.8

Truths of Our Catholic Faith

Like sheep seeking a shepherd, cohesive groups of people have a natural need for a competent leader. In no way demeaning the dignity of individual persons, groups of people benefit from inspired leadership.

Jesus knew that His Church would need leadership throughout history. And so He called apostles to Himself, forming them in leadership, establishing an apostolic succession that continues to this very day.

> *The Church is apostolic. She is built on a lasting foundation: "the twelve apostles of the Lamb"* (Rev *21:14). She is indestructible (cf.* Mt *16:18). She is upheld infallibly in the truth: Christ governs her through Peter and the other apostles, who are present in their successors, the Pope and the college of bishops. (CCC 869)*

Saint Peter was called first to be the overseer of the overseers—the primary bishop among his brother bishops/apostles. While it took a few years to reach clarity on these terms and concepts, their origins are evident in all four Gospels.

The twelve apostles (except Judas of course) ministered in early Church communities—dioceses, if you will. Jesus' basic plan for His Body's leadership continues in the Bishop of Rome and all Catholic bishops throughout our world.

> *The bishop receives the fullness of the sacrament of Holy Orders, which integrates him into the episcopal college and makes him the visible head of the particular Church entrusted to him. As successors of the apostles and members of the college, the bishops share in the apostolic responsibility and mission of the whole Church under the authority of the Pope, successor of St. Peter. (CCC 1594)*

A Question for Me

Why was Jesus' heart moved with pity for the crowds? In what ways are the crowds of today troubled if not abandoned?

For a Child in My Life

Which apostle did Jesus call first? Why?

My Role in the Community

What young man in my community is most likely being called by God to the sacrament of Holy Orders? How will I inform this young man that I perceive the potential for this vocation in him?

For Depth and Further Life Application

Exodus 19:2–6a
Psalm 100
Romans 5:6–11

📖 United States Catholic Catechism for Adults, pages 261–262

REFLECTION

The kingdom of God is at hand. Repent and believe the Gospel.

—Mark 1:15

A Twelfth Sunday of Ordinary Time

The Gospel

Jesus said to the Twelve:
"Fear no one.
Nothing is concealed that will not be revealed,
nor secret that will not be known.
What I say to you in the darkness, speak in the light;
what you hear whispered, proclaim on the housetops.
And do not be afraid of those who kill the body
but cannot kill the soul;
rather, be afraid of the one who can destroy
both soul and body in Gehenna.
Are not two sparrows sold for a small coin?
Yet not one of them falls to the ground without
your Father's knowledge.
Even all the hairs of your head are counted.
So do not be afraid; you are worth more than many sparrows.
Everyone who acknowledges me before others
I will acknowledge before my heavenly Father.
But whoever denies me before others,
I will deny before my heavenly Father."

—Matthew 10:26–33

Truths of Our Catholic Faith

Jesus respects the Twelve too much not to be honest with them about hell. Rather than avoid the topic out of misguided concern (and certainly not overemphasizing it) Jesus presents His apostles with the reality of hell, knowing that because of Him they have the potential to be acknowledged before our heavenly Father.

> *Following the example of Christ, the Church warns the faithful of the "sad and lamentable reality of eternal death"* (GCD 69), *also called "hell."* (CCC 1056)

Denying God, either explicitly or implicitly, can constitute the sin of atheism. The First Commandment draws our attention to the one, true God. When we verbally deny Him or for all practical purposes live as if He doesn't exist, we lead an atheistic life. An "atheistic life" is certainly a contradictory term, for without God, ultimately, we cannot live.

> *Since it rejects or denies the existence of God, atheism is a sin against the first commandment.* (CCC 2140)

A Question for Me

In what ways do I acknowledge Jesus before others? How might I be denying Him, and more importantly, what can I do to change this behavior?

For a Child in My Life

What's hell? Where would you rather live forever?

My Role in the Community

What, if any, atheistic influences do I see in my community. How might I reverse or prevent atheism's effects?

For Depth and Further Life Application

Jeremiah 20:10–13
Psalm 69
Romans 5:12–15

📖 United States Catholic Catechism for Adults, pages 341–346

REFLECTION

The Spirit of truth will testify to me, says the Lord; and you also will testify.

—John 15:26b, 27a

A Thirteenth Sunday of Ordinary Time

The Gospel

Jesus said to his apostles:
"Whoever loves father or mother more than me is not worthy of me,
and whoever loves son or daughter more than me
is not worthy of me;
and whoever does not take up his cross
and follow after me is not worthy of me.
Whoever finds his life will lose it,
and whoever loses his life for my sake will find it.

"Whoever receives you receives me,
and whoever receives me receives the one who sent me.
Whoever receives a prophet because he is a prophet
will receive a prophet's reward,
and whoever receives a righteous man
because he is a righteous man
will receive a righteous man's reward.
And whoever gives only a cup of cold water
to one of these little ones to drink
because the little one is a disciple—
amen, I say to you, he will surely not lose his reward."

—Matthew 10:37–42

Truths of Our Catholic Faith

Taking up your cross means different things at different points in your life. Eventually most people experience illness and old age. The Sacrament of Anointing of the Sick can help you follow after Jesus more closely when you must take up certain crosses.

> *The sacrament of Anointing of the Sick has as its purpose the conferral of a special grace on the Christian experiencing the difficulties inherent in the condition of grave illness or old age.* (CCC 1527)

Giving a bit of cold water isn't an enormously costly act; yet to the one badly in need of hydration, it must seem like love in a cup. There are times when someone around you clearly needs a little help. There are ways that you can make charitable contributions to provide genuine assistance to the poor and support other ministries within our Church.

> *Giving alms to the poor is a witness to fraternal charity: it is also a work of justice pleasing to God.* (CCC 2462)

A Question for Me

How should a Christian face old age or serious sickness?

For a Child in My Life

How does God feel when you help a poor person?

My Role in the Community

In what ways can I show my appreciation of those who fulfill various ministries at my parish? (e.g., pastor, director of religious education, youth minister, principal, etc.)

For Depth and Further Life Application

2 Kings 4:8–11, 14–16a
Psalm 89
Romans 6:3–4, 8–11

📖 United States Catholic Catechism for Adults, pages 424–425

REFLECTION

You are a chosen race, a royal priesthood, a holy nation; announce the praises of him who called you out of darkness into his wonderful light.

—1 Peter 2:9

A Fourteenth Sunday of Ordinary Time

The Gospel

At that time Jesus exclaimed:
"I give praise to you, Father, Lord of heaven and earth,
for although you have hidden these things
from the wise and the learned
you have revealed them to little ones.
Yes, Father, such has been your gracious will.
All things have been handed over to me by my Father.
No one knows the Son except the Father,
and no one knows the Father except the Son
and anyone to whom the Son wishes to reveal him."

"Come to me, all you who labor and are burdened,
and I will give you rest.
Take my yoke upon you and learn from me,
for I am meek and humble of heart;
and you will find rest for yourselves.
For my yoke is easy, and my burden light."

—Matthew 11:25–30

Truths of Our Catholic Faith

It may seem an exaggeration to say that no one knows the Father except the Son; yet in the deepest sense this is entirely true. Only Jesus is both divine and human. For this reason He is uniquely qualified to intercede on our behalf, and in turn to reveal God's own truth to us for our eternal benefit.

> *Jesus Christ is true God and true man, in the unity of his divine person; for this reason he is the one and only mediator between God and men. (CCC 480)*

In giving praise to our Father, Jesus demonstrates one of five basic prayer forms. Along with blessing, petition, intercession and thanksgiving, praise forms the basis for each Christian's prayer life. The Holy Spirit helps us express prayers of several sorts to the living God who the Son has revealed to us.

> *The Holy Spirit who teaches the Church and recalls to her all that Jesus said also instructs her in the life of prayer, inspiring new expressions of the same basic forms of prayer: blessing, petition, intercession, thanksgiving, and praise.* (CCC 2644)

A Question for Me

What basic prayer form occupies most of my prayer time, and to what form ought I pay a bit more attention?

For a Child in My Life

Why is Jesus the best person to go between God and us?

My Role in the Community

For whom in my communities do I need to engage in intercessory prayer?

For Depth and Further Life Application

Zechariah 9:9–10
Psalm 145
Romans 8:9, 11–13

📖 United States Catholic Catechism for Adults, pages 476–478

REFLECTION

Blessed are you, Father, Lord of heaven and earth; you have revealed to little ones the mysteries of the kingdom.

—cf. Matthew 11:25

A Fifteenth Sunday of Ordinary Time

The Gospel

On that day, Jesus went out of the house and sat down by the sea.
Such large crowds gathered around him
that he got into a boat and sat down,
and the whole crowd stood along the shore.
And he spoke to them at length in parables, saying:
"A sower went out to sow.
And as he sowed, some seed fell on the path,
and birds came and ate it up.
Some fell on rocky ground, where it had little soil.
It sprang up at once because the soil was not deep,
and when the sun rose it was scorched,
and it withered for lack of roots.
Some seed fell among thorns, and the thorns grew up and choked it.
But some seed fell on rich soil and produced fruit,
a hundred or sixty or thirtyfold.
Whoever has ears ought to hear."

—Matthew 13:1–9

Truths of Our Catholic Faith

If you use your ears, chances are you'll be able to hear. Similarly, when you become and remain aware of all the signs of God around you and within you, a sense of certitude about His abiding presence can stay with you, helping you to bear abundant fruit.

> *When he listens to the message of creation and to the voice of conscience, man can arrive at certainty about the existence of God, the cause and the end of everything. (CCC 46)*

To produce fruit and remain on the path of goodness, you must listen for and hear the voice of your conscience. In the end, the conscience is a very practical faculty, helping you make the right decisions in ordinary and even some extraordinary instances.

Conscience is a judgment of reason by which the human person recognizes the moral quality of a concrete act. (CCC 1796)

A Question for Me
What traits of God are evident simply by looking at all He has created?

For a Child in My Life
What can you tell about God just by looking at everything He's made?

My Role in the Community
To whom in my communities should I listen more closely?

For Depth and Further Life Application

Isaiah 55:10–11
Psalm 65
Romans 8:18–23

📖 United States Catholic Catechism for Adults, pages 570–576

REFLECTION

The seed is the word of God, Christ is the sower. All who come to him will have life forever.

A Sixteenth Sunday of Ordinary Time

The Gospel

Jesus proposed another parable to the crowds, saying:
"The kingdom of heaven may be likened to a man
who sowed good seed in his field.
While everyone was asleep his enemy came
and sowed weeds all through the wheat, and then went off.
When the crop grew and bore fruit, the weeds appeared as well.
The slaves of the householder came to him and said,
'Master, did you not sow good seed in your field?
Where have the weeds come from?'
He answered, 'An enemy has done this.'
His slaves said to him, 'Do you want us to go and pull them up?'
He replied, 'No, if you pull up the weeds
you might uproot the wheat along with them.
Let them grow together until harvest;
then at harvest time I will say to the harvesters,
"First collect the weeds and tie them in bundles for burning;
but gather the wheat into my barn."'"

—Matthew 13:24–30

Truths of Our Catholic Faith

The harvest time. Time for the harvesters to gather the wheat and collect the weeds to burn them.

It is probably a good idea to recall, at least every now and then, that you will be harvested one day. What will the Master do with you?

> *Every man receives his eternal recompense in his immortal soul from the moment of his death in a particular judgment by Christ, the judge of the living and the dead. (CCC 1051)*

In the wheatfield of your moral life, you may experience a serious crop disease. If you are like many people, though, your main problem is going to be weeds.

Just as even a single, small weed should not be entirely

ignored, any sin if left unattended can repeat itself and lead to very serious problems—maybe even a bad harvest.

> *The repetition of sins—even venial ones—engenders vices, among which are the capital sins.* (CCC 1876)

A Question for Me

Of the seven capital sins—pride, covetousness, lust, anger, greed, envy and sloth—which troubles me the most? How might I amend my life to do better in this area?

For a Child in My Life

What happens to the weeds at the end of Jesus' parable? What happens to the wheat? What do you suppose this all means for you and me?

My Role in the Community

How might I help raise awareness of what contributes to the seven capital sins' prominence in my community?

For Depth and Further Life Application

Wisdom 12:13, 16–19
Psalm 86
Romans 8:26–27

📖 United States Catholic Catechism for Adults, pages 509–511

REFLECTION

Blessed are you, Father, Lord of heaven and earth; you have revealed to little ones the mysteries of the kingdom.

—cf. Matthew 11:25

A Seventeenth Sunday of Ordinary Time

The Gospel

Jesus said to his disciples:
"The kingdom of heaven is like a treasure buried in a field,
which a person finds and hides again,
and out of joy goes and sells all that he has and buys that field.
Again, the kingdom of heaven is like a merchant
searching for fine pearls.
When he finds a pearl of great price,
he goes and sells all that he has and buys it.
Again, the kingdom of heaven is like a net thrown into the sea,
which collects fish of every kind.
When it is full they haul it ashore
and sit down to put what is good into buckets.
What is bad they throw away.
Thus it will be at the end of the age.
The angels will go out and separate the wicked from the righteous
and throw them into the fiery furnace,
where there will be wailing and grinding of teeth.

"Do you understand all these things?"
They answered, "Yes."
And he replied,
"Then every scribe who has been instructed
in the kingdom of heaven
is like the head of a household
who brings from his storeroom both the new and the old."

—Matthew 13:44–52

Truths of Our Catholic Faith

The treasure in this parable is not created by the person finding it. Similarly, although your collaboration may allow you to attain eternal life in God's heavenly kingdom, His grace is ultimately the only thing that makes eternal life possible in the first place.

We can have merit in God's sight only because of God's free plan to associate man with the work of his grace. Merit is to be ascribed in the first place to the grace of God, and secondly to man's collaboration. Man's merit is due to God. (CCC 2025)

A scribe instructed in the kingdom would be familiar with salvation history up to the time of Jesus, plus be open to the Good News proclaimed by this God-Man. The law of the Old Testament prepares the way in many ways for the saving message and action of our Lord Jesus.

The Old Law is a preparation for the Gospel. (CCC 1982)

A Question for Me

When I consider that all my merit is due to God, what thoughts and feelings come to my mind and heart?

For a Child in My Life

What word does Jesus use to express the feeling of the person who finds the treasure buried in a field? How do you think Jesus might want you to feel as one of His friends and followers?

My Role in the Community

The words liberal and conservative are mistakenly used in relation to Catholic belief and practice. Like the household head who draws from both old and new, orthodox Catholics are neither moderate, conservative nor liberal; they are simply orthodox, which makes them liberal to some and conservative to others. Next time you hear these terms bandied about in a conversation about Catholicism, consider a polite challenge along these lines.

For Depth and Further Life Application

1 Kings 3:5, 7–12
Psalm 119
Romans 8:28–30

📖 United States Catholic Catechism for Adults, page 533

REFLECTION

Blessed are you Father, Lord of heaven and earth; for you have revealed to little ones the mysteries of the kingdom.

—cf. Matthew 11:25

 Eighteenth Sunday of Ordinary Time

The Gospel

When Jesus heard of the death of John the Baptist,
he withdrew in a boat to a deserted place by himself.
The crowds heard of this and followed him on foot from their towns.
When he disembarked and saw the vast crowd,
his heart was moved with pity for them, and he cured their sick.
When it was evening, the disciples approached him and said,
"This is a deserted place and it is already late;
dismiss the crowds so that they can go to the villages
and buy food for themselves."
Jesus said to them, "There is no need for them to go away;
give them some food yourselves."
But they said to him,
"Five loaves and two fish are all we have here."
Then he said, "Bring them here to me, "
and he ordered the crowds to sit down on the grass.
Taking the five loaves and the two fish, and looking up to heaven,
he said the blessing, broke the loaves,
and gave them to the disciples,
who in turn gave them to the crowds.
They all ate and were satisfied,
and they picked up the fragments left over—
twelve wicker baskets full.
Those who ate were about five thousand men,
not counting women and children.

—Matthew 14:13–21

Truths of Our Catholic Faith

Jesus' heart was moved when He saw the people. The warmth of His love showed itself in miraculous cures and the feeding of over 5,000 children, women and men.

Our Church has a warm invitation for us. She encourages us to receive the Bread of Life—Jesus in the Most Holy Eucharist—on a regular basis.

> *The Church warmly recommends that the faithful receive Holy Communion when they participate in the celebration of the Eucharist; she obliges them to do so at least once a year. (CCC 1417)*

The connection you feel to your fellow human persons is known as solidarity. Solidarity obliges us to be concerned with the well-being of all our sisters and brothers in the human family.

In living out solidarity, physical well-being isn't our exclusive or even our primary concern. Because human persons consist of both body and soul, the spiritual health of others is an area where we can and should try to be of help.

> *Solidarity is an eminently Christian virtue. It practices the sharing of spiritual goods even more than material ones. (CCC 1948)*

A Question for Me

What is my comfort level with Jesus performing miracles? Do I try to explain them away, or can I accept the fact that the author of nature's laws can choose to alter them occasionally for a good purpose?

For a Child in My Life

Jesus takes bread, blesses it, breaks it and gives it to people. When else do you see a man take bread, bless it, break it and give it out?

My Role in the Community

What does the sharing of spiritual goods mean? How can I share spiritual goods with sisters and brothers in my community?

For Depth and Further Life Application

Isaiah 55:1–3
Psalm 145
Romans 8:35, 37–39

📖 United States Catholic Catechism for Adults, pages 577–583

REFLECTION

One does not live on bread alone, but on every word that comes forth from the mouth of God.

—Matthew 4:4b

A Nineteenth Sunday of Ordinary Time

The Gospel

After he had fed the people, Jesus made the disciples get into a boat
and precede him to the other side,
while he dismissed the crowds.
After doing so, he went up on the mountain by himself to pray.
When it was evening he was there alone.
Meanwhile the boat, already a few miles offshore,
was being tossed about by the waves, for the wind was against it.
During the fourth watch of the night,
he came toward them walking on the sea.
When the disciples saw him walking on the sea they were terrified.
"It is a ghost," they said, and they cried out in fear.
At once Jesus spoke to them, "Take courage, it is I; do not be afraid."
Peter said to him in reply,
"Lord, if it is you, command me to come to you on the water."
He said, "Come."
Peter got out of the boat and began to walk on the water toward
Jesus.
But when he saw how strong the wind was he became frightened;
and, beginning to sink, he cried out, "Lord, save me!"
Immediately Jesus stretched out his hand and caught Peter,
and said to him, "O you of little faith, why did you doubt?"
After they got into the boat, the wind died down.
Those who were in the boat did him homage, saying,
"Truly, you are the Son of God."

—Matthew 14:22–33

Truths of Our Catholic Faith

Jesus chastises Peter for having little faith. Let your faith be big! Jesus tells you not to be afraid. Be attentive to His words and deeds. Ask Him to save you, and Jesus will continue revealing Himself to you as being truly and faithfully God's beloved Son.

> *Faith is a personal adherence of the whole man to God who reveals himself. It involves an assent of the intellect*

> *and will to the self-revelation God has made through his deeds and words.* (CCC 176)

Distractions could have been plenty for Jesus. He remained vigilant against being sidetracked from His prayer relationship with the Father.

You, too, can make the sacrifices necessary for a vibrant prayer life—benefiting far more than anything you might give up to help this occur. Turning away from sin, turning toward our Father, you will weather the strong winds, caught by Jesus' outstretched hand.

> *The principal difficulties in the practice of prayer are distraction and dryness. The remedy lies in faith, conversion, and vigilance of heart.* (CCC 2754)

A Question for Me

How might I better follow Jesus' example of making time to pray?

For a Child in My Life

Why did Jesus go up on the mountain? What did Peter cry out when he began to sink? What did everyone in the boat say after the wind died down?

My Role in the Community

What example do I set for those around me regarding the priority of prayer? How do I encourage and allow others to have an active, healthy prayer life?

For Depth and Further Life Application

1 Kings 19:9a, 11–13a
Psalm 85
Romans 9:1–5

📖 United States Catholic Catechism for Adults, pages 478–480

REFLECTION

I wait for the Lord; my soul waits for his word.

—cf. Psalm 130:5

A Twentieth Sunday of Ordinary Time

The Gospel

At that time, Jesus withdrew to the region of Tyre and Sidon.
And behold, a Canaanite woman of that district came and called out,
"Have pity on me, Lord, Son of David!
My daughter is tormented by a demon."
But Jesus did not say a word in answer to her.
Jesus' disciples came and asked him,
"Send her away, for she keeps calling out after us."
He said in reply,
"I was sent only to the lost sheep of the house of Israel."
But the woman came and did Jesus homage, saying, "Lord, help me."
He said in reply,
"It is not right to take the food of the children
and throw it to the dogs."
She said, "Please, Lord, for even the dogs eat the scraps
that fall from the table of their masters."
Then Jesus said to her in reply,
"O woman, great is your faith!
Let it be done for you as you wish."
And the woman's daughter was healed from that hour.

—Matthew 15:21–28

Truths of Our Catholic Faith

Women of great faith were no strangers to Jesus. He was raised by a woman who possessed and enjoyed a tremendous faith life.

In a sense, Mary had been a coworker with her Son for many years. Like the woman in this Gospel passage who intercedes on behalf of her daughter, our Blessed Mother continually takes our needs and concerns to her Son, our brother Jesus.

> *By pronouncing her "fiat" at the Annunciation and giving her consent to the Incarnation, Mary was already collaborating with the whole work her Son was to accomplish. She is mother wherever he is Savior and head of the Mystical Body. (CCC 973)*

The Canaanite woman invited Jesus in to her home, figuratively at least, to make it whole, healthy and happy. Our homes need to be places where the Lord is welcome—sought after, actually.

Family life can be tough in its own way. The grace of Holy Matrimony, though, when we are open to it, can combat demons that sometimes wreak havoc on society by attacking its most basic building blocks: families. Jesus will do for us as we wish, when we wish to make our homes virtuous, loving and prayerful.

> *The Christian home is the place where children receive the first proclamation of the faith. For this reason the family home is rightly called "the domestic church," a community of grace and prayer, a school of human virtues and of Christian charity. (CCC 1666)*

A Question for Me

Being assertive is not the same as being aggressive. The Canaanite woman is assertive. How assertive am I when I need to be in order to help God's will be done?

For a Child in My Life

Who said yes and allowed the baby Jesus to be born?

My Role in the Community

My family is my primary community, and the building block on whom the stability of every other community essentially depends. How's my role in the family going?

For Depth and Further Life Application

Isaiah 56:1, 6–7
Psalm 67
Romans 11:13–15, 29–32

📖 United States Catholic Catechism for Adults, pages 277–278

REFLECTION

Jesus proclaimed the Gospel of the kingdom and cured every disease among the people.

—cf. Matthew 4:23

A Twenty-first Sunday of Ordinary Time

The Gospel

Jesus went into the region of Caesarea Philippi and
he asked his disciples,
"Who do people say that the Son of Man is?"
They replied, "Some say John the Baptist, others Elijah,
still others Jeremiah or one of the prophets."
He said to them, "But who do you say that I am?"
Simon Peter said in reply,
"You are the Christ, the Son of the living God."
Jesus said to him in reply,
"Blessed are you, Simon son of Jonah.
For flesh and blood has not revealed this to you,
but my heavenly Father.
And so I say to you, you are Peter,
and upon this rock I will build my church,
and the gates of the netherworld shall not prevail against it.
I will give you the keys to the kingdom of heaven.
Whatever you bind on earth shall be bound in heaven;
and whatever you loose on earth shall be loosed in heaven."
Then he strictly ordered his disciples
to tell no one that he was the Christ.

—Matthew 16:13–20

Truths of Our Catholic Faith

Jewish people of Jesus' time were waiting for the Christ, the Messiah, the Anointed One. They weren't in complete agreement among themselves exactly what the Christ would be like, but they knew that God was sending them someone very special.

Peter makes the connection that this Christ is somehow on the same level as God almighty. This mystery forms the basis of a whole religion, Christianity. Christians believe that Jesus, the Son of God, is THE Anointed One, the promised Messiah, the Christ.

The title "Christ" means "Anointed One" (Messiah). Jesus is the Christ, for "God anointed Jesus of Nazareth with the Holy Spirit and with power" (Acts *10:38). He*

> *was the one "who is to come"* (Lk *7:19), the object of "the hope of Israel"* (Acts *28:20). (CCC 453)*

To say that Jesus gives Peter tremendous power and authority is an understatement. Had Jesus not modeled the way that power needs to be used—in service of others, spiritually even more so than physically—the thought of Him giving such power to one man might be frightening.

Catholics take comfort in knowing that one man—a man, yes, but a man guided in an entirely unique way by the Holy Spirit—has been entrusted by our Church's founder with the authority to shepherd souls toward the heavenly pasture. Flesh and blood has not so endowed the successor of Peter, the Bishop of Rome, but rather this arrangement is instituted by our heavenly Father.

> *The Pope enjoys, by divine institution, "supreme, full, immediate, and universal power in the care of souls"* (CD *2). (CCC 937)*

A Question for Me

I don't use the word Christ in any non-prayerful situations, now, do I?

For a Child in My Life

Who revealed to Peter that Jesus is the Christ, the Son of the living God?

My Role in the Community

Next time you're in a social setting, depending on how adventurous you're feeling, pose the question—who would you say that Jesus is?

For Depth and Further Life Application

Isaiah 22:19–23
Psalm 138
Romans 11:33–36

United States Catholic Catechism for Adults, pages125–126

REFLECTION

You are Peter and upon this rock I will build my Church and the gates of the netherworld shall not prevail against it.

—Matthew 16:18

A Twenty-second Sunday of Ordinary Time

The Gospel

Jesus began to show his disciples
that he must go to Jerusalem and suffer greatly
from the elders, the chief priests, and the scribes,
and be killed and on the third day be raised.
Then Peter took Jesus aside and began to rebuke him,
"God forbid, Lord! No such thing shall ever happen to you."
He turned and said to Peter,
"Get behind me, Satan! You are an obstacle to me.
You are thinking not as God does, but as human beings do."

Then Jesus said to his disciples,
"Whoever wishes to come after me must deny himself,
take up his cross, and follow me.
For whoever wishes to save his life will lose it,
but whoever loses his life for my sake will find it.
What profit would there be for one to gain the whole world
and forfeit his life?
Or what can one give in exchange for his life?
For the Son of Man will come with his angels in his Father's glory,
and then he will repay all according to his conduct."

—Matthew 16:21–27

Truths of Our Catholic Faith

Peter was understandably shocked at the thought of Jesus suffering and dying. Peter's way of thinking could have led to Jesus foregoing the suffering and death that was His Father's mysterious will.

Jesus didn't refuse to do what was asked of Him. He embraced His own Paschal mystery—His suffering, death, and resurrection—out of love for you.

> *To the benefit of every man, Jesus Christ tasted death (cf.* Heb 2:9*). It is truly the Son of God made man who died and was buried.* (CCC 629)

If you gain the whole world, then another person or persons must lose it. Our world offers enough resources for all. It all comes down to providing for yourself without making it overly difficult for others to do the same.

When you see unhealthy grabbing for money and power, you are obligated to say or do something to reverse that trend for the sake of the haves as well as the have-nots. You do not do people a favor by allowing them to live in unhealthy excess. After all, their eternity might not go so well without a change of heart.

> *The equal dignity of human persons requires the effort to reduce excessive social and economic inequalities. It gives urgency to the elimination of sinful inequalities. (CCC 1947)*

A Question for Me

Apparently God does not always think the way human beings think. What current events or issues come to mind that make this clear?

For a Child in My Life

What does Jesus say he will repay you according to?

My Role in the Community

What are some ways I can work to reduce or eliminate excessive and sinful social and economic inequalities?

For Depth and Further Life Application

Jeremiah 20:7–9
Psalm 63
Romans 12:1–2

📖 United States Catholic Catechism for Adults, pages 323–324

REFLECTION

May the Father of our Lord Jesus Christ enlighten the eyes of our hearts, that we may know what is the hope that belongs to our call.

—cf. Ephesians 1:17–18

A Twenty-third Sunday of Ordinary Time

The Gospel

Jesus said to his disciples:
"If your brother sins against you,
go and tell him his fault between you and him alone.
If he listens to you, you have won over your brother.
If he does not listen,
take one or two others along with you,
so that 'every fact may be established
on the testimony of two or three witnesses.'
If he refuses to listen to them, tell the church.
If he refuses to listen even to the church,
then treat him as you would a Gentile or a tax collector.
Amen, I say to you,
whatever you bind on earth shall be bound in heaven,
and whatever you loose on earth shall be loosed in heaven.
Again, amen, I say to you,
if two of you agree on earth
about anything for which they are to pray,
it shall be granted to them by my heavenly Father.
For where two or three are gathered together in my name,
there am I in the midst of them."

—Matthew 18:15–20

Truths of Our Catholic Faith

Jesus gives His apostles the power to forgive sins in His name. His Church makes available to you the normal, ordinary means of addressing sins that you commit after baptism. It is His will that you celebrate the Sacrament of Penance.

> *By Christ's will, the Church possesses the power to forgive the sins of the baptized and exercises it through bishops and priests normally in the sacrament of Penance. (CCC 986)*

Celebrating the Sacrament of Penance requires a careful examination of conscience. Because sin involves both your relationship with God and your responsibilities in the Body of Christ, sacramental confession is the ordinary means—the normal way—that God wills you to seek reconciliation for mortal as well as venial sins.

> *One who desires to obtain reconciliation with God and with the Church, must confess to a priest all the unconfessed grave sins he remembers after having carefully examined his conscience. The confession of venial faults, without being necessary in itself, is nevertheless strongly recommended by the Church.* (CCC 1493)

A Question for Me

How often and how carefully do I examine my conscience?

For a Child in My Life

Who gives bishops and priests the power to forgive sins in the Sacrament of Penance?

My Role in the Community

When someone sins against me, do I first go to that person and that person alone to address the situation?

For Depth and Further Life Application

Ezekiel 33:7–9
Psalm 95
Romans 13:8–10

📖 United States Catholic Catechism for Adults, pages 233–234

REFLECTION

God was reconciling the world to himself in Christ and entrusting to us the message of reconciliation.

—2 Corinthians 5:19

A Twenty-fourth Sunday of Ordinary Time

The Gospel

Peter approached Jesus and asked him,
"Lord, if my brother sins against me,
how often must I forgive?
As many as seven times?"
Jesus answered, "I say to you, not seven times
but seventy-seven times.
That is why the kingdom of heaven may be likened to a king
who decided to settle accounts with his servants.
When he began the accounting,
a debtor was brought before him who owed him a huge amount.
Since he had no way of paying it back,
his master ordered him to be sold,
along with his wife, his children, and all his property,
in payment of the debt.
At that, the servant fell down, did him homage, and said,
'Be patient with me, and I will pay you back in full.'
Moved with compassion the master of that servant
let him go and forgave him the loan.
When that servant had left, he found one of his fellow servants
who owed him a much smaller amount.
He seized him and started to choke him, demanding,
'Pay back what you owe.'
Falling to his knees, his fellow servant begged him,
'Be patient with me, and I will pay you back.'
But he refused.
Instead, he had the fellow servant put in prison
until he paid back the debt.
Now when his fellow servants saw what had happened,
they were deeply disturbed, and went to their master
and reported the whole affair.
His master summoned him and said to him, 'You wicked servant!
I forgave you your entire debt because you begged me to.
Should you not have had pity on your fellow servant,
as I had pity on you?'
Then in anger his master handed him over to the torturers
until he should pay back the whole debt.

> So will my heavenly Father do to you,
> unless each of you forgives your brother from your heart."
>
> —Matthew 18:21–35

Truths of Our Catholic Faith

The first debtor forgot that he was shown an excellent work of mercy, or he chose to ignore it out of self-centeredness. None-the-less he, like us, has been treated most mercifully in an undeservedly good way.

Through Jesus, our Father freely gives us His gift of everlasting life. He asks that we live lives of great gratitude, forgiving our sisters and brothers from our heart.

> *Justification has been merited for us by the Passion of Christ. It is granted us through Baptism. It conforms us to the righteousness of God, who justifies us. It has for its goal the glory of God and of Christ, and the gift of eternal life. It is the most excellent work of God's mercy. (CCC 2020)*

Many of Jesus' parables help us understand the personality of the Father in hopes that we will imitate Him as well as following the example of Jesus. The Holy Spirit can enkindle in us the desire to live a more Godly life. Through prayer—especially the Lord's Prayer—our hearts can learn to trust in healthy humility, open to receiving and giving in turn great forgiveness and mercy.

> *Praying to our Father should develop in us the will to become like him and foster in us a humble and trusting heart. (CCC 2800)*

A Question for Me

How would I describe my heart in terms of it being humble and trusting?

For a Child in My Life

What are some ways you and I can be like God?

My Role in the Community

Recall a person who has shown you forgiveness to some significant degree. Go out of your way to thank that person within the next couple of days.

For Depth and Further Life Application

Sirach 27:30–28:9
Psalm 103
Romans 14:7–9

📖 United States Catholic Catechism for Adults, pages 483–490

REFLECTION

I give you a new commandment, says the Lord; love one another as I have loved you.

—John 13:34

A Twenty-fifth Sunday of Ordinary Time

The Gospel

Jesus told his disciples this parable:
"The kingdom of heaven is like a landowner
who went out at dawn to hire laborers for his vineyard.
After agreeing with them for the usual daily wage,
he sent them into his vineyard.
Going out about nine o'clock,
the landowner saw others standing idle in the marketplace,
and he said to them, 'You too go into my vineyard,
and I will give you what is just.'
So they went off.
And he went out again around noon,
and around three o'clock, and did likewise.
Going out about five o'clock,
the landowner found others standing around, and said to them,
'Why do you stand here idle all day?'
They answered, 'Because no one has hired us.'
He said to them, 'You too go into my vineyard.'
When it was evening the owner of the vineyard said to his foreman,
'Summon the laborers and give them their pay,
beginning with the last and ending with the first.'
When those who had started about five o'clock came,
each received the usual daily wage.
So when the first came, they thought that they would receive more,
but each of them also got the usual wage.
And on receiving it they grumbled against the landowner, saying,
'These last ones worked only one hour,
and you have made them equal to us,
who bore the day's burden and the heat.'
He said to one of them in reply,
'My friend, I am not cheating you.
Did you not agree with me for the usual daily wage?
Take what is yours and go.
What if I wish to give this last one the same as you?
Or am I not free to do as I wish with my own money?
Are you envious because I am generous?'
Thus, the last will be first, and the first will be last."

—Matthew 20:1–16a

Truths of Our Catholic Faith

God is indeed generous. Sheer generosity and love motivated God to create our universe and rests behind the fact that He sustains our existence day-by-day.

The Lord God is free to do as He wishes, and God chooses to love you.

> *By love, God has revealed himself and given himself to man. He has thus provided the definitive, superabundant answer to the questions that man asks himself about the meaning and purpose of his life.* (CCC 68)

Being envious is a problem. Grumbling against others. Inappropriately wanting to have what another possesses.

Envy is an attitude that often leads to action—bad action. That is why the Ten Commandments end with a warning against this dangerous vice.

> *Envy is sadness at the sight of another's goods and the immoderate desire to have them for oneself. It is a capital sin.* (CCC 2553)

A Question for Me

How hard do I try to be first at various endeavors? Do I do so with an awareness that God doesn't always judge things the way we do?

For a Child in My Life

Why has God revealed himself and given himself to us?

My Role in the Community

What effects do I see envy having in my various communities? What role might envy play in my own life?

For Depth and Further Life Application

Isaiah 55:6–9
Psalm 145
Philippians 1:20c–24, 27a

United States Catholic Catechism for Adults, pages 454–455

REFLECTION

Open our hearts, O Lord, to listen to the words of your Son.

—cf. Acts of the Apostles 16:14b

Twenty-sixth Sunday of Ordinary Time

The Gospel

Jesus said to the chief priests and elders of the people:
"What is your opinion?
A man had two sons.
He came to the first and said,
'Son, go out and work in the vineyard today.'
He said in reply, 'I will not, '
but afterwards changed his mind and went.
The man came to the other son and gave the same order.
He said in reply, 'Yes, sir, 'but did not go.
Which of the two did his father's will?"
They answered, "The first."
Jesus said to them, "Amen, I say to you,
tax collectors and prostitutes
are entering the kingdom of God before you.
When John came to you in the way of righteousness,
you did not believe him;
but tax collectors and prostitutes did.
Yet even when you saw that,
you did not later change your minds and believe him."

—Matthew 21:28–32

Truths of Our Catholic Faith

Sinners of various sorts took John the Baptist's words to heart. They changed their hearts, their minds, their ways. They experienced significant spiritual effects.

When we turn from sin toward a fuller citizenship in God's kingdom, we enjoy spiritual effects as well. God's will for how we address our sin, the Sacrament of Penance, helps us in several noticeable ways.

The spiritual effects of the Sacrament of Penance are:

† *reconciliation with God by which the penitent recovers grace;*

† *reconciliation with the Church;*

- † *remission of the eternal punishment incurred by mortal sins;*
- † *remission, at least in part, of temporal punishments resulting from sin;*
- † *peace and serenity of conscience, and spiritual consolation;*
- † *an increase of spiritual strength for the Christian battle.* (CCC 1496)

Cheating people out of money, as these tax collectors did, is wrong. Even if such a tax collector used this ill-gotten money to do something good, such as providing for his family, the act of cheating is still morally evil.

The temptation to justify an objectively evil act by using it for good has been around for a long time, and it is still a temptation toward something sinful. These are human actions that are always wrong to pursue; therefore, they should be avoided as either a goal or a means to an end.

> *There are concrete acts that it is always wrong to choose, because their choice entails a disorder of the will, i.e., a moral evil. One may not do evil so that good may result from it.* (CCC 1761)

A Question for Me

Although it can be hard, how willing am I to change my mind and admit I have changed it when I am wrong about something.

For a Child in My Life

Tell me some of the effects of celebrating the Sacrament of Penance.

My Role in the Community

What evil acts are permitted by law in my various communities? What action might I take to alter these laws for the better?

For Depth and Further Life Application

Ezekiel 18:25–28
Psalm 103:25
Philippians 2:1–11

📖 United States Catholic Catechism for Adults, pages 324–331

REFLECTION

My sheep hear my voice, says the Lord; I know them, and they follow me.

—John 10:27

A Twenty-seventh Sunday of Ordinary Time

The Gospel

Jesus said to the chief priests and the elders of the people:
"Hear another parable.
There was a landowner who planted a vineyard,
put a hedge around it, dug a wine press in it, and built a tower.
Then he leased it to tenants and went on a journey.
When vintage time drew near,
he sent his servants to the tenants to obtain his produce.
But the tenants seized the servants and one they beat,
another they killed, and a third they stoned.
Again he sent other servants, more numerous than the first ones,
but they treated them in the same way.
Finally, he sent his son to them, thinking,
'They will respect my son.'
But when the tenants saw the son, they said to one another,
'This is the heir.
Come, let us kill him and acquire his inheritance.'
They seized him, threw him out of the vineyard, and killed him.
What will the owner of the vineyard do to those tenants
when he comes?"
They answered him,
"He will put those wretched men to a wretched death
and lease his vineyard to other tenants
who will give him the produce at the proper times."
Jesus said to them, "Did you never read in the Scriptures:
The stone that the builders rejected
has become the cornerstone;
by the Lord has this been done,
and it is wonderful in our eyes?
Therefore, I say to you,
the kingdom of God will be taken away from you
and given to a people that will produce its fruit."

—Matthew 21:33–43

Truths of Our Catholic Faith

Jesus' harsh words to the Jewish leaders are sometimes misinterpreted as a rejection of Jewish people as an entire group.

Understanding the context of Jesus' remarks can help you keep all people of Jewish faith in a proper perspective.

> *. . . [N]either all Jews indiscriminately at that time, nor Jews today, can be charged with the crimes committed during his Passion. . . . [T]he Jews should not be spoken of as rejected or accursed as if this followed from holy Scripture.[1] (CCC 597)*

The tenants in Jesus' parable did something instantly recognized as sinful by His hearers. Murder has a tendency to be abhorrent because it seizes a power that belongs rightfully to God—that of determining when a person's life should end. The perpetrators in this parable are considered wretched due to their sinful act.

> *The murder of a human being is gravely contrary to the dignity of the person and the holiness of the Creator. (CCC 2320)*

A Question for Me

In what ways am I producing the fruit of God's kingdom?

For a Child in My Life

What does it mean to say that the stone rejected by the builders has become the cornerstone of the building?

My Role in the Community

What signs of anti-Semitism are present in my communities, and what is my role in alleviating this unjust attitude?

For Depth and Further Life Application

Isaiah 5:1–7
Psalm 80
Philippians 4:6–9

United States Catholic Catechism for Adults, pages 387–398

REFLECTION

I have chosen you from the world, says the Lord, to go and bear fruit that will remain.

—cf. John 15:16

A Twenty-eighth Sunday of Ordinary Time

The Gospel

Jesus again in reply spoke to the chief priests and elders of the people
in parables, saying,
"The kingdom of heaven may be likened to a king
who gave a wedding feast for his son.
He dispatched his servants
to summon the invited guests to the feast,
but they refused to come.
A second time he sent other servants, saying,
'Tell those invited: "Behold, I have prepared my banquet,
my calves and fattened cattle are killed,
and everything is ready; come to the feast."'
Some ignored the invitation and went away,
one to his farm, another to his business.
The rest laid hold of his servants,
mistreated them, and killed them.
The king was enraged and sent his troops,
destroyed those murderers, and burned their city.
Then he said to his servants, 'The feast is ready,
but those who were invited were not worthy to come.
Go out, therefore, into the main roads
and invite to the feast whomever you find.'
The servants went out into the streets
and gathered all they found, bad and good alike,
and the hall was filled with guests."

—Matthew 22:1–10

Truths of Our Catholic Faith

Like the king who tells his servants to invite large numbers of people to the feast, God wants us to share the Good News of salvation through His Son with as many people as we can. Trying to find ways—some subtle, some a bit more obvious—to inform and encourage people to journey with Jesus is not really optional for those who would claim membership in the Church that He founded.

> The missionary mandate. *"Having been divinely sent to the nations that she might be 'the universal sacrament of salvation,' the Church, in obedience to the command of her founder and because it is demanded by her own essential universality, strives to preach the Gospel to all men":*[2] *"Go therefore and make disciples of all nations, baptizing them in the name of the Father and of the Son and of the Holy Spirit, teaching them to observe all that I have commanded you; and Lo, I am with you always, until the close of the age."*[3] *(CCC 849)*

God invites all of us to develop the potential that He's given to each of us. In order to develop fully in a healthy way, we need to live in community with the other guests at the banquet hall. When we help each other reach fulfillment as daughters and sons of our heavenly Father, we are seeing to the presence of what is known as the common good.

> *The common good comprises "the sum total of social conditions which allow people, either as groups or as individuals, to reach their fulfillment more fully and more easily"* (GS 26 § 1). *(CCC 1924)*

A Question for Me

What might it mean to reach my fulfillment? How well, how fully, am I attaining this goal?

For a Child in My Life

Who insists that Church members tell other people about Jesus and salvation?

My Role in the Community

Preaching the Gospel to all men is a tall order, but you have to start somewhere. What are some ways I can share the good news of salvation through Jesus with sizable numbers of people in my communities?

For Depth and Further Life Application

Isaiah 25:6–10a
Psalm 23
Philippians 4:12–14, 19–20

📖 United States Catholic Catechism for Adults, pages 332–335

REFLECTION

May the Father of our Lord Jesus Christ enlighten the eyes of your hearts, so that we may know what is the hope that belongs to our call.

—cf. Ephesians 1:17–18

A Twenty-ninth Sunday of Ordinary Time

The Gospel

The Pharisees went off
and plotted how they might entrap Jesus in speech.
They sent their disciples to him, with the Herodians, saying,
"Teacher, we know that you are a truthful man
and that you teach the way of God in accordance with the truth.
And you are not concerned with anyone's opinion,
for you do not regard a person's status.
Tell us, then, what is your opinion:
Is it lawful to pay the census tax to Caesar or not?"
Knowing their malice, Jesus said,
"Why are you testing me, you hypocrites?
Show me the coin that pays the census tax."
Then they handed him the Roman coin.
He said to them, "Whose image is this and whose inscription?"
They replied, "Caesar's."
At that he said to them,
"Then repay to Caesar what belongs to Caesar
and to God what belongs to God."

—Matthew 22:15–21

Truths of Our Catholic Faith

Even Caesar belongs to God. And while it is tempting to separate Godly or religious things or people from the people and activities that supposedly make up the rest of life, the fact is that all of us are called to holiness. Lay people especially are expected to take into the realm of Caesar that which reflects God's loving will—to permeate society with love and life as our holy, mighty, immortal Father sees them.

> *Lay people share in Christ's priesthood: ever more united with him, they exhibit the grace of Baptism and Confirmation in all dimensions of their personal, family, social, and ecclesial lives, and so fulfill the call to holiness addressed to all the baptized. (CCC 941)*

Repaying to God what belongs to God is lived out in part by observing the Lord's Day. The importance of resting from worldly pursuits so as to keep a proper perspective cannot be overstated.

Keeping Sunday holy helps keep you healthy. Rest. Enjoy. Receive the blessings of your generous God.

> *Sunday, the "Lord's Day," is the principal day for the celebration of the Eucharist because it is the day of the Resurrection. It is the pre-eminent day of the liturgical assembly, the day of the Christian family, and the day of joy and rest from work. Sunday is "the foundation and kernel of the whole liturgical year"* (SC 106). *(CCC 1193)*

A Question for Me

How do I share in the priesthood of Jesus, fulfilling the call to holiness addressed to me through baptism?

For a Child in My Life

Why do we call Sunday the Lord's Day?

My Role in the Community

How honest am I when it comes to taxes—paying my fair share without overdoing it or taking dishonest deductions/credits?

For Depth and Further Life Application

Isaiah 45:1, 4–6
Psalm 96
Thessalonians 1:1–5b

United States Catholic Catechism for Adults, pages 165–166

REFLECTION

Shine like lights in the world as you hold on to the word of life.

—Philippians 2:15d, 16a

A Thirtieth Sunday of Ordinary Time

The Gospel

When the Pharisees heard that Jesus had silenced the Sadducees,
they gathered together, and one of them,
a scholar of the law tested him by asking,
"Teacher, which commandment in the law is the greatest?"
He said to him,
"You shall love the Lord, your God,
with all your heart,
with all your soul,
and with all your mind.
This is the greatest and the first commandment.
The second is like it:
You shall love your neighbor as yourself.
The whole law and the prophets depend on
these two commandments."

—Matthew 22:34–40

Truths of Our Catholic Faith

Jesus mentions the soul, distinguishing it from other aspects of the human person. Without your soul, you are not you. You consist of a soul that will live forever with your resurrected body.

> *"Man, though made of body and soul, is a unity"* (GS 14 § 1). *The doctrine of the faith affirms that the spiritual and immortal soul is created immediately by God. (CCC 382)*

Because we are all daughters and sons of God, each neighbor is in a sense your sister or brother. It pleases parents when children interact harmoniously. It pleases our Father when you love your sister and brother as yourself.

Together with your sisters and brothers, through the work of liturgy you express your all-encompassing love for the Lord, our God. By worshipping with the People of God you involve your mind, soul and heart in adoring and blessing the Father through our Brother and Savior, Jesus.

In the liturgy of the Church, God the Father is blessed and adored as the source of all the blessings of creation and salvation with which he has blessed us in his Son, in order to give us the Spirit of filial adoption. (CCC 1110)

A Question for Me

In what way do I love myself? Is it a healthy love that spills over to others? Or is my self love really a self-centeredness that harms the ability to love my neighbor?

For a Child in My Life

What did Jesus say when He was asked which commandment is the greatest?

My Role in the Community

What are some ways I will show an authentic love of neighbor this week?

For Depth and Further Life Application

Exodus 22:20–26
Psalm 18
Thessalonians 1:5c–10

📖 United States Catholic Catechism for Adults, pages 166–175

REFLECTION

Whoever loves me will keep my word, says the Lord, and my Father will love him and we will come to him.

—John 14:23

A Thirty-first Sunday of Ordinary Time

The Gospel

Jesus spoke to the crowds and to his disciples, saying,
"The scribes and the Pharisees
have taken their seat on the chair of Moses.
Therefore, do and observe all things whatsoever they tell you,
but do not follow their example.
For they preach but they do not practice.
They tie up heavy burdens hard to carry
and lay them on people's shoulders,
but they will not lift a finger to move them.
All their works are performed to be seen.
They widen their phylacteries and lengthen their tassels.
They love places of honor at banquets, seats of honor in synagogues,
greetings in marketplaces, and the salutation 'Rabbi.'
As for you, do not be called 'Rabbi.'
You have but one teacher, and you are all brothers.
Call no one on earth your father;
you have but one Father in heaven.
Do not be called 'Master';
you have but one master, the Christ.
The greatest among you must be your servant.
Whoever exalts himself will be humbled;
but whoever humbles himself will be exalted."

—Matthew 23:1–12

Truths of Our Catholic Faith

Jesus' words about calling no one father are sometimes taken out of context and used as an argument against ordained ministerial priesthood. The Lord certainly would not want you to consider any priest of God as being on the same level as God. In prayerfully choosing and calling the twelve Apostles, though, Jesus clearly had in mind a special role of service to His people.

The ministerial priesthood differs in essence from the common priesthood of the faithful because it confers a sacred power for the service of the faithful. The ordained ministers exercise their service for the People of God by

> *teaching* (munus docendi), *divine worship* (munus liturgicum) *and pastoral governance* (munus regendi). *(CCC 1592)*

The Lord chose His words very carefully. It was important to Him that the image of God as Father soaked deep in to the hearts of His listeners. Because of Jesus' revelation of truth about God's very nature—that of perfect parent who uses power to serve—we can affectionately think of the Exalted One essentially as our Dad in heaven.

> *We can invoke God as "Father" because the Son of God made man has revealed him to us. In this Son, through Baptism, we are incorporated and adopted as sons of God. (CCC 2798)*

A Question for Me

A hypocrite holds everyone to the highest of standards except her- or himself. Do I engage in any hypocrisy and, if so, how can I best put an end to it immediately?

For a Child in My Life

Who taught us to think of God as our heavenly Dad and to call him Father?

My Role in the Community

How might I do at least one good deed for others behind the scenes in order not to seek or receive any public recognition?

For Depth and Further Life Application

Malachi 1:14b–2:2b, 8–10
Psalm 131
Thessalonians 2:7b–9, 13

📖 United States Catholic Catechism for Adults, pages 490–492

REFLECTION

You have but one Father in heaven and one master, the Christ.

—Matthew 23:9b, 10b

A Thirty-second Sunday of Ordinary Time

The Gospel

Jesus told his disciples this parable:
"The kingdom of heaven will be like ten virgins
who took their lamps and went out to meet the bridegroom.
Five of them were foolish and five were wise.
The foolish ones, when taking their lamps,
brought no oil with them,
but the wise brought flasks of oil with their lamps.
Since the bridegroom was long delayed,
they all became drowsy and fell asleep.
At midnight, there was a cry,
'Behold, the bridegroom! Come out to meet him!'
Then all those virgins got up and trimmed their lamps.
The foolish ones said to the wise,
'Give us some of your oil,
for our lamps are going out.'
But the wise ones replied,
'No, for there may not be enough for us and you.
Go instead to the merchants and buy some for yourselves.'
While they went off to buy it,
the bridegroom came
and those who were ready went into the wedding feast with him.
Then the door was locked.
Afterwards the other virgins came and said,
'Lord, Lord, open the door for us!'
But he said in reply,
'Amen, I say to you, I do not know you.'
Therefore, stay awake,
for you know neither the day nor the hour."

—Matthew 25:1–13

Truths of Our Catholic Faith

Oil was quite a commodity in Jesus' day. In some ways things haven't changed.

Today, we also use oil for some of our sacraments, most notably, the Sacrament Confirmation. In this sacrament, we receive the Holy Spirit in a uniquely powerful way.

> *The essential rite of Confirmation is anointing the forehead of the baptized with sacred chrism (in the East other sense-organs as well), together with the laying on of the minister's hand and the words:* "Accipe signaculum doni Spiritus Sancti" *(Be sealed with the Gift of the Holy Spirit.) in the Roman rite, or:* Signaculum doni Spiritus Sancti *(the seal of the gift of the Holy Spirit) in the Byzantine rite. (CCC 1320)*

Jesus tells us to stay awake, to be mindful of His presence at all times. While it may not be feasible to pray in a formal sense during every waking moment of your life, you can certainly cultivate an awareness of God's presence and an appreciation of His many gifts. Christian life simply involves an attitude of prayerfulness.

> *"Pray constantly"* (1 Thess *5:17). It is always possible to pray. It is even a vital necessity. Prayer and Christian life are inseparable. (CCC 2757)*

A Question for Me

What are some ways that I can move closer to the idea of praying constantly?

For a Child in My Life

What words are said when a person receives the Sacrament of Confirmation?

My Role in the Community

What person or persons in my communities might I pray with this coming week? (e.g., if I have a meeting scheduled, can I begin it with a brief prayer?)

For Depth and Further Life Application

Wisdom 6:12–16
Psalm 63
Thessalonians 4:13–18

📖 United States Catholic Catechism for Adults, pages 207–210

REFLECTION

Stay awake and be ready! For you do not know in what day your Lord will come.

—Matthew 24:42a, 44

A Thirty-third Sunday of Ordinary Time

The Gospel

Jesus told his disciples this parable:
"A man going on a journey
called in his servants and entrusted his possessions to them.
To one he gave five talents; to another, two; to a third, one—
to each according to his ability.
Then he went away.

After a long time
the master of those servants came back
and settled accounts with them.
The one who had received five talents came forward
bringing the additional five.
He said, 'Master, you gave me five talents.
See, I have made five more.'
His master said to him, 'Well done, my good and faithful servant.
Since you were faithful in small matters,
I will give you great responsibilities.
Come, share your master's joy.'"

—Matthew 25:14–15, 19–21

Truths of Our Catholic Faith

It has been a long time since Jesus ascended to heaven. His Church meanwhile has taken all Jesus has given Her and tried using it wisely. Entrusted with great responsibility, our Church strives constantly, guided by the Holy Spirit, to share Her Master's joy with all generations.

> *"The Church, in her doctrine, life, and worship, perpetuates and transmits to every generation all that she herself is, all that she believes"* (DV *8 §1). (CCC 98)*

God made you male or female for a reason. Your sexuality is a gift from God to be used faithfully in whatever specific way He calls you (e.g. married life or Holy Orders). Sexuality is no small matter.

> *By creating the human being man and woman, God gives personal dignity equally to the one and the other. Each of them, man and woman, should acknowledge and accept his sexual identity. (CCC 2393)*

A Question for Me

What talents has God given me? How am I using God's gifts?

For a Child in My Life

What talent has God given you? How can you use it to help others?

My Role in the Community

Do I ever hear others make male-chauvinistic remarks or, on the other hand, engage in male-bashing? What will I do next time this occurs?

For Depth and Further Life Application

Proverbs 31:10–13, 19–20, 30–31
Psalm 128
Thessalonians 5:1–6

📖 United States Catholic Catechism for Adults, pages 403–404

REFLECTION

Remain in me as I remain in you, says the Lord. Whoever remains in me bears much fruit.

—John 15:4a, 5b

A Christ the King

The Gospel

Jesus said to his disciples:
"When the Son of Man comes in his glory,
and all the angels with him,
he will sit upon his glorious throne,
and all the nations will be assembled before him.
And he will separate them one from another,
as a shepherd separates the sheep from the goats.
He will place the sheep on his right and the goats on his left.
Then the king will say to those on his right,
'Come, you who are blessed by my Father.
Inherit the kingdom prepared for you from
the foundation of the world.
For I was hungry and you gave me food,
I was thirsty and you gave me drink,
a stranger and you welcomed me,
naked and you clothed me,
ill and you cared for me,
in prison and you visited me.'
Then the righteous will answer him and say,
'Lord, when did we see you hungry and feed you,
or thirsty and give you drink?
When did we see you a stranger and welcome you,
or naked and clothe you?
When did we see you ill or in prison, and visit you?'
And the king will say to them in reply,
'Amen, I say to you, whatever you did
for one of the least brothers of mine, you did for me.'
Then he will say to those on his left,
'Depart from me, you accursed,
into the eternal fire prepared for the devil and his angels.
For I was hungry and you gave me no food,
I was thirsty and you gave me no drink,
a stranger and you gave me no welcome,
naked and you gave me no clothing,
ill and in prison, and you did not care for me.'
Then they will answer and say,

'Lord, when did we see you hungry or thirsty
or a stranger or naked or ill or in prison,
and not minister to your needs?'
He will answer them, 'Amen, I say to you,
what you did not do for one of these least ones,
you did not do for me.'
And these will go off to eternal punishment,
but the righteous to eternal life."

—Matthew 25:31–46

Truths of Our Catholic Faith

The devil and his angels are acknowledged in this Gospel passage. The evil one has been contributing to trouble for a long time, enticing us to abuse our freedom. May we end up like the sheep in this passage, sharing the eternal life prepared for the righteous.

> *"Although set by God in a state of rectitude, man, enticed by the evil one, abused his freedom at the very start of history. He lifted himself up against God and sought to attain his goal apart from him"* (GS 13 § 1). (CCC 415)

There is no such thing as in insignificant person. No matter how big the social organization, every individual person within it has profound dignity and deserves unconditional respect. Every member of each community, even the least ones, puts us in contact with Jesus Himself.

> *"The human person . . . is and ought to be the principle, the subject, and the object of every social organization"* (GS 25 § 1). (CCC 1892)

A Question for Me

How do I use my freedom? If I abuse it in any way, how might I turn this tendency around?

For a Child in My Life

How can you do something nice to Jesus every day?

My Role in the Community

Which of the good deeds Jesus talks about do I do most often? Which ones may be an area for me to improve at least a bit?

For Depth and Further Life Application

Ezekiel 34:11–12, 15–17
Psalm 23
Corinthians 15:20–26, 28

United States Catholic Catechism for Adults, pages 335–338

REFLECTION

Blessed is he who comes in the name of the Lord! Blessed is the kingdom of our father David that is to come!

—Mark 11:9, 10

B First Sunday of Advent

The Gospel

Jesus said to his disciples:
"Be watchful! Be alert!
You do not know when the time will come.
It is like a man traveling abroad.
He leaves home and places his servants in charge,
each with his own work,
and orders the gatekeeper to be on the watch.
Watch, therefore;
you do not know when the Lord of the house is coming,
whether in the evening, or at midnight,
or at cockcrow, or in the morning.
May he not come suddenly and find you sleeping.
What I say to you, I say to all: 'Watch!'"

—Mark 13:33–37

Truths of Our Catholic Faith

When the time comes, your body and soul will separate temporarily. (Unless, that is, Jesus comes again in glory before you experience physical death.) At any rate, when the Lord of the house comes your body will have incorruptible life. Be alert so that your everlasting life will be pleasant.

> *By death the soul is separated from the body, but in the resurrection God will give incorruptible life to our body, transformed by reunion with our soul. Just as Christ is risen and lives forever, so all of us will rise at the last day. (CCC 1016)*

Sometimes we know in advance that we are going to meet the Lord. Even if death is not imminent, a serious sickness or even advanced age makes a person well-suited to celebrate the Sacrament of Anointing of the Sick. Knowing that the time is coming can be a blessing.

> *The proper time for receiving this holy anointing has certainly arrived when the believer begins to be in danger of death because of illness or old age.* (CCC 1528)

A Question for Me

What are some ways I can treat my body that show I expect it to be with me forever?

For a Child in My Life

Who is the oldest person you know personally? When could you go to visit her or him soon?

My Role in the Community

What aged person might I visit in the near future?

For Depth and Further Life Application

Isaiah 63:16b–17, 19b; 64:2–7
Psalm 80
Corinthians 1:3–9

📖 United States Catholic Catechism for Adults, pages 249–251

REFLECTION

Show us, Lord, your love; and grant us your salvation.

—Psalm 85:8

B Second Sunday of Advent

The Gospel

The beginning of the gospel of Jesus Christ the Son of God.

As it is written in Isaiah the prophet:
Behold, I am sending my messenger ahead of you;
he will prepare your way.
A voice of one crying out in the desert:
"Prepare the way of the Lord,
make straight his paths."
John the Baptist appeared in the desert
proclaiming a baptism of repentance for the forgiveness of sins.
People of the whole Judean countryside
and all the inhabitants of Jerusalem
were going out to him
and were being baptized by him in the Jordan River
as they acknowledged their sins.
John was clothed in camel's hair,
with a leather belt around his waist.
He fed on locusts and wild honey.
And this is what he proclaimed:
"One mightier than I is coming after me.
I am not worthy to stoop and loosen the thongs of his sandals.
I have baptized you with water;
he will baptize you with the Holy Spirit."

—Mark 1:1–8

Truths of Our Catholic Faith

John's baptism certainly had significance. Yet he acknowledged that another baptism was coming, one mightier than his. Christian baptism brings with it several awe-inspiring effects.

> *The fruit of Baptism, or baptismal grace, is a rich reality that includes forgiveness of original sin and all personal sins, birth into the new life by which man becomes an adoptive son of the Father, a member of Christ and a temple of the Holy Spirit. By this very fact the person baptized is incorporated into the Church, the Body of*

> *Christ, and made a sharer in the priesthood of Christ. (CCC 1279)*

Those who John baptized apparently had functioning consciences. They acknowledged their sins. We have an obligation to form our conscience well so that if we sin we will know it and, ideally, we will make judgments that will help us avoid wrongdoing.

> *A well-formed conscience is upright and truthful. It formulates its judgments according to reason, in conformity with the true good willed by the wisdom of the Creator. Everyone must avail himself of the means to form his conscience. (CCC 1798)*

A Question for Me

What are the means of forming my conscience, and how do I avail myself to them?

For a Child in My Life

Tell me about one result of being baptized.

My Role in the Community

How well and how often do I defer to others when it's appropriate, acknowledging that "one mightier than I is coming."

For Depth and Further Life Application

Isaiah 40:1–5, 9–11
Psalm 85
2 Peter 3:8–14

United States Catholic Catechism for Adults, pages 181–182

REFLECTION

Prepare the way of the Lord, make straight his paths: all flesh shall see the salvation of God

—Luke 3:4, 6

B Third Sunday of Advent

The Gospel

A man named John was sent from God.
He came for testimony, to testify to the light,
so that all might believe through him.
He was not the light,
but came to testify to the light.

And this is the testimony of John.
When the Jews from Jerusalem sent priests
and Levites to him
to ask him, "Who are you?"
He admitted and did not deny it,
but admitted, "I am not the Christ."
So they asked him,
"What are you then? Are you Elijah?"
And he said, "I am not."
"Are you the Prophet?"
He answered, "No."
So they said to him,
"Who are you, so we can give an answer to those who sent us?
What do you have to say for yourself?"
He said:
"I am the voice of one crying out in the desert,
'make straight the way of the Lord,'"
as Isaiah the prophet said."
Some Pharisees were also sent.
They asked him,
"Why then do you baptize
if you are not the Christ or Elijah or the Prophet?"
John answered them,
"I baptize with water;
but there is one among you whom you do not recognize,
the one who is coming after me,
whose sandal strap I am not worthy to untie."
This happened in Bethany across the Jordan,
where John was baptizing.

—John 1:6–8, 19–28

Truths of Our Catholic Faith

We need baptism in the first place because without it we can not live the holiness to which God calls us; we can not attain the degree of justice that He intends. Ever since the first sin of the first human person, all of creation waited breathlessly for Light to come into our world, dispelling sin's darkness forever.

> *By his sin Adam, as the first man, lost the original holiness and justice he had received from God, not only for himself but for all human beings. (CCC 416)*

Jesus is the Word of God. God speaks His Word to us in various ways, especially through Scripture and Church teaching. Reflecting on God's Word, and acting upon it, helps to keep us on a good path.

> *The Word of God is a light for our path. We must assimilate it in faith and prayer and put it into practice. This is how moral conscience is formed. (CCC 1802)*

A Question for Me

How does original sin influence me?

For a Child in My Life

Who is affected by the sin of Adam?

My Role in the Community

What are some ways I might put the Word of God into practice in my community this week?"

For Depth and Further Life Application

Isaiah 61:1–2a, 10–11
Luke 1:46–54
Thessalonians 5:16–24

📖 United States Catholic Catechism for Adults, pages 65–67

REFLECTION

The Spirit of the Lord is upon me, because he has anointed me to bring glad tidings to the poor.

—Isaiah 61:1 cited in Luke 4:18

B Fourth Sunday of Advent

The Gospel

The angel Gabriel was sent from God
to a town of Galilee called Nazareth,
to a virgin betrothed to a man named Joseph,
of the house of David,
and the virgin's name was Mary.
And coming to her, he said,
"Hail, full of grace! The Lord is with you."
But she was greatly troubled at what was said
and pondered what sort of greeting this might be.
Then the angel said to her,
"Do not be afraid, Mary,
for you have found favor with God.

"Behold, you will conceive in your womb and bear a son,
and you shall name him Jesus.
He will be great and will be called Son of the Most High,
and the Lord God will give him the throne of David his father,
and he will rule over the house of Jacob forever,
and of his kingdom there will be no end."
But Mary said to the angel,
"How can this be,
since I have no relations with a man?"
And the angel said to her in reply,
"The Holy Spirit will come upon you,
and the power of the Most High will overshadow you.
Therefore the child to be born
will be called holy, the Son of God.
And behold, Elizabeth, your relative,
has also conceived a son in her old age,
and this is the sixth month for her who was called barren;
for nothing will be impossible for God."
Mary said, "Behold, I am the handmaid of the Lord.
May it be done to me according to your word."
Then the angel departed from her.

—Luke 1:26–38

Truths of Our Catholic Faith

Everything we believe about Mary essentially relates to our faith in her Son. As we hope one day to be filled with grace according to the potential for holiness that God gives us, so Mary lived her whole life. Sinless, she conceived, bore and raised the One who conquers sin forever.

> *From among the descendants of Eve, God chose the Virgin Mary to be the mother of his Son. "Full of grace," Mary is "the most excellent fruit of redemption" (SC 103): from the first instant of her conception, she was totally preserved from the stain of original sin and she remained pure from all personal sin throughout her life. (CCC 508)*

Mary's parents no doubt taught her to pray by word and example. Mary in turn, together with Saint Joseph, provided Jesus with excellent models of closeness to the Father through prayer. And so praying passes from one generation to the next. Those taught to pray, in turn, teach others by example and word the life of prayer.

> *The Christian family is the first place for education in prayer. (CCC 2694)*

A Question for Me

How often do I pray the Hail Mary? How might I do so more often?

For a Child in My Life

What words does the angel Gabriel use to greet Mary?

My Role in the Community

How is prayer taught and modeled in my family?

For Depth and Further Life Application

Samuel 7:1–5, 8b–12, 14a, 16
Psalm 89
Romans 16:25–27

United States Catholic Catechism for Adults, pages 77–78

REFLECTION

Behold, I am the handmaid of the Lord. May it be done to me according to your word.

—Luke 1:38

B The Holy Family

The Gospel

When the days were completed for their purification
according to the law of Moses,
they took him up to Jerusalem
to present him to the Lord.

When they had fulfilled all the prescriptions
of the law of the Lord,
they returned to Galilee,
to their own town of Nazareth.
The child grew and became strong, filled with wisdom;
and the favor of God was upon him.

—Luke 2:22, 39–40

Truths of Our Catholic Faith

In theory, Joseph and Mary could have waited until Jesus was older, then let him decide whether to present himself to the Lord. Rather, they fulfilled their duty as parents, presenting the infant Jesus before taking him back home to help him grow in strength and wisdom, blessed with God's favor.

Jesus established His Church to make disciples and to baptize all—not just adults. In the New Testament we read of entire households becoming members of Christ's body. Bringing children to the Lord for the life-giving gift of Christian baptism is eminently reasonable, proper, and firmly established as a practice of Faith.

> *Since the earliest times, Baptism has been administered to children, for it is a grace and a gift of God that does not presuppose any human merit; children are baptized in the faith of the Church. Entry into Christian life gives access to true freedom. (CCC 1282)*

Joseph and Mary saw to the needs of Jesus. They knew that physical strength was not their only goal for Jesus in providing for His well-being. Mary and Joseph truly modeled good parenting for us all.

> *Parents have the first responsibility for the education of their children in the faith, prayer, and all the virtues. They have the duty to provide as far as possible for the physical and spiritual needs of their children. (CCC 2252)*

A Question for Me

How might I explain the practice of infant baptism to a person who disagrees with or does not understand it?

For a Child in My Life

What are the most important things for parents to teach their children?

My Role in the Community

When does my parish usually baptize infants? Can I make it a point to attend one such baptism in the near future, as a sign of my loving support?

For Depth and Further Life Application

Sirach 3:2–7, 12–14
Psalm 128
Colossians 3:12–21

United States Catholic Catechism for Adults, pages 380–385

REFLECTION

Let the peace of Christ control your hearts; let the word of Christ dwell in you richly.

—Colossians 3:15a, 16a

B The Baptism of the Lord

The Gospel

This is what John the Baptist proclaimed:
"One mightier than I is coming after me.
I am not worthy to stoop and loosen the thongs of his sandals.
I have baptized you with water;
he will baptize you with the Holy Spirit."

It happened in those days that Jesus came from Nazareth of Galilee
and was baptized in the Jordan by John.
On coming up out of the water he saw the heavens being torn open
and the Spirit, like a dove, descending upon him.
And a voice came from the heavens,
"You are my beloved Son; with you I am well pleased."

—Mark 1:7–11

Truths of Our Catholic Faith

The Spirit is present when God acknowledges Jesus as His beloved Son. This same Holy Spirit helps us, too, to acknowledge the Lord God and all He has revealed to us. The gift of faith is one that our Father is pleased to offer.

> *Faith is a supernatural gift from God. In order to believe, man needs the interior helps of the Holy Spirit. (CCC 179)*

Christian baptism is very much focused on forgiveness. Exactly why Jesus submitted to John's baptism we do not know for sure. Certainly, Jesus had no reason to seek forgiveness of sins. The cleansing waters of baptism link us to Jesus and pour out upon us the Holy Spirit, the third Person of the Blessed Trinity.

> *Baptism is the first and chief sacrament of the forgiveness of sins: it unites us to Christ, who died and rose, and gives us the Holy Spirit. (CCC 985)*

A Question for Me

How often do I pray for the gift of faith? How might I ask the Holy Spirit more consistently to help strengthen my belief?

For a Child in My Life

What words came from the heavens after Jesus was baptized?

My Role in the Community

God offers words of affirmation to Jesus. Who in my community needs my affirmation, and how soon will I give it?

For Depth and Further Life Application

Isaiah 42:1–4, 6–7
Psalm 29
Acts 10:34–38

📖 United States Catholic Catechism for Adults, pages 36–41

REFLECTION

The heavens were opened and the voice of the Father thundered: This is my beloved Son, listen to him.

—cf. Mark 9:7

OR

REFLECTION

John saw Jesus approaching him, and said: Behold the Lamb of God who takes away the sin of the world.

—cf. John 1:29

B First Sunday of Lent

The Gospel

The Spirit drove Jesus out into the desert,
and he remained in the desert for forty days,
tempted by Satan.
He was among wild beasts,
and the angels ministered to him.

After John had been arrested,
Jesus came to Galilee proclaiming the gospel of God:
"This is the time of fulfillment.
The kingdom of God is at hand.
Repent, and believe in the gospel."

—Mark 1:12–15

Truths of Our Catholic Faith

In the Church year or liturgical calendar, Lent marks a time between early Ordinary Time and the observance of Jesus' death, resurrection and ascension. When we are mindful of the liturgical year, we are mindful of the life, teaching and actions of Jesus. Our Church year helps us journey with and get to know the Lord better and better as these years pass.

The Church, "in the course of the year, . . . unfolds the whole mystery of Christ from his Incarnation and Nativity through his Ascension, to Pentecost and the expectation of the blessed hope of the coming of the Lord" (SC 102 § 2). (CCC 1194)

Jesus uses His freedom wisely and well. He expects us to respect others' freedom and to use our freedom in service to God's kingdom. When we abuse this freedom we are to repent and recommit ourselves to the Good News of our salvation in Him—to believe in the gospel.

The right to the exercise of freedom, especially in religious and moral matters, is an inalienable requirement of the dignity of man. But the exercise of freedom does not entail the putative right to say or do anything. (CCC 1747)

A Question for Me

How am I at avoiding near occasions of sin, those times when I drive myself to the desert of temptation?

For a Child in My Life

What are some special things you could do, or not do, during Lent?

My Role in the Community

In my communities, do I use my freedom responsibly or take it as the right to do and say anything?

For Depth and Further Life Application

Genesis 9:8–15
Psalm 25
1 Peter 3:18–22

United States Catholic Catechism for Adults, pages 584–590

REFLECTION

One does not live on bread alone, but on every word that comes forth from the mouth of God.

—Matthew 4:4b

B Second Sunday of Lent

The Gospel

Jesus took Peter, James, and John
and led them up a high mountain apart by themselves.
And he was transfigured before them,
and his clothes became dazzling white,
such as no fuller on earth could bleach them.
Then Elijah appeared to them along with Moses,
and they were conversing with Jesus.
Then Peter said to Jesus in reply,
"Rabbi, it is good that we are here!
Let us make three tents:
one for you, one for Moses, and one for Elijah."
He hardly knew what to say, they were so terrified.
Then a cloud came, casting a shadow over them;
from the cloud came a voice,
"This is my beloved Son. Listen to him."
Suddenly, looking around, they no longer saw anyone
but Jesus alone with them.

As they were coming down from the mountain,
he charged them not to relate what they had seen to anyone,
except when the Son of Man had risen from the dead.
So they kept the matter to themselves,
questioning what rising from the dead meant.

—Mark 9:2–10

Truths of Our Catholic Faith

Sometimes we take the resurrection for granted. To Peter, James and John, Jesus talking about the Son of Man rising from the dead must have sounded utterly mysterious. Yet rise from the dead He did, paving the way for us all.

> *Christ, "the first-born from the dead"* (Col *1:18), is the principle of our own resurrection, even now by the justification of our souls (cf.* Rom *6:4), and one day by the new life he will impart to our bodies (cf.* Rom *8:11). (CCC 658)*

Jesus rightfully instructed the three to keep the transfiguration a secret, at least for the time being. Although exceptions of course occur, there are times when keeping secrets is absolutely the right thing to do.

> *"The sacramental seal is inviolable" (CIC, can. 983 § 1). Professional secrets must be kept. Confidences prejudicial to another are not to be divulged. (CCC 2511)*

A Question for Me

There is an old saying, "It is better to remain silent and be thought a fool than to speak and remove all doubt." How good am I at remaining silent when the situation implies that it is the most appropriate course of action?

For a Child in My Life

When someone does something bad and asks you or tells you to keep it a secret, do you have to keep it a secret? (Note: the answer is essentially no; this is an important distinction for kids to understand in order to be protected from abusive exploitation by poorly behaved adults.)

My Role in the Community

How susceptible am I to the gossip urge? What might I do to maintain better control of my conversations in this regard?

For Depth and Further Life Application

Genesis 22:1–2, 9a, 10–13, 15–18
Psalm 116
Romans 8:31b–34

📖 United States Catholic Catechism for Adults, pages 429–430

REFLECTION

From the shining cloud the Father's voice is heard: This is my beloved Son, listen to him.

—cf. Matthew 17:5

B Third Sunday of Lent

The Gospel

Since the Passover of the Jews was near,
Jesus went up to Jerusalem.
He found in the temple area those who sold oxen, sheep, and doves,
as well as the money changers seated there.
He made a whip out of cords
and drove them all out of the temple area, with the sheep and oxen,
and spilled the coins of the money changers
and overturned their tables,
and to those who sold doves he said,
"Take these out of here,
and stop making my Father's house a marketplace."
His disciples recalled the words of Scripture,
Zeal for your house will consume me.
At this the Jews answered and said to him,
"What sign can you show us for doing this?"
Jesus answered and said to them,
"Destroy this temple and in three days I will raise it up."
The Jews said,
"This temple has been under construction for forty-six years,
and you will raise it up in three days?"
But he was speaking about the temple of his body.
Therefore, when he was raised from the dead,
his disciples remembered that he had said this,
and they came to believe the Scripture
and the word Jesus had spoken.

While he was in Jerusalem for the feast of Passover,
many began to believe in his name
when they saw the signs he was doing.
But Jesus would not trust himself to them because he knew them all,
and did not need anyone to testify about human nature.
He himself understood it well.

—John 2:13–25

Truths of Our Catholic Faith

Jesus needed no one to explain human nature to Him. He experienced human nature firsthand. And even though He got annoyed at people occasionally (such as clearing the Temple), Jesus loves each of us infinitely and wants us all to share the divine life of our Triune God—Father, Son and Holy Spirit.

> *The Word became flesh to make us* "partakers of the divine nature":[4] *"For this is why the Word became man, and the Son of God became the Son of man: so that man, by entering into communion with the Word and thus receiving divine sonship, might become a son of God."*[5] *"For the Son of God became man so that we might become God."*[6] *"The only-begotten Son of God, wanting to make us sharers in his divinity, assumed our nature, so that he, made man, might make men gods."*[7] *(CCC 460)*

The vendors and currency exchangers were not showing good judgment by plying their trade within the Temple area. They were not being fair or loving to God, in a sense, by taking up His space. The Lord does not mind us dealing in earthly goods—working for a living, buying and selling what we need. He insists, though, that we are charitable and just in doing so.

> *The seventh commandment enjoins the practice of justice and charity in the administration of earthly goods and the fruits of men's labor. (CCC 2451)*

A Question for Me

How good am I at being assertive (like Jesus clearing the Temple) without being aggressive (saying intentionally hurtful things or initiating physical harm)?

For a Child in My Life

Why does Jesus know and understand us all so well?

My Role in the Community
Fairness and love should characterize my behavior as an employee, employer, customer, vendor etc. How charitable and just am I in my daily business/temporal affairs?

For Depth and Further Life Application

Exodus 20:1–3, 7–8, 12–17
Psalm 19
Corinthians 1:22–25

📖 United States Catholic Catechism for Adults, pages 426–428

REFLECTION

God so loved the world that he gave his only Son, so that everyone who believes in him might have eternal life.

—John 3:16

B Fourth Sunday of Lent

The Gospel

Jesus said to Nicodemus:
"Just as Moses lifted up the serpent in the desert,
so must the Son of Man be lifted up,
so that everyone who believes in him may have eternal life."

For God so loved the world that he gave his only Son,
so that everyone who believes in him might not perish
but might have eternal life.
For God did not send his Son into the world to condemn the world,
but that the world might be saved through him.
Whoever believes in him will not be condemned,
but whoever does not believe has already been condemned,
because he has not believed in the name of the only Son of God.
And this is the verdict,
that the light came into the world,
but people preferred darkness to light,
because their works were evil.
For everyone who does wicked things hates the light
and does not come toward the light,
so that his works might not be exposed.
But whoever lives the truth comes to the light,
so that his works may be clearly seen as done in God.

—John 3:14–21

Truths of Our Catholic Faith

God wants no person to suffer eternal punishment. He is not out to get any person in a negative sense. Rather, God wants us all to enjoy eternal life. And you can help.

> Missionary motivation. *It is from God's love for all men that the Church in every age receives both the obligation and the vigor of her missionary dynamism, "for the love of Christ urges us on."[8] Indeed, God "desires all men to be saved and to come to the knowledge of the truth";[9] that is, God wills the salvation of everyone through the knowledge of the truth. Salvation is found in the truth. Those who obey the prompting of the Spirit of*

> *truth are already on the way of salvation. But the Church, to whom this truth has been entrusted, must go out to meet their desire, so as to bring them the truth. Because she believes in God's universal plan of salvation, the Church must be missionary. (CCC 851)*

Sometimes we seem to prefer darkness to the light of our Lord. Sometimes our works are evil. Sometimes we do wicked things.

The first step toward rising above sin, is knowing what sin is, born on the grace of God, toward the saving light that is Jesus. God wants us to avoid sin; this includes recognizing it for what it is.

> *Sin is an utterance, a deed, or a desire contrary to the eternal law (St. Augustine,* Faust *22: PL 42, 418). It is an offense against God. It rises up against God in a disobedience contrary to the obedience of Christ. (CCC 1871)*

A Question for Me

How might I describe my quest for knowledge of the truth?

For a Child in My Life

What does God want for all people?

My Role in the Community

What is my level of missionary dynamism? I.e., how hard do I work at helping others come to the knowledge of the truth so that through the truth they might enjoy salvation?

For Depth and Further Life Application

2 Chronicles 36:14–16, 19–23
Psalm 137
Ephesians 2:4–10

📖 United States Catholic Catechism for Adults, pages 512–513

REFLECTION

God so loved the world that he gave his only Son, so that everyone who believes in him might have eternal life.

—John 3:16

B Fifth Sunday of Lent

The Gospel

Some Greeks who had come to worship at the Passover Feast
came to Philip, who was from Bethsaida in Galilee,
and asked him, "Sir, we would like to see Jesus."
Philip went and told Andrew;
then Andrew and Philip went and told Jesus.
Jesus answered them,
"The hour has come for the Son of Man to be glorified.
Amen, amen, I say to you,
unless a grain of wheat falls to the ground and dies,
it remains just a grain of wheat;
but if it dies, it produces much fruit.
Whoever loves his life loses it,
and whoever hates his life in this world
will preserve it for eternal life.
Whoever serves me must follow me,
and where I am, there also will my servant be.
The Father will honor whoever serves me.

"I am troubled now. Yet what should I say?
'Father, save me from this hour'?
But it was for this purpose that I came to this hour.
Father, glorify your name."
Then a voice came from heaven,
"I have glorified it and will glorify it again."
The crowd there heard it and said it was thunder;
but others said, "An angel has spoken to him."
Jesus answered and said,
"This voice did not come for my sake but for yours.
Now is the time of judgment on this world;
now the ruler of this world will be driven out.
And when I am lifted up from the earth,
I will draw everyone to myself."
He said this indicating the kind of death he would die.

—John 12:20–33

Truths of Our Catholic Faith

Preserving your life for eternity. Once you have really heard the Good News of salvation through Jesus, it is important to become and remain a member of His Body in the ways revealed by God. Through initiation into the Christian community, you embark on and remain faithful through your journey in this world and on to eternal life.

> *Christian initiation is accomplished by three sacraments together: Baptism which is the beginning of new life; Confirmation which is its strengthening; and the Eucharist which nourishes the disciple with Christ's Body and Blood for his transformation in Christ. (CCC 1275)*

Whoever serves Jesus must follow Him. Serving Jesus often means making decisions guided by conscience. Following Jesus may occasionally mean making judgments that require some sacrifice.

It is true that there is no higher authority than your informed conscience. You really must inform your conscience with God's Word in Scripture and the teachings of His Church; that way, in your judgments you will be more certain to serve and follow Jesus. Even if sacrificing, you will produce much fruit.

> *A human being must always obey the certain judgment of his conscience. (CCC 1800)*

A Question for Me

In what ways can a person gain life by dying—by sacrificing greatly, gain something even greater in return?

For a Child in My Life

What does Jesus say He will do when He is lifted up from the earth?

My Role in the Community

Into what groups have I been initiated or otherwise formally received? What does this teach me about the three Sacraments of Christian Initiation? (I.e., similarities in the initiation processes? differences?)

For Depth and Further Life Application

Jeremiah 31:31–34
Psalm 51
Hebrews 5:7–9

United States Catholic Catechism for Adults, pages 183–195

REFLECTION

Whoever serves me must follow me, says the Lord; and where I am, there also will my servant be.

—John 12:26

B Palm Sunday

The Gospel

As soon as morning came,
the chief priests with the elders and the scribes,
that is, the whole Sanhedrin held a council.
They bound Jesus, led him away, and handed him over to Pilate.
Pilate questioned him,
"Are you the king of the Jews?"
He said to him in reply, "You say so."
The chief priests accused him of many things.
Again Pilate questioned him,
"Have you no answer?
See how many things they accuse you of."
Jesus gave him no further answer, so that Pilate was amazed.

Now on the occasion of the feast he used to release to them
one prisoner whom they requested.
A man called Barabbas was then in prison
along with the rebels who had committed murder in a rebellion.
The crowd came forward and began to ask him
to do for them as he was accustomed.
Pilate answered,
"Do you want me to release to you the king of the Jews?"
For he knew that it was out of envy
that the chief priests had handed him over.
But the chief priests stirred up the crowd
to have him release Barabbas for them instead.
Pilate again said to them in reply,
"Then what do you want me to do
with the man you call the king of the Jews?"
They shouted again, "Crucify him."
Pilate said to them, "Why? What evil has he done?"
They only shouted the louder, "Crucify him."
So Pilate, wishing to satisfy the crowd,
released Barabbas to them and, after he had Jesus scourged,
handed him over to be crucified.

The soldiers led him away inside the palace,
that is, the praetorium, and assembled the whole cohort.

They clothed him in purple and,
weaving a crown of thorns, placed it on him.
They began to salute him with, "Hail, King of the Jews!"
and kept striking his head with a reed and spitting upon him.
They knelt before him in homage.
And when they had mocked him,
they stripped him of the purple cloak,
dressed him in his own clothes,
and led him out to crucify him.
They pressed into service a passer-by, Simon,
a Cyrenian, who was coming in from the country,
the father of Alexander and Rufus,
to carry his cross.

They brought him to the place of Golgotha
—which is translated Place of the Skull—
They gave him wine drugged with myrrh,
but he did not take it.
Then they crucified him and divided his garments
by casting lots for them to see what each should take.
It was nine o'clock in the morning when they crucified him.
The inscription of the charge against him read,
"The King of the Jews."
With him they crucified two revolutionaries,
one on his right and one on his left.
Those passing by reviled him,
shaking their heads and saying,
"Aha! You who would destroy the temple
and rebuild it in three days,
save yourself by coming down from the cross."
Likewise the chief priests, with the scribes,
mocked him among themselves and said,
"He saved others; he cannot save himself.
Let the Christ, the King of Israel,
come down now from the cross
that we may see and believe."
Those who were crucified with him also kept abusing him.

At noon darkness came over the whole land
until three in the afternoon.
And at three o'clock Jesus cried out in a loud voice,

"Eloi, Eloi, lema sabachthani?"
which is translated,
"My God, my God, why have you forsaken me?"
Some of the bystanders who heard it said,
"Look, he is calling Elijah."
One of them ran, soaked a sponge with wine, put it on a reed
and gave it to him to drink saying,
"Wait, let us see if Elijah comes to take him down."
Jesus gave a loud cry and breathed his last.

Here all kneel and pause for a short time.

The veil of the sanctuary was torn in two from top to bottom.
When the centurion who stood facing him
saw how he breathed his last he said,
"Truly this man was the Son of God!"

—Mark 15:1–39

Truths of Our Catholic Faith

The centurion makes an act of faith. He is not alone, nor is he standing with Jesus only. This centurion is surrounded by saints and sinners, by those who believe in Jesus and those who, God–willing, might believe at some future point. The centurion's expression of belief occurs within a community.

> *"Believing" is an ecclesial act. The Church's faith precedes, engenders, supports, and nourishes our faith. The Church is the mother of all believers. "No one can have God as Father who does not have the Church as Mother" (St. Cyprian,* De unit. *6: PL 4, 519). (CCC 181)*

It is all too easy to vilify those involved with Jesus' death. And granted, some of these agents may well have been acting with consciously evil intent.

Others, though, may honestly not have known better. Some, maybe a soldier or two, may have felt forced or fearful if not compliant. While we can certainly judge the goodness or badness of an act, we must be careful about presuming that all perpetrators always do so knowingly and willingly enough to be morally responsible in all cases.

> *The imputability or responsibility for an action can be diminished or nullified by ignorance, duress, fear, and other psychological or social factors.* (CCC 1746)

A Question for Me
To what extent is my faith an ecclesial act, one that occurs in the context of our Church?

For a Child in My Life
What did the centurion say when he say how Jesus died?

My Role in the Community
How much do I allow for the possibility of ignorance, duress, fear or other factors, regarding the misdeeds of others?

For Depth and Further Life Application

Isaiah 50:4–7
Psalm 22
Philippians 2:6–10

United States Catholic Catechism for Adults, pages 41–44

REFLECTION

Christ became obedient to the point of death, even death on a cross. Because of this, God greatly exalted him and bestowed on him the name which is above every name.

—Philippians 2:8–9

B Second Sunday of Easter

The Gospel

On the evening of that first day of the week,
when the doors were locked, where the disciples were,
for fear of the Jews,
Jesus came and stood in their midst
and said to them, "Peace be with you."
When he had said this, he showed them his hands and his side.
The disciples rejoiced when they saw the Lord.
Jesus said to them again, "Peace be with you.
As the Father has sent me, so I send you."
And when he had said this, he breathed on them and said to them,
"Receive the Holy Spirit.
Whose sins you forgive are forgiven them,
and whose sins you retain are retained."

Thomas, called Didymus, one of the Twelve,
was not with them when Jesus came.
So the other disciples said to him, "We have seen the Lord."
But he said to them,
"Unless I see the mark of the nails in his hands
and put my finger into the nailmarks
and put my hand into his side, I will not believe."

Now a week later his disciples were again inside
and Thomas was with them.
Jesus came, although the doors were locked,
and stood in their midst and said, "Peace be with you."
Then he said to Thomas, "Put your finger here and see my hands,
and bring your hand and put it into my side,
and do not be unbelieving, but believe."
Thomas answered and said to him, "My Lord and my God!"
Jesus said to him, "Have you come to believe because
you have seen me?
Blessed are those who have not seen and have believed."

Now Jesus did many other signs in the presence of his disciples
that are not written in this book.

But these are written that you may come to believe
that Jesus is the Christ, the Son of God,
and that through this belief you may have life in his name.

—John 20:19–31

Truths of Our Catholic Faith

The Holy Spirit was given to and received by Jesus' friends and followers. This had to be so that the infant Church could continue Jesus' mission of forgiveness and peace.

> Missionary paths. *The Holy Spirit is the protagonist, "the principal agent of the whole of the Church's mission."*[10] *It is he who leads the Church on her missionary paths. "This mission continues and, in the course of history, unfolds the mission of Christ, who was sent to evangelize the poor; so the Church, urged on by the Spirit of Christ, must walk the road Christ himself walked, a way of poverty and obedience, of service and self-sacrifice even to death, a death from which he emerged victorious by his resurrection."*[11] *So it is that "the blood of martyrs is the seed of Christians."*[12] *(CCC 852)*

Thomas' exclamation "My Lord and my God!" is one to make our own. When we address Jesus as Lord, we proclaim that while sharing our human nature He is at the same time, indeed, God.

> *The title "Lord" indicates divine sovereignty. To confess or invoke Jesus as Lord is to believe in his divinity. "No one can say 'Jesus is Lord' except by the Holy Spirit"* (1 Cor *12:3). (CCC 455)*

A Question for Me

How is my life different because Jesus is my Lord?

For a Child in My Life

Why do we call Jesus "Lord?"

My Role in the Community
What signs do I see of the Holy Spirit's work in my community? How might I further this work?

For Depth and Further Life Application

Acts of the Apostles 4:32–35
Psalm 118
1 John 5:1–6

United States Catholic Catechism for Adults, pages 79–83

REFLECTION

You believe in me, Thomas, because you have seen me, says the Lord; blessed are those who have not seen, but still believe!

—John 20:29

B Third Sunday of Easter

The Gospel

The two disciples recounted what had taken place on the way,
and how Jesus was made known to them
in the breaking of bread.

While they were still speaking about this,
he stood in their midst and said to them,
"Peace be with you."
But they were startled and terrified
and thought that they were seeing a ghost.
Then he said to them, "Why are you troubled?
And why do questions arise in your hearts?
Look at my hands and my feet, that it is I myself.
Touch me and see, because a ghost does not have flesh and bones
as you can see I have."
And as he said this,
he showed them his hands and his feet.
While they were still incredulous for joy and were amazed,
he asked them, "Have you anything here to eat?"
They gave him a piece of baked fish;
he took it and ate it in front of them.

He said to them,
"These are my words that I spoke to you while I was still with you,
that everything written about me in the law of Moses
and in the prophets and psalms must be fulfilled."
Then he opened their minds to understand the Scriptures.
And he said to them,
"Thus it is written that the Christ would suffer
and rise from the dead on the third day
and that repentance, for the forgiveness of sins,
would be preached in his name
to all the nations, beginning from Jerusalem.
You are witnesses of these things."

—Luke 24:35–48

Truths of Our Catholic Faith

Those who had witnessed the ministry of Jesus from the very beginning had a place of honor in the very early Church. When a disciple was to be elevated to an Apostle (to replace Judas Iscariot) this witnessing was one of the criteria. A structure was evident in our Church from the earliest of days.

> *Since the beginning, the ordained ministry has been conferred and exercised in three degrees: that of bishops, that of presbyters, and that of deacons. The ministries conferred by ordination are irreplaceable for the organic structure of the Church: without the bishop, presbyters, and deacons, one cannot speak of the Church (cf. St. Ignatius of Antioch,* Ad Trall. *3,1). (CCC 1593)*

Repentance is a vital ingredient of the Good News. This repentance consists mainly of listening to the moral law, and turning away from evil. The voice that beckons us toward goodness is our conscience.

> *Man is obliged to follow the moral law, which urges him "to do what is good and avoid what is evil" (cf.* GS *16). This law makes itself heard in his conscience. (CCC 1713)*

A Question for Me

How might you respond to a criticism that the Church is not very democratic?

For a Child in My Life

What are the three degrees of Holy Orders?

My Role in the Community

In what ways do I witness to my community of the great deeds God has done?

For Depth and Further Life Application

Acts of the Apostles 3:13–15, 17–19
Psalm 4
1 John 2:1–5a

📖 United States Catholic Catechism for Adults, pages 262–270

REFLECTION

Lord Jesus, open the Scriptures to us; make our hearts burn while you speak to us.

—cf. Luke 24:32

B Fourth Sunday of Easter

The Gospel

Jesus said:
"I am the good shepherd.
A good shepherd lays down his life for the sheep.
A hired man, who is not a shepherd
and whose sheep are not his own,
sees a wolf coming and leaves the sheep and runs away,
and the wolf catches and scatters them.
This is because he works for pay and has no concern for the sheep.
I am the good shepherd,
and I know mine and mine know me,
just as the Father knows me and I know the Father;
and I will lay down my life for the sheep.
I have other sheep that do not belong to this fold.
These also I must lead, and they will hear my voice,
and there will be one flock, one shepherd.
This is why the Father loves me,
because I lay down my life in order to take it up again.
No one takes it from me, but I lay it down on my own.
I have power to lay it down, and power to take it up again.
This command I have received from my Father."

—John 10:11–18

Truths of Our Catholic Faith

To serve the way Jesus serves is a unique calling. Certainly all Christians are called to participate in Jesus' ministry through a variety of means. Yet, in order to serve the entire community, God calls specific men to participate in the life of the community in the person of the God-Man, Jesus, as well as in His name. Thus the ordained, ministerial priesthood complements the way all of the baptized share in Jesus' priestly ministry.

The whole Church is a priestly people. Through Baptism all the faithful share in the priesthood of Christ. This participation is called the "common priesthood of the faithful." Based on this common priesthood and ordered to its service, there exists another participation in the mission of Christ: the ministry conferred by the sacrament of Holy Orders, where the task is to serve in the name and in the person of Christ the Head in the midst of the community. (CCC 1591)

Who are these other sheep that do not belong to the fold? Whoever they are, in God's eyes there will eventually be one shepherd leading one flock; the key is to listen for the voice of Jesus, allowing Him to lead.

Certainly the closest earthly image to the united flock that our Father desires is the Church led by Christ's vicar, the Bishop of Rome. Bits and pieces of the fullness of truth can be found outside the visible structure of Catholicism; it can be helpful when interacting with people of various faiths to keep this in mind.

"The sole Church of Christ which in the Creed we profess to be one, holy, catholic, and apostolic, . . . subsists in the Catholic Church, which is governed by the successor of Peter and by the bishops in communion with him. Nevertheless, many elements of sanctification and of truth are found outside its visible confines"(LG *8). (CCC 870)*

A Question for Me

How might I explain the similarities and differences between an ordained priest and the rest of the baptized?

For a Child in My Life

Who serves the Church in the name of Jesus and in the person of Jesus?

My Role in the Community

How might I deepen my interaction with people of faiths other than Catholicism without taking anything away from my own Catholic faith and practice?

For Depth and Further Life Application

Acts of the Apostles 4:8–12
Psalm 118
1 John 3:1–2

📖 United States Catholic Catechism for Adults, pages 126–134

REFLECTION

I am the good shepherd, says the Lord; I know my sheep, and mine know me.

—John 10:14

B Fifth Sunday of Easter

The Gospel

Jesus said to his disciples:
"I am the true vine, and my Father is the vine grower.
He takes away every branch in me that does not bear fruit,
and every one that does he prunes so that it bears more fruit.
You are already pruned because of the word that I spoke to you.
Remain in me, as I remain in you.
Just as a branch cannot bear fruit on its own
unless it remains on the vine,
so neither can you unless you remain in me.
I am the vine, you are the branches.
Whoever remains in me and I in him will bear much fruit,
because without me you can do nothing.
Anyone who does not remain in me
will be thrown out like a branch and wither;
people will gather them and throw them into a fire
and they will be burned.
If you remain in me and my words remain in you,
ask for whatever you want and it will be done for you.
By this is my Father glorified,
that you bear much fruit and become my disciples."

—John 15:1–8

Truths of Our Catholic Faith

Being thrown into a fire and burned brings to mind thoughts of hell. What exactly is hell like? Because we are made to be united with God, hell is that place where we are cut off from God forever. More than any physical pain, the torment of estrangement from the source of our happiness would be a hopelessly agonizing punishment.

> *Hell's principal punishment consists of eternal separation from God in whom alone man can have the life and happiness for which he was created and for which he longs. (CCC 1057)*

How do we remain in Jesus, and He in us? There are many ways;

prominent among them is prayer. When we pray, we follow Jesus' example and enjoy the relationship that He has with our Father. Filled with the Holy Spirit we can, like Jesus, ask our Father to help us bear fruit as disciples of His only Son. And the words of the Son will remain in us.

> *"Prayer is the raising of one's mind and heart to God or the requesting of good things from God" (St. John Damascene,* De fide orth. *3, 24: PG 94, 1089C). (CCC 2590)*

A Question for Me

Along with the vine/branch analogy, what other comparisons can I think of that convey the relationship between Jesus and me?

For a Child in My Life

What is the main punishment in hell?

My Role in the Community

For whom in my community can I, right now, request good things from God?

For Depth and Further Life Application

Acts of the Apostles 9:26–31
Psalm 22
1 John 3:18–24

📖 United States Catholic Catechism for Adults, pages 153–158

REFLECTION

Remain in me as I remain in you, says the Lord. Whoever remains in me will bear much fruit.

—John 15:4a, 5b

B Sixth Sunday of Easter

The Gospel

Jesus said to his disciples:
"As the Father loves me, so I also love you.
Remain in my love.
If you keep my commandments, you will remain in my love,
just as I have kept my Father's commandments
and remain in his love.

"I have told you this so that my joy may be in you
and your joy might be complete.
This is my commandment: love one another as I love you.
No one has greater love than this,
to lay down one's life for one's friends.
You are my friends if you do what I command you.
I no longer call you slaves,
because a slave does not know what his master is doing.
I have called you friends,
because I have told you everything I have heard from my Father.
It was not you who chose me, but I who chose you
and appointed you to go and bear fruit that will remain,
so that whatever you ask the Father in my name he may give you.
This I command you: love one another."

—John 15:9–17

Truths of Our Catholic Faith

God initiates love; He makes the first move. The Father inspires virtues. We respond to our immeasurable benefit. We enjoy the life of Father, Son and Holy Spirit.

> *The theological virtues dispose Christians to live in a relationship with the Holy Trinity. They have God for their origin, their motive, and their object—God known by faith, God hoped in and loved for his own sake. (CCC 1840)*

Jesus reveals the greatest expression of love. His teaching had been hinted at for centuries, especially in the Decalogue or Ten

Commandments. Everything Jesus heard from His Father, from of old, culminates in His command and example of love.

> *The Old Law is the first stage of revealed law. Its moral prescriptions are summed up in the Ten Commandments. (CCC 1980)*

A Question for Me

With which of the three theological virtues does God seem to have blessed me most? For which of the three do I need to pray with a special intensity?

For a Child in My Life

How does Jesus say you will remain in His love? How does He say you can be His friend?

My Role in the Community

Who in your community do you find it difficult to love as Jesus loves this person? Ask our Father in Jesus' name to help you love all people as Jesus does.

For Depth and Further Life Application

Acts of the Apostles 10:25–26, 34–35, 44–48
Psalm 98
1 John 4:7–10

📖 United States Catholic Catechism for Adults, page 534

REFLECTION

Whoever loves me will keep my word, says the Lord, and my Father will love him and we will come to him.

—John 14:23

B Seventh Sunday of Easter

The Gospel

Lifting up his eyes to heaven, Jesus prayed saying:
"Holy Father, keep them in your name that you have given me,
so that they may be one just as we are one.
When I was with them I protected them in your name
that you gave me,
and I guarded them, and none of them was lost
except the son of destruction,
in order that the Scripture might be fulfilled.
But now I am coming to you.
I speak this in the world
so that they may share my joy completely.
I gave them your word, and the world hated them,
because they do not belong to the world
any more than I belong to the world.
I do not ask that you take them out of the world
but that you keep them from the evil one.
They do not belong to the world
any more than I belong to the world.
Consecrate them in the truth. Your word is truth.
As you sent me into the world,
so I sent them into the world.
And I consecrate myself for them,
so that they also may be consecrated in truth."

—John 17:11b–19

Truths of Our Catholic Faith

Jesus clearly desires that His followers be united. For this reason we know that a clear sign or mark of the Church established by Jesus is that she is united. The Church is one.

> *The Church is one: she acknowledges one Lord, confesses one faith, is born of one Baptism, forms only one Body, is given life by the one Spirit, for the sake of one hope (cf.* Eph 4:3–5*), at whose fulfillment all divisions will be overcome. (CCC 866)*

Unity or oneness transcends in some ways the Church's visible membership. More and more, unity among human persons has visible international or global dimensions. Because all human persons share a bond through their Creator, it is fitting that at the international level efforts are underway to build community.

> *It is the role of the state to defend and promote the common good of civil society. The common good of the whole human family calls for an organization of society on the international level. (CCC 1927)*

A Question for Me

How is my level of oneness with the people with whom I most need to be united (spouse, for example)? What might I do to enhance the degree of this unity?

For a Child in My Life

What does it mean to say the Church is one?

My Role in the Community

What are some ways I can be an agent of unity (a peacemaker, even) within my community?

For Depth and Further Life Application

Acts of the Apostles 1:15–17, 20a, 20c–26
Psalm 103
1 John 4:11–16

📖 United States Catholic Catechism for Adults, pages 134–137

REFLECTION

I will not leave you orphans, says the Lord. I will come back to you, and your hearts will rejoice.

—cf. John 14:18

B Pentecost Sunday

The Gospel

Jesus said to his disciples:
"When the Advocate comes whom I will send you from the Father,
the Spirit of truth that proceeds from the Father,
he will testify to me.
And you also testify,
because you have been with me from the beginning.

"I have much more to tell you, but you cannot bear it now.
But when he comes, the Spirit of truth,
he will guide you to all truth.
He will not speak on his own,
but he will speak what he hears,
and will declare to you the things that are coming.
He will glorify me,
because he will take from what is mine and declare it to you.
Everything that the Father has is mine;
for this reason I told you that he will take from what is mine
and declare it to you."

—John 15:26–27, 16:12–15

Truths of Our Catholic Faith

The Holy Spirit is crucially important in interpreting the Bible. In many cases, there are true interpretations of Scripture and those that are simply inaccurate. The Spirit, working in the magisterium or teaching authority of our Church, helps us understand and apply what is in the Bible to our everyday life.

> *Interpretation of the inspired Scripture must be attentive above all to what God wants to reveal through the sacred authors for our salvation. What comes from the Spirit is not fully "understood except by the Spirit's action" (cf. Origen,* Hom. *in* Ex. *4, 5: PG 12, 320). (CCC 137)*

When the Spirit guides you to all truth, the Spirit may occasionally steer you away from television, the internet, etc., which does not always offer the clear truth. In seeking the truth we must be mindful that not all media programming puts priority on justice, truth and freedom. We need prudence and other virtues to be wise consumers of media.

> *Society has a right to information based on truth, freedom, and justice. One should practice moderation and discipline in the use of the social communications media. (CCC 2512)*

A Question for Me
What degree of moderation and discipline do I practice in using social communications media?

For a Child in My Life
What does it mean to practice moderation and discipline in using social communications media?

My Role in the Community
How involved am I in a good, Catholic Bible study group? Might I increase my involvement—or begin it?

For Depth and Further Life Application

Acts of the Apostles 2:1–11
Psalm 104
Galatians 5:16–25

📖 United States Catholic Catechism for Adults, pages 431–434

REFLECTION

Come, Holy Spirit, fill the hearts of your faithful and kindle in them the fire of your love.

B Trinity Sunday

The Gospel

The eleven disciples went to Galilee,
to the mountain to which Jesus had ordered them.
When they all saw him, they worshiped, but they doubted.
Then Jesus approached and said to them,
"All power in heaven and on earth has been given to me.
Go, therefore, and make disciples of all nations,
baptizing them in the name of the Father,
and of the Son, and of the Holy Spirit,
teaching them to observe all that I have commanded you.
And behold, I am with you always, until the end of the age."

—Matthew 28:16–20

Truths of Our Catholic Faith

To observe all that Jesus has commanded. Jesus continues to command action through His teaching voice, the holy Catholic Church. Our Church offers a few practical guidelines or precepts to help us express our faith concretely day in and day out; when we do so, we become better disciples and by our example help make disciples of all the nations.

The first precept ("You shall attend Mass on Sundays and on holy days of obligation and rest from servile labor") requires the faithful to sanctify the day commemorating the Resurrection of the Lord as well as the principal liturgical feasts honoring the mysteries of the Lord, the Blessed Virgin Mary, and the saints; in the first place, by participating in the Eucharistic celebration, in which the Christian community is gathered, and by resting from those works and activities which could impede such a sanctification of these days.[13]

The second precept ("You shall confess your sins at least once a year.") ensures preparation for the Eucharist by the reception of the sacrament of reconciliation, which continues Baptism's work of conversion and forgiveness.[14]

The third precept ("You shall receive the sacrament of the Eucharist at least during the Easter season") guarantees as a minimum the reception of the Lord's Body and Blood in connection with the Paschal feasts, the origin and center of the Christian liturgy.[15]

The fourth precept ("You shall observe the days of fasting and abstinence established by the Church") ensures the times of ascesis and penance which prepare us for the liturgical feasts and help us acquire mastery over our instincts and freedom of heart.[16]

The fifth precept ("You shall help to provide for the needs of the Church") means that the faithful are obliged to assist with the material needs of the Church, each according to his own ability.[17]

The faithful also have the duty of providing for the material needs of the Church, each according to his abilities.[18]
(CCC 2042, 2043)

A Question for Me

Do I have an occasional doubt or two about some aspect of the Faith? (Recall that even the Eleven doubted; but they obeyed, took action and persevered to glory.)

For a Child in My Life

What are some ways Jesus is with us always, until the end of the age?

My Role in the Community

Would I consider taking Holy Days of Obligation off of work as a personal or vacation day? When coworkers know the reason for this (holy days are to be treated as Sunday) it can be a powerful witness.

For Depth and Further Life Application

Deuteronomy 4:32–34, 39–40
Psalm 33
Romans 8:14–17

📖 United States Catholic Catechism for Adults, pages 514–515

REFLECTION

Glory to the Father, the Son, and the Holy Spirit; to God who is, who was, and who is to come.

—Revelation 1:8

B Corpus Christi

The Gospel

On the first day of the Feast of Unleavened Bread,
when they sacrificed the Passover lamb,
Jesus' disciples said to him,
"Where do you want us to go
and prepare for you to eat the Passover?"
He sent two of his disciples and said to them,
"Go into the city and a man will meet you,
carrying a jar of water.
Follow him.
Wherever he enters, say to the master of the house,
'The Teacher says, "Where is my guest room
where I may eat the Passover with my disciples?"'
Then he will show you a large upper room furnished and ready.
Make the preparations for us there."
The disciples then went off, entered the city,
and found it just as he had told them;
and they prepared the Passover.
While they were eating,
he took bread, said the blessing,
broke it, gave it to them, and said,
"Take it; this is my body."
Then he took a cup, gave thanks, and gave it to them,
and they all drank from it.
He said to them,
"This is my blood of the covenant,
which will be shed for many.
Amen, I say to you,
I shall not drink again the fruit of the vine
until the day when I drink it new in the kingdom of God."
Then, after singing a hymn,
they went out to the Mount of Olives.

—Mark 14:12–16, 22–26

Truths of Our Catholic Faith

The Passover celebrates God keeping His promise—His covenant—with Abraham. Through Moses, God delivers His people from the slavery of Egypt. Through Jesus' sacrifice, our heavenly Father delivers us from the slavery of sin and death.

> *God chose Abraham and made a covenant with him and his descendants. By the covenant God formed his people and revealed his law to them through Moses. Through the prophets, he prepared them to accept the salvation destined for all humanity. (CCC 72)*

It was bread that Jesus took, blessed, broke and gave. Wine as well. And priests to this day take bread, bless it, break it and give it to us, our saving feast of passing over from death and sin to new life in Jesus.

> *The essential signs of the Eucharistic sacrament are wheat bread and grape wine, on which the blessing of the Holy Spirit is invoked and the priest pronounces the words of consecration spoken by Jesus during the Last Supper: "This is my body which will be given up for you. . . . This is the cup of my blood. . . ." (CCC 1412)*

A Question for Me

How am I at keeping my promises? What might I do to improve in this regard?

For a Child in My Life

What did Jesus say when He gave His Body and Blood to the Apostles at the Last Supper?

My Role in the Community

How might I learn more about Judaism, or at least get to know a person of Jewish faith a little better?

For Depth and Further Life Application

Exodus 24:3–8
Psalm 116
Hebrews 9:11–15

📖 United States Catholic Catechism for Adults, pages 228–232

REFLECTION

I am the living bread that came down from heaven, says the Lord; whoever eats this bread will live forever.

—John 6:51

B Sacred Heart

The Gospel

Since it was preparation day,
in order that the bodies might not remain on the cross
on the sabbath,
for the sabbath day of that week was a solemn one,
the Jews asked Pilate that their legs be broken
and they be taken down.
So the soldiers came and broke the legs of the first
and then of the other one who was crucified with Jesus.
But when they came to Jesus and saw that he was already dead,
they did not break his legs,
but one soldier thrust his lance into his side,
and immediately blood and water flowed out.
An eyewitness has testified, and his testimony is true;
he knows that he is speaking the truth,
so that you also may come to believe.
For this happened so that the Scripture passage might be fulfilled:
Not a bone of it will be broken.
And again another passage says:
They will look upon him whom they have pierced.

—John 19:31–37

Truths of Our Catholic Faith

From something sacred, the heart of Jesus, flowed something important—both blood and water. The presence of both indicated Jesus' death, the definitive step toward His resurrection and our salvation.

Our first parents experienced something sacred, too: intimate friendship with God. From this holy relationship flowed an important sense of happiness, which is important because it reminds us of what once was and of what in a sense can be again thanks to Jesus' sacrifice.

> *Revelation makes known to us the state of original holiness and justice of man and woman before sin: from their friendship with God flowed the happiness of their existence in paradise.* (CCC 384)

For the soldier, this was an unforgettable—unrepeatable—experience. Similarly, when the waters of baptism bring God's life into us, we are forever changed. There is no such thing as rebaptism.

> *Baptism imprints on the soul an indelible spiritual sign, the character, which consecrates the baptized person for Christian worship. Because of the character Baptism cannot be repeated (cf. DS 1609 and DS 1624). (CCC 1280)*

A Question for Me

In what ways am I different because I am baptized?

For a Child in My Life

How do we know about the things that happened in this Gospel reading?

My Role in the Community

Having been an eyewitness to God doing great things for me, how well do I testify to this in the presence of other community members?

For Depth and Further Life Application

Hosea 11:1, 3–4, 8c–9
Isaiah 12:2–6
Ephesians 3:8–12, 14–19

📖 United States Catholic Catechism for Adults, pages 67–71

REFLECTION

Take my yoke upon you, says the Lord; and learn from me, for I am meek and humble of heart.

—Matthew 11:29ab

OR

REFLECTION

God first loved us and sent his Son as expiation for our sins.

—1 John 4:10b

B Second Sunday of Ordinary Time

The Gospel

John was standing with two of his disciples,
and as he watched Jesus walk by, he said,
"Behold, the Lamb of God."
The two disciples heard what he said and followed Jesus.
Jesus turned and saw them following him and said to them,
"What are you looking for?"
They said to him, "Rabbi" — which translated means Teacher —,
"where are you staying?"
He said to them, "Come, and you will see."
So they went and saw where Jesus was staying,
and they stayed with him that day.
It was about four in the afternoon.
Andrew, the brother of Simon Peter,
was one of the two who heard John and followed Jesus.
He first found his own brother Simon and told him,
"We have found the Messiah" — which is translated Christ —.
Then he brought him to Jesus.
Jesus looked at him and said,
"You are Simon the son of John;
you will be called Cephas"—which is translated Peter.

—John 1:35–42

Truths of Our Catholic Faith

Jesus takes initiative when He interacts with the disciples in this Gospel passage. He invites their free response. In cooperating with Jesus, Andrew and Peter start on their journey toward true freedom.

> *The divine initiative in the work of grace precedes, prepares, and elicits the free response of man. Grace responds to the deepest yearnings of human freedom, calls freedom to cooperate with it, and perfects freedom. (CCC 2022)*

Jesus is an authentic teacher. The disciples acknowledge Him as such. Authentic teachers can not help but teach, and those who follow in the footsteps of the Apostles today—the Bishop of Rome and all bishops united with him—continue offering what we are looking for: clear teaching about life, freedom and what it means to be truly human.

> *The Roman Pontiff and the bishops, as authentic teachers, preach to the People of God the faith which is to be believed and applied in moral life. It is also encumbent on them to pronounce on moral questions that fall within the natural law and reason.* (CCC 2050)

A Question for Me

What does it mean to say that grace perfects freedom by calling freedom to cooperate with it?

For a Child in My Life

What did Saint John the Baptist say to his two friends when Jesus walked by?

My Role in the Community

To whom could I say "Come, and you will see," meaning who in my community might I invite to learn more about Jesus and His Church?

For Depth and Further Life Application

Samuel 3:3b–10, 19
Psalm 40
Corinthians 6:13c–15a, 17–20

📖 United States Catholic Catechism for Adults, pages 591–598

REFLECTION

We have found the Messiah: Jesus Christ, who brings us truth and grace.

—John 1:41, 17b

B Third Sunday of Ordinary Time

The Gospel

After John had been arrested,
Jesus came to Galilee proclaiming the gospel of God:
"This is the time of fulfillment.
The kingdom of God is at hand.
Repent, and believe in the gospel."

As he passed by the Sea of Galilee,
he saw Simon and his brother Andrew casting their nets into the sea;
they were fishermen.
Jesus said to them,
"Come after me, and I will make you fishers of men."
Then they abandoned their nets and followed him.
He walked along a little farther
and saw James, the son of Zebedee, and his brother John.
They too were in a boat mending their nets.
Then he called them.
So they left their father Zebedee in the boat
along with the hired men and followed him.

—Mark 1:14–20

Truths of Our Catholic Faith

Jesus called them. He called twelve men from among all His female and male followers. The Church that Jesus established, like Him, recognizes a suitability for priestly ministry in a small but important group of men; She, like Jesus, calls them.

> *The Church confers the sacrament of Holy Orders only on baptized men (*viri*), whose suitability for the exercise of the ministry has been duly recognized. Church authority alone has the responsibility and right to call someone to receive the sacrament of Holy Orders. (CCC 1598)*

They followed Him. Peter and Andrew, James and John fulfilled the first calling of the Christian—to follow Jesus. Zebedee did not prevent the latter two from answering Jesus' call. For all we know, he may have encouraged them. Parents must always encourage children to listen for and to answer their vocation call from God.

> *Parents should respect and encourage their children's vocations. They should remember and teach that the first calling of the Christian is to follow Jesus.* (CCC 2253)

A Question for Me
What is Jesus' basic message?

For a Child in My Life
What did Jesus proclaim when He came to Galilee?

My Role in the Community
In what ways do I or should I encourage and respect my children's vocations?

For Depth and Further Life Application

Jonah 3:1–5, 10
Psalm 25
Corinthians 7:29–31

📖 United States Catholic Catechism for Adults, pages 546–547

REFLECTION

The kingdom of God is at hand. Repent and believe in the Gospel.

—Mark 1:15

B Fourth Sunday of Ordinary Time

The Gospel

Then they came to Capernaum,
 and on the sabbath Jesus entered the synagogue and taught.
The people were astonished at his teaching,
 for he taught them as one having authority and not as the scribes.
In their synagogue was a man with an unclean spirit;
 he cried out, "What have you to do with us, Jesus of Nazareth?
Have you come to destroy us?
I know who you are—the Holy One of God!"
Jesus rebuked him and said,
 "Quiet! Come out of him!"
The unclean spirit convulsed him and with a loud cry came out of him.
All were amazed and asked one another,
 "What is this?
A new teaching with authority.
He commands even the unclean spirits and they obey him."
His fame spread everywhere throughout the whole region of Galilee.

—Mark 1:21–28

Truths of Our Catholic Faith

The unclean spirit, interestingly, knew Jesus—not as a rival of God, but as One with an entirely unique relationship to our Father. Even a demon had sense enough to know that, ultimately, God is One.

> *"Hear, O Israel, the LORD our God is one LORD . . ."* (Deut *6:4;* Mk *12:29). "The supreme being must be unique, without equal. . . . If God is not one, he is not God" (Tertullian,* Adv. Marc.*, 1, 3, 5: PL 2, 274). (CCC 228)*

Jesus kept the Sabbath. He also had no problem using and delegating authority. The Church that Jesus founded authoritatively teaches that each and every Sunday, one way or another, Catholics had better participate in Mass.

> *"Sunday . . . is to be observed as the foremost holy day of obligation in the universal Church" (CIC, can. 1246 § 1). "On Sundays and other holy days of obligation the faithful are bound to participate in the Mass" (CIC, can. 1247). (CCC 2192)*

A Question for Me

What is my overall attitude toward legitimate authority? Keeping in mind Jesus' example of authority exercised appropriately, how might my attitude in this area improve?

For a Child in My Life

How many Gods are there? (One is the answer. If a discussion on the Trinity occurs, explain that they are one God. The point is that there is no such thing as gods and goddesses per se; even very young children appreciate this.)

My Role in the Community

How might I be influencing my community by my example of participating in Mass every Sunday no matter what, within reason?

For Depth and Further Life Application

Deuteronomy 18:15–20
Psalm 95
Corinthians 7:32–35

United States Catholic Catechism for Adults, pages 499–502

REFLECTION

The people who sit in darkness have seen a great light; on those dwelling in a land overshadowed by death, light has arisen.

—Matthew 4:16

B Fifth Sunday of Ordinary Time

The Gospel

On leaving the synagogue
Jesus entered the house of Simon and Andrew with James and John.
Simon's mother-in-law lay sick with a fever.
They immediately told him about her.
He approached, grasped her hand, and helped her up.
Then the fever left her and she waited on them.

When it was evening, after sunset,
they brought to him all who were ill or possessed by demons.
The whole town was gathered at the door.
He cured many who were sick with various diseases,
and he drove out many demons,
not permitting them to speak because they knew him.

Rising very early before dawn, he left
and went off to a deserted place, where he prayed.
Simon and those who were with him pursued him
and on finding him said, "Everyone is looking for you."
He told them, "Let us go on to the nearby villages
that I may preach there also.
For this purpose have I come."
So he went into their synagogues,
preaching and driving out demons throughout the whole of Galilee.

—Mark 1:29–39

Truths of Our Catholic Faith

Jesus could have asked an apostle to grasp the hand of Peter's mother-in-law and help her up. Rather, He approached and did it Himself, just as He cured many others who were sick. In the Sacrament of the Anointing of the Sick, the priest acts in the person of Jesus, facilitating a unique encounter with our living Risen Lord.

Only priests (presbyters and bishops) can give the sacrament of the Anointing of the Sick, using oil blessed by the bishop, or if necessary by the celebrating presbyter himself. (CCC 1530)

A pattern of prayer is obvious in Jesus' life. The Church He founded calls us to follow Jesus' example in various ways, establishing a healthy, holy habit of prayer.

The Church invites the faithful to regular prayer: daily prayers, the Liturgy of the Hours, Sunday Eucharist, the feasts of the liturgical year. (CCC 2720)

A Question for Me

When do I go off to a deserted place and pray? How might I find time to do this more often?

For a Child in My Life

What did Jesus do when He rose very early before dawn, left and went off to a deserted place?

My Role in the Community

The Liturgy of the Hours connects me with my Church community throughout the entire world. How might I learn more about this type of prayer, and consider practicing it in some form?

For Depth and Further Life Application

Job 7:1–4, 6–7
Psalm 147
Corinthians 9:16–19, 22–23

📖 United States Catholic Catechism for Adults, preface, pages ix–xii

REFLECTION

Christ took away our infirmities and bore our diseases.

—Matthew 8:17

B Sixth Sunday of Ordinary Time

The Gospel

A leper came to Jesus and kneeling down begged him and said,
"If you wish, you can make me clean."
Moved with pity, he stretched out his hand,
touched him, and said to him,
"I do will it. Be made clean."
The leprosy left him immediately, and he was made clean.
Then, warning him sternly, he dismissed him at once.

He said to him, "See that you tell no one anything,
but go, show yourself to the priest
and offer for your cleansing what Moses prescribed;
that will be proof for them."

The man went away and began to publicize the whole matter.
He spread the report abroad
so that it was impossible for Jesus to enter a town openly.
He remained outside in deserted places,
and people kept coming to him from everywhere.

—Mark 1:40–45

Truths of Our Catholic Faith

Jesus knows the limitations of being a bodily person—injury, fatigue, leprosy, etc. When we call the Church Christ's Body, we tap into a deep wellspring of understanding this great mystery. Jesus can and does heal bodies, making them clean. He offers cleansing and genuine health to us constantly, individually and as a community of persons.

> *The Church is the Body of Christ. Through the Spirit and his action in the sacraments, above all the Eucharist, Christ, who once was dead and is now risen, establishes the community of believers as his own Body.* (CCC 805)

"I do will it," says Jesus. He knows what it means to enjoy freedom. Would that we readily took responsibility for all of our freely chosen acts. Would that we all used our freedom as perfectly as the Son of God who challenges us and helps us live lives in which we can take appropriate pride.

> *Freedom characterizes properly human acts. It makes the human being responsible for acts of which he is the voluntary agent. His deliberate acts properly belong to him.* (CCC 1745)

A Question for Me

How am I at taking responsibility for acts of which I am the voluntary agent? What, if any, persistent sinful acts do I need to take to Jesus, saying "You can make me clean"?

For a Child in My Life

What does it mean to say that the Church is the Body of Christ?

My Role in the Community

Lepers were outcasts in Jesus' day. Who are the societal outcasts of my community? What might I do to show genuine concern for them?

For Depth and Further Life Application

Leviticus 13:1–2, 44–46
Psalm 32
Corinthians 10:31–11:1

📖 United States Catholic Catechism for Adults, introduction, pages xv–xxiv

REFLECTION

A great prophet has arisen in our midst, God has visited his people.

—Luke 7:16

B Seventh Sunday of Ordinary Time

The Gospel

When Jesus returned to Capernaum after some days,
it became known that he was at home.
Many gathered together so that there was no longer room for them,
not even around the door,
and he preached the word to them.
They came bringing to him a paralytic carried by four men.
Unable to get near Jesus because of the crowd,
they opened up the roof above him.
After they had broken through,
they let down the mat on which the paralytic was lying.
When Jesus saw their faith, he said to the paralytic,
"Child, your sins are forgiven."
Now some of the scribes were sitting there asking themselves,
"Why does this man speak that way? He is blaspheming.
Who but God alone can forgive sins?"
Jesus immediately knew in his mind
what they were thinking to themselves,
so he said, "Why are you thinking such things in your hearts?
Which is easier, to say to the paralytic,
'Your sins are forgiven,'
or to say, 'Rise, pick up your mat and walk?'
But that you may know
that the Son of Man has authority to forgive sins on earth"
—he said to the paralytic,
"I say to you, rise, pick up your mat, and go home."
He rose, picked up his mat at once,
and went away in the sight of everyone.
They were all astounded
and glorified God, saying, "We have never seen anything like this."

—Mark 2:1–12

Truths of Our Catholic Faith

The four men carrying the paralytic had a goal. They chose an alternate means of reaching their end and, presuming they fixed the roof afterward, one could assert that they performed a morally good act. Both a good goal and a good method as well as circumstances permitting sufficient knowledge and freedom are required to call an act morally good.

> *A morally good act requires the goodness of its object, of its end, and of its circumstances together.* (CCC 1760)

Jesus did not hang up a sign saying Entry Through Door Preferred. He did not expressly reveal His will in this case. At other times Jesus did articulate ordinary means of behavior, and His Church occasionally does so as well, expressing God's will with as much certainty as feasible this side of heaven. The way that mortal sin gets addressed is one of these instances.

> *Individual and integral confession of grave sins followed by absolution remains the only ordinary means of reconciliation with God and with the Church.* (CCC 1497)

A Question for Me

What are some of the ordinary means—the ways God wills—that He has revealed to us how we ought to express and live out our faith? (This phrase often refers to sacraments and matters related to them.)

For a Child in My Life

How do we make peace with God and our fellow Church members if we commit a very serious sin?

My Role in the Community

How would I explain the Sacrament of Penance to one who thinks it is unnecessary? (The phrase "ordinary means" may help.)

For Depth and Further Life Application

Isaiah 43:18–19, 21–22, 24b–25
Psalm 41
Corinthians 1:18–22

📖 United States Catholic Catechism for Adults, pages 234–241

REFLECTION

The Lord sent me to bring glad tidings to the poor, and to proclaim liberty to captives.

—cf. Luke 4:18

B Eighth Sunday of Ordinary Time

The Gospel

The disciples of John and of the Pharisees were accustomed to fast.
People came to him and objected,
"Why do the disciples of John and the disciples of the Pharisees fast,
but your disciples do not fast?"
Jesus answered them,
"Can the wedding guests fast while the bridegroom is with them?
As long as they have the bridegroom with them they cannot fast.
But the days will come when the bridegroom is
taken away from them,
and then they will fast on that day.
No one sews a piece of unshrunken cloth on an old cloak.
If he does, its fullness pulls away,
the new from the old, and the tear gets worse.
Likewise, no one pours new wine into old wineskins.
Otherwise, the wine will burst the skins,
and both the wine and the skins are ruined.
Rather, new wine is poured into fresh wineskins."

—Mark 2:18–22

Truths of Our Catholic Faith

Jesus seems fond of weddings. How fitting, then, that one way of grasping the mystery that is our Church is to consider Her as the Bride of Christ.

> *The Church is the Bride of Christ: he loved her and handed himself over for her. He has purified her by his blood and made her the fruitful mother of all God's children. (CCC 808)*

Our bridegroom, Jesus, is with us at every liturgy. We do not fast at the Eucharistic liturgy; we are fed there. Liturgy helps strengthen us to live morally as friends of Jesus Christ—to understand and act upon our Church's precepts and other moral teachings.

> *The precepts of the Church concern the moral and Christian life united with the liturgy and nourished by it. (CCC 2048)*

A Question for Me

To what degree is my life as a Christian united with the liturgy and nourished by it? How might I make a positive adjustment here?

For a Child in My Life

What does it mean to say that the Church is the Bride of Christ?

My Role in the Community

When I am invited to a wedding, do I attend the ceremony as well as the reception to show that I believe the ceremony is as or more important then the reception?

For Depth and Further Life Application

Hosea 2:16b, 17b, 21–22
Psalm 103
Corinthians 3:1b–6

📖 United States Catholic Catechism for Adults, pages 599–605

REFLECTION

The Father willed to give us birth by the word of truth that we may be a kind of firstfruits of his creatures.

—James 1:18

B Ninth Sunday of Ordinary Time

The Gospel

As Jesus was passing through a field of grain on the sabbath,
his disciples began to make a path while picking the heads of grain.
At this the Pharisees said to him,
"Look, why are they doing what is unlawful on the sabbath?"
He said to them, "Have you never read what David did
when he was in need and he and his companions were hungry?
How he went into the house of God when Abiathar was high priest
and ate the bread of offering
that only the priests could lawfully eat,
and shared it with his companions?"
Then he said to them,
"The sabbath was made for man, not man for the sabbath.
That is why the Son of Man is lord even of the sabbath."

—Mark 2:23–28

Truths of Our Catholic Faith

The sabbath was made for man. Sometimes people think they can get ahead by doing extra things on Sunday. Extra work. Extra shopping. Sometimes they will even sacrifice going to Mass to get these things done.

When we fail to observe the Lord's Day, we hurt ourselves. God gives us Sunday as a gift. God made Sunday for you.

> *"On Sundays and other holy days of obligation the faithful are bound . . . to abstain from those labors and business concerns which impede the worship to be rendered to God, the joy which is proper to the Lord's Day, or the proper relaxation of mind and body" (CIC, can. 1247). (CCC 2193)*

David's deeds say a lot in this instance. Jesus' words in turn reveal true teaching from God Himself. God, out of love, chose to start revealing Himself to human persons. He did so to and through David. He does so in the teaching, action and Person of Jesus.

God has revealed himself to man by gradually communicating his own mystery in deeds and in words. (CCC 69)

A Question for Me

Jesus uses an example from Scripture to make a point. How often do I do this? How might I familiarize myself with the Bible more deeply in order to be more like Jesus in this regard?

For a Child in My Life

Tell me everything you can think of that we are supposed to do on Sunday. What should we avoid on Sunday?

My Role in the Community

In what ways do I see God acting within my communities? How might I help make His presence more noticeable?

For Depth and Further Life Application

Deuteronomy 5:12–15
Psalm 81
Corinthians 4:6–11

📖 United States Catholic Catechism for Adults, pages 11–15

REFLECTION

Your word, O Lord, is truth; consecrate us in the truth.

—cf. John 17:17b, 17a

B Tenth Sunday of Ordinary Time

The Gospel

Jesus came home with his disciples.
Again the crowd gathered,
making it impossible for them even to eat.
When his relatives heard of this they set out to seize him,
for they said, "He is out of his mind."
The scribes who had come from Jerusalem said,
"He is possessed by Beelzebul,"
and "By the prince of demons he drives out demons."

Summoning them, he began to speak to them in parables,
"How can Satan drive out Satan?
If a kingdom is divided against itself,
that kingdom cannot stand.
And if a house is divided against itself,
that house will not be able to stand.
And if Satan has risen up against himself
and is divided, he cannot stand;
that is the end of him.
But no one can enter a strong man's house to plunder his property
unless he first ties up the strong man.
Then he can plunder the house.
Amen, I say to you,
all sins and all blasphemies that people utter will be forgiven them.
But whoever blasphemes against the Holy Spirit
will never have forgiveness,
but is guilty of an everlasting sin."
For they had said, "He has an unclean spirit."

His mother and his brothers arrived.
Standing outside they sent word to him and called him.
A crowd seated around him told him,
"Your mother and your brothers and your sisters
are outside asking for you."
But he said to them in reply,
"Who are my mother and my brothers?"
And looking around at those seated in the circle he said,
"Here are my mother and my brothers.

For whoever does the will of God
is my brother and sister and mother."

—Mark 3:20–35

Truths of Our Catholic Faith

The Father, the Son and the Holy Spirit desire us to be in communion with them. United with the Blessed Trinity, no power can ultimately harm us. Our Church is an entirely unique place and way to encounter the Triune God, learning and doing His will.

> *The Holy Spirit, whom Christ the head pours out on his members, builds, animates, and sanctifies the Church. She is the sacrament of the Holy Trinity's communion with men. (CCC 747)*

Jesus makes it abundantly clear: doing the will of God is profoundly important if we desire closeness with Him. Moral teachings like the Ten Commandments are to be taken very seriously; when we strive to live them we experience joy and peace that no one other than a loving God could create.

> *The Ten Commandments, in their fundamental content, state grave obligations. However, obedience to these precepts also implies obligations in matter which is, in itself, light. (CCC 2081)*

A Question for Me

How familiar am I with the Church's teaching regarding Mary's perpetual virginity? What are some ways I might deepen my appropriation of the Faith in this regard?

For a Child in My Life

What role should the Ten Commandments play in our life?

My Role in the Community

Some Christians assert that Mary had biological children in addition to Jesus. How might I help dispel this misconception?

For Depth and Further Life Application

Genesis 3:9–15
Psalm 130
2 Corinthians 4:13–5:1

📖 United States Catholic Catechism for Adults, pages 102–106

REFLECTION

Now the ruler of this world will be driven out, says the Lord; and when I am lifted up from the earth, I will draw everyone to myself.

—John 12:31b–32

B Eleventh Sunday of Ordinary Time

The Gospel

Jesus said to the crowds:
"This is how it is with the kingdom of God;
it is as if a man were to scatter seed on the land
and would sleep and rise night and day
and through it all the seed would sprout and grow,
he knows not how.
Of its own accord the land yields fruit,
first the blade, then the ear, then the full grain in the ear.
And when the grain is ripe, he wields the sickle at once,
for the harvest has come."

He said,
"To what shall we compare the kingdom of God,
or what parable can we use for it?
It is like a mustard seed that, when it is sown in the ground,
is the smallest of all the seeds on the earth.
But once it is sown, it springs up and becomes the largest of plants
and puts forth large branches,
so that the birds of the sky can dwell in its shade."
With many such parables
he spoke the word to them as they were able to understand it.
Without parables he did not speak to them,
but to his own disciples he explained everything in private.

—Mark 4:26–34

Truths of Our Catholic Faith

When the grain is ripe, Jesus will use the sickle. Jesus will judge the living and dead based on faithful citizenship in God's kingdom. Sometimes what seems insignificant to kings and rulers of this world may, like the mustard seed, make an enormous difference in terms of our eternity.

> *When he comes at the end of time to judge the living and the dead, the glorious Christ will reveal the secret disposition of hearts and will render to each man according to his works and according to his acceptance or refusal of grace. (CCC 682)*

In God's kingdom, human life and concern for its respect—for the dignity of each person without exception—receives a very high priority. Although this Kingdom is never fully realized during our earthly life, we are obliged to take steps that will provide shelter, shade and sustenance for as many people as feasible.

> *The dignity of the human person requires the pursuit of the common good. Everyone should be concerned to create and support institutions that improve the conditions of human life.* (CCC 1926)

A Question for Me

Knowing that the secret disposition of my heart is known to Jesus, what in my heart is most in need of positive change?

For a Child in My Life

How is God's kingdom like a tiny seed?

My Role in the Community

What examples of the common good being pursued do I see in my communities? How might I help more in this pursuit?

For Depth and Further Life Application

Ezekiel 17:22–24
Psalm 92
2 Corinthians 5:6–10

📖 United States Catholic Catechism for Adults, pages 91–96

REFLECTION

The seed is the word of God, Christ is the sower. All who come to him will live forever.

B Twelfth Sunday of Ordinary Time

The Gospel

On that day, as evening drew on, Jesus said to his disciples:
"Let us cross to the other side."
Leaving the crowd, they took Jesus with them in the boat
just as he was.
And other boats were with him.
A violent squall came up and waves were breaking over the boat,
so that it was already filling up.
Jesus was in the stern, asleep on a cushion.
They woke him and said to him,
"Teacher, do you not care that we are perishing?"
He woke up,
rebuked the wind, and said to the sea, "Quiet! Be still!"
The wind ceased and there was great calm.
Then he asked them, "Why are you terrified?
Do you not yet have faith?"
They were filled with great awe and said to one another,
"Who then is this whom even wind and sea obey?"

—Mark 4:35–41

Truths of Our Catholic Faith

Jesus is Lord of creation. He is Lord over all creation. The fact that God created us shows our Father's great love. Jesus, present from the beginning, fulfills our Father's ultimate plan and exercises loving dominion over all of creation. Even sea and wind obey our loving Lord Jesus.

> *In the creation of the world and of man, God gave the first and universal witness to his almighty love and his wisdom, the first proclamation of the "plan of his loving goodness," which finds its goal in the new creation in Christ. (CCC 315)*

Like Jesus' nature miracles, the miracle of the Most Holy Eucharist brings about some awe-inspiring effects. He who the wind and sea obey can certainly pour out miraculous blessings through this great sacrament.

> *Communion with the Body and Blood of Christ increases the communicant's union with the Lord, forgives his venial sins, and preserves him from grave sins. Since receiving this sacrament strengthens the bonds of charity between the communicant and Christ, it also reinforces the unity of the Church as the Mystical Body of Christ. (CCC 1416)*

A Question for Me

How might I explain to another the effects of receiving Holy Communion?

For a Child in My Life

What are some results of receiving Holy Communion?

My Role in the Community

What indications in my community do I see of God's almighty love and His wisdom? How might I help point these out to others more clearly?

For Depth and Further Life Application

Job 38:1, 8–11
Psalm 107
2 Corinthians 5:14–17

📖 United States Catholic Catechism for Adults, pages 49–50

REFLECTION

A great prophet has arisen in our midst. God has visited his people.

—Luke 7:16

B Thirteenth Sunday of Ordinary Time

The Gospel

When Jesus had crossed again in the boat
to the other side,
a large crowd gathered around him, and he stayed close to the sea.
One of the synagogue officials, named Jairus, came forward.
Seeing him he fell at his feet and pleaded earnestly with him, saying,
"My daughter is at the point of death.
Please, come lay your hands on her
that she may get well and live."
He went off with him,
and a large crowd followed him and pressed upon him.

While he was still speaking, people from the synagogue
official's house arrived and said,
"Your daughter has died; why trouble the teacher any longer?"
Disregarding the message that was reported,
Jesus said to the synagogue official,
"Do not be afraid; just have faith."
He did not allow anyone to accompany him inside
except Peter, James, and John, the brother of James.
When they arrived at the house of the synagogue official,
he caught sight of a commotion,
people weeping and wailing loudly.
So he went in and said to them,
"Why this commotion and weeping?
The child is not dead but asleep."
And they ridiculed him.
Then he put them all out.
He took along the child's father and mother
and those who were with him
and entered the room where the child was.
He took the child by the hand and said to her, "Talitha koum,"
which means, "Little girl, I say to you, arise!"
The girl, a child of twelve, arose immediately and walked around.
At that they were utterly astounded.
He gave strict orders that no one should know this
and said that she should be given something to eat.

—Mark 5:21–24, 35b–43

Truths of Our Catholic Faith

If this child were not dead, it would be appropriate in our time for a priest to administer the Sacrament of Anointing of the Sick. This Sacrament is certainly not to be reserved only for times when death is imminent. Acting in the person of Christ, priests anoint the seriously ill so that if God wills it they may get well and live.

> *Each time a Christian falls seriously ill, he may receive the Anointing of the Sick, and also when, after he has received it, the illness worsens. (CCC 1529)*

God's Son commands a little girl to arise. His healing grace allows this to occur. God does not command the impossible. Grace helps us fulfill His commandments.

> *What God commands he makes possible by his grace. (CCC 2082)*

A Question for Me

Have I ever been ridiculed for my faith? What was my reaction? How does Jesus react in this Gospel passage? How might I become more like Him in this respect?

For a Child in My Life

When may a Christian receive the Anointing of the Sick?

My Role in the Community

Have I ever been guilty of ridiculing another for her or his faith? What are some of the results when this sort of thing happens? How can I avoid this sort of behavior from this time forth?

For Depth and Further Life Application

Wisdom 1:13–15; 2:23–24
Psalm 30
2 Corinthians 8:7, 9, 13–15

📖 United States Catholic Catechism for Adults, pages 251–255

REFLECTION

Our Savior Jesus Christ destroyed death and brought life to light through the Gospel.

—cf. 2 Timothy 1:10

B Fourteenth Sunday of Ordinary Time

The Gospel

Jesus departed from there and came to his native place,
accompanied by his disciples.
When the sabbath came he began to teach in the synagogue,
and many who heard him were astonished.
They said, "Where did this man get all this?
What kind of wisdom has been given him?
What mighty deeds are wrought by his hands!
Is he not the carpenter, the son of Mary,
and the brother of James and Joses and Judas and Simon?
And are not his sisters here with us?"
And they took offense at him.
Jesus said to them,
"A prophet is not without honor except in his native place
and among his own kin and in his own house."
So he was not able to perform any mighty deed there,
apart from curing a few sick people by laying his hands on them.
He was amazed at their lack of faith.

—Mark 6:1–6

Truths of Our Catholic Faith

There are several theories about references to sisters and brothers of Jesus even though we know that Mary herself never bore a child other than Jesus. The main point here is that when something at face value seems to contradict a Church teaching, it is important to dig a little deeper and get all the facts so that the truth of Church teaching is understood, communicated and in fact spread.

> *Mary "remained a virgin in conceiving her Son, a virgin in giving birth to him, a virgin in carrying him, a virgin in nursing him at her breast, always a virgin" (St. Augustine,* Serm. *186, 1: PL 38, 999): with her whole being she is "the handmaid of the Lord"* (Lk *1:38). (CCC 510)*

Jesus regularly observed the Sabbath. As His friends and followers we celebrate His Resurrection on the Lord's Day, Sunday. In order to imitate Him and deepen our relationship with Him we observe the Lord's Day and all that it entails.

> *The Church celebrates the day of Christ's Resurrection on the "eighth day," Sunday, which is rightly called the Lord's Day (cf.* SC 106*). (CCC 2191)*

A Question for Me

Have I ever heard someone make derogatory remarks about Mary? What are some ways I might help others better understand Mary's importance and great love for us all?

For a Child in My Life

Why is Sunday so special? Why do we call Sunday the Lord's Day?

My Role in the Community

Along with helping out in the broader community, how am I at offering my time, talent and treasure in my parish and at my home?

For Depth and Further Life Application

Ezekiel 2:2–5
Psalm 123
2 Corinthians 12:7–10

📖 United States Catholic Catechism for Adults, pages 363–367

REFLECTION

The Spirit of the Lord is upon me for he sent me to bring glad tidings to the poor.

—cf. Luke 4:18

B Fifteenth Sunday of Ordinary Time

The Gospel

> Jesus summoned the Twelve and began to send them out two by two
> and gave them authority over unclean spirits.
> He instructed them to take nothing for the journey
> but a walking stick—
> no food, no sack, no money in their belts.
> They were, however, to wear sandals
> but not a second tunic.
> He said to them,
> "Wherever you enter a house, stay there until you leave.
> Whatever place does not welcome you or listen to you,
> leave there and shake the dust off your feet
> in testimony against them."
> So they went off and preached repentance.
> The Twelve drove out many demons,
> and they anointed with oil many who were sick and cured them.
>
> —Mark 6:7–13

Truths of Our Catholic Faith

Jesus sent the Twelve. He gave them special authority and instructions. Although democracy has proven itself to be an effective means of civil government, and although there are certainly some elements of democratic process in our Catholic Church (e.g., cardinals elect a pope), we need to recall occasionally that from the Church's infancy special authority and a unique role was given the apostles by Jesus Himself. The Spirit-guided men who fill this role today are our bishops.

> *The Bishops, established by the Holy Spirit, succeed the apostles. They are "the visible source and foundation of unity in their own particular Churches"* (LG 23). *(CCC 938)*

They anointed with oil many who were sick. This practice, grace-filled anointing, continues today each time the Sacrament of

Anointing of the Sick is celebrated. When a priest or bishop liturgically prays for the unique grace that this sacrament offers, his holy anointing facilitates an encounter with the soothing, often healing, Jesus.

> *The celebration of the Anointing of the Sick consists essentially in the anointing of the forehead and hands of the sick person (in the Roman Rite) or of other parts of the body (in the Eastern rite), the anointing being accompanied by the liturgical prayer of the celebrant asking for the special grace of this sacrament.* (CCC 1531)

A Question for Me

What comes to mind when I ponder the fact that my bishop is a successor to the original apostles?

For a Child in My Life

Who takes the place of the apostles in our world today?

My Role in the Community

What are some of my bishop's priorities? (Often these are described on diocesan websites.) How might I help my bishop pursue those goals he currently considers most important in the diocese?

For Depth and Further Life Application

Amos 7:12–15
Psalm 85
Ephesians 1:3–10

📖 United States Catholic Catechism for Adults, pages 256–259

REFLECTION

May the Father of our Lord Jesus Christ enlighten the eyes of our hearts, that we may know what is the hope that belongs to our call.

—cf. Ephesians 1:17–18

B Sixteenth Sunday of Ordinary Time

The Gospel

The apostles gathered together with Jesus
 and reported all they had done and taught.
He said to them,
 "Come away by yourselves to a deserted place and rest a while."
People were coming and going in great numbers,
 and they had no opportunity even to eat.
So they went off in the boat by themselves to a deserted place.
People saw them leaving and many came to know about it.
They hastened there on foot from all the towns
 and arrived at the place before them.

When he disembarked and saw the vast crowd,
 his heart was moved with pity for them,
 for they were like sheep without a shepherd;
and he began to teach them many things.

—Mark 6:30–34

Truths of Our Catholic Faith

The apostles needed a day of recollection. Their hearts, minds, bodies and souls needed to rest a while.

Time for prayer helps us to learn from the Master Teacher. Whether it is speaking to God (vocal prayer), reflecting on something He said (meditation) or simply and wordlessly enjoying His presence (contemplation), making time to pray keeps us focused on what and Who truly gives us life.

> *The Christian tradition comprises three major expressions of the life of prayer: vocal prayer, meditation, and contemplative prayer. They have in common the recollection of the heart. (CCC 2721)*

The Sacred Heart of Jesus felt pity for the crowd. They had a right to know the truth about life, both earthly and eternal. They had a dignity that was not being lived out fully. Jesus respects us too much to let us live in darkness; so through His Church, He teaches us many things.

> *Respect for the human person considers the other "another self." It presupposes respect for the fundamental rights that flow from the dignity intrinsic of the person. (CCC 1944)*

A Question for Me

How might I move toward practicing contemplative prayer? (Bear in mind that this differs dramatically from the "mind-emptying" approach to meditation that you may have encountered.)

For a Child in My Life

What does it mean to consider a person as "another self"?

My Role in the Community

Who do I know that is like sheep without a shepherd? While recalling that I myself am in need of shepherding, how might I help this person or these people get the guidance they need?

For Depth and Further Life Application

Jeremiah 23:1–6
Psalm 23
Ephesians 2:13–18

📖 United States Catholic Catechism for Adults, page 535

REFLECTION

My sheep hear my voice, says the Lord; I know them, and they follow me.

—John 10:27

B Seventeenth Sunday of Ordinary Time

The Gospel

Jesus went across the Sea of Galilee.
A large crowd followed him,
because they saw the signs he was performing on the sick.
Jesus went up on the mountain,
and there he sat down with his disciples.
The Jewish feast of Passover was near.
When Jesus raised his eyes
and saw that a large crowd was coming to him,
he said to Philip,
"Where can we buy enough food for them to eat?"
He said this to test him,
because he himself knew what he was going to do.
Philip answered him,
"Two hundred days' wages worth of food would not be enough
for each of them to have a little."
One of his disciples,
Andrew, the brother of Simon Peter, said to him,
"There is a boy here who has five barley loaves and two fish;
but what good are these for so many?"
Jesus said, "Have the people recline."
Now there was a great deal of grass in that place.
So the men reclined, about five thousand in number.
Then Jesus took the loaves, gave thanks,
and distributed them to those who were reclining,
and also as much of the fish as they wanted.
When they had had their fill, he said to his disciples,
"Gather the fragments left over,
so that nothing will be wasted."
So they collected them,
and filled twelve wicker baskets with fragments
from the five barley loaves
that had been more than they could eat.
When the people saw the sign he had done, they said,
"This is truly the Prophet, the one who is to come into the world."

> Since Jesus knew that they were going to come and carry him off
> to make him king,
> he withdrew again to the mountain alone.
>
> —John 6:1–15

Truths of Our Catholic Faith

Jesus could have distributed this food in a variety of ways. Yet He Himself took, blessed, broke and gave the loaves to the people. Today, through our priests, Jesus offers His sacrifice of thanks and praise, giving us Himself as the Bread of Life.

> *It is Christ himself, the eternal high priest of the New Covenant who, acting through the ministry of the priests, offers the Eucharistic sacrifice. And it is the same Christ, really present under the species of bread and wine, who is the offering of the Eucharistic sacrifice. (CCC 1410)*

The Lord wanted nothing to be wasted. Squandering resources is irresponsible, disrespectful and bothersome to God. We have a moral obligation to use creation's bounty wisely, both for present purposes and with respect to future generations.

> *The dominion granted by the Creator over the mineral, vegetable, and animal resources of the universe cannot be separated from respect for moral obligations, including those toward generations to come. (CCC 2456)*

A Question for Me

What does the fact that Christ Himself offers the Eucharistic sacrifice have to do with who receives the Sacrament of Holy Orders?

For a Child in My Life

Why did Jesus withdraw to the mountain?

My Role in the Community

How might one abuse dominion over mineral, vegetable and animal resources? How could one be excessive in fulfilling perceived obligations toward generations to come? What are some suitable ways to show respect for future generations regarding our universe's resources?

For Depth and Further Life Application

2 Kings 4:42–44
Psalm 145
Ephesians 4:1–6

📖 United States Catholic Catechism for Adults, pages 516–517

REFLECTION

A great prophet has risen in our midst. God has visited his people.

—Luke 7:16

B Eighteenth Sunday of Ordinary Time

The Gospel

When the crowd saw that neither Jesus nor his disciples were there,
they themselves got into boats
and came to Capernaum looking for Jesus.
And when they found him across the sea they said to him,
"Rabbi, when did you get here?"
Jesus answered them and said,
"Amen, amen, I say to you,
you are looking for me not because you saw signs
but because you ate the loaves and were filled.
Do not work for food that perishes
but for the food that endures for eternal life,
which the Son of Man will give you.
For on him the Father, God, has set his seal."
So they said to him,
"What can we do to accomplish the works of God?"
Jesus answered and said to them,
"This is the work of God, that you believe in the one he sent."
So they said to him,
"What sign can you do, that we may see and believe in you?
What can you do?
Our ancestors ate manna in the desert, as it is written:
He gave them bread from heaven to eat."
So Jesus said to them,
"Amen, amen, I say to you,
it was not Moses who gave the bread from heaven;
my Father gives you the true bread from heaven.
For the bread of God is that which comes down from heaven
and gives life to the world."

So they said to him,
"Sir, give us this bread always."
Jesus said to them,
"I am the bread of life;
whoever comes to me will never hunger,
and whoever believes in me will never thirst."

—John 6:24–35

Truths of Our Catholic Faith

Jesus isn't shy in this Gospel passage. He clearly communicates His importance, and in the process alludes to the Eucharist.

The importance of the Eucharist is crystal clear in our Catholic faith. A bishop, above all other duties related to worship, must see to it that the Eucharist is available and celebrated throughout his diocese in accordance with the resources accessible to him.

> *Helped by the priests, their co-workers, and by the deacons, the bishops have the duty of authentically teaching the faith, celebrating divine worship, above all the Eucharist, and guiding their Churches as true pastors. Their responsibility also includes concern for all the Churches, with and under the Pope. (CCC 939)*

Sometimes we eat and are filled. Other times we receive our fair share on any given day and may be less than full. Always we are entitled to be treated fairly so that we have a reasonable chance to obtain sufficient resources for ourselves and any dependents. This is justice in the social or societal setting.

> *Society ensures social justice by providing the conditions that allow associations and individuals to obtain their due. (CCC 1943)*

A Question for Me

How is Jesus the bread of life?

For a Child in My Life

What does Jesus mean when He says "I am the bread of life"?

My Role in the Community

In what ways do I contribute to providing conditions that allow individuals and associations to get their due?

For Depth and Further Life Application

Exodus 16:2–4, 12–15
Psalm 78
Ephesians 4:17, 20–24

📖 United States Catholic Catechism for Adults, pages 138–139

REFLECTION

One does not live on bread alone, but by every word that comes forth from the mouth of God.

—Matthew 4:4b

B Nineteenth Sunday of Ordinary Time

The Gospel

The Jews murmured about Jesus because he said,
"I am the bread that came down from heaven, "
and they said,
"Is this not Jesus, the son of Joseph?
Do we not know his father and mother?
Then how can he say,
'I have come down from heaven'?"
Jesus answered and said to them,
"Stop murmuring among yourselves.
No one can come to me unless the Father who sent me draw him,
and I will raise him on the last day.
It is written in the prophets:
They shall all be taught by God.
Everyone who listens to my Father and learns from him comes to me.
Not that anyone has seen the Father
except the one who is from God;
he has seen the Father.
Amen, amen, I say to you,
whoever believes has eternal life.
I am the bread of life.
Your ancestors ate the manna in the desert, but they died;
this is the bread that comes down from heaven
so that one may eat it and not die.
I am the living bread that came down from heaven;
whoever eats this bread will live forever;
and the bread that I will give is my flesh for the life of the world."

—John 6:41–51

Truths of Our Catholic Faith

None of us has seen the Father. God is in a sense invisible. Yet those who met Jesus got a glimpse of divinity. And as we become more Christ-like we show the world that God is real, even though a leap of faith is required to allow ourselves to be drawn to the Father, to be taught by Him, to receive God into our heart and home.

> *Man is predestined to reproduce the image of God's Son made man, the "image of the invisible God"* (Col *1:15), so that Christ shall be the first-born of a multitude of brothers and sisters (cf.* Eph *1:3-6;* Rom *8:29). (CCC 381)*

To justify our life entirely to God would be an impossibility. We all fall short and need to be renewed by God's grace. Placing our faith in the Father, believing the effectiveness of Jesus' sacrifice, adhering to the ordinary means of salvation revealed by our Triune God acquire for us justification and, ultimately, eternal life.

> *Justification includes the remission of sins, sanctification, and the renewal of the inner man. (CCC 2019)*

A Question for Me

In what ways does God teach me?

For a Child in My Life

What does Jesus say is the bread that He will give? For what reason does He give it to us?

My Role in the Community

How much murmuring do I do? In what ways might I use my gift of speech more constructively?

For Depth and Further Life Application

1 Kings 19:4–8
Psalm 34
Ephesians 4:30–5:2

United States Catholic Catechism for Adults, pages 71–73

REFLECTION

I am the living bread that came down from heaven, says the Lord; whoever eats this bread will live forever.

—John 6:51

B Twentieth Sunday of Ordinary Time

The Gospel

Jesus said to the crowds:
"I am the living bread that came down from heaven;
whoever eats this bread will live forever;
and the bread that I will give
is my flesh for the life of the world."

The Jews quarreled among themselves, saying,
"How can this man give us his flesh to eat?"
Jesus said to them,
"Amen, amen, I say to you,
unless you eat the flesh of the Son of Man and drink his blood,
you do not have life within you.
Whoever eats my flesh and drinks my blood
has eternal life,
and I will raise him on the last day.
For my flesh is true food,
and my blood is true drink.
Whoever eats my flesh and drinks my blood
remains in me and I in him.
Just as the living Father sent me
and I have life because of the Father,
so also the one who feeds on me
will have life because of me.
This is the bread that came down from heaven.
Unlike your ancestors who ate and still died,
whoever eats this bread will live forever."

—John 6:51–58

Truths of Our Catholic Faith

The apostles were there when Jesus delivered these unambiguous words. They eventually came to know that one major uniting factor among the followers of Jesus is Holy Communion. Even today, amidst legitimate diversity, the witness of our apostles and their successors, the bishops, helps draw all together in Jesus.

The criterion that assures unity amid the diversity of liturgical traditions is fidelity to apostolic Tradition, i.e., the communion in the faith and the sacraments received from the apostles, a communion that is both signified and guaranteed by apostolic succession. (CCC 1209)

Not just anyone can effect the change that occurs in ordinary bread and wine, making them the Body, Blood, Soul and Divinity of Jesus. Those who were with Him from the beginning, the apostles, were first to confect the Eucharist. Eventually, hands were laid on presbyters (priests) to help make this great sacrament more widely available.

Only validly ordained priests can preside at the Eucharist and consecrate the bread and the wine so that they become the Body and Blood of the Lord. (CCC 1411)

A Question for Me

What are the benefits of the apostolic succession?

For a Child in My Life

Who can consecrate bread and wine so they become the Lord's Body and Blood?

My Role in the Community

How might I explain my belief in the real presence of Jesus in the Eucharist to one who has yet to make that leap of faith?

For Depth and Further Life Application

Proverbs 9:1–6
Psalm 34
Ephesians 5:15–20

📖 United States Catholic Catechism for Adults, pages 175–177

REFLECTION

Whoever eats my flesh and drinks my blood remains in me and I in him, says the Lord.

—John 6:56

B Twenty-first Sunday of Ordinary Time

The Gospel

Many of Jesus' disciples who were listening said,
"This saying is hard; who can accept it?"
Since Jesus knew that his disciples were murmuring about this,
he said to them, "Does this shock you?
What if you were to see the Son of Man ascending
to where he was before?
It is the spirit that gives life,
while the flesh is of no avail.
The words I have spoken to you are Spirit and life.
But there are some of you who do not believe."
Jesus knew from the beginning the ones who would not believe
and the one who would betray him.
And he said,
"For this reason I have told you that no one can come to me
unless it is granted him by my Father."

As a result of this,
many of his disciples returned to their former way of life
and no longer accompanied him.
Jesus then said to the Twelve, "Do you also want to leave?"
Simon Peter answered him, "Master, to whom shall we go?
You have the words of eternal life.
We have come to believe
and are convinced that you are the Holy One of God."

—John 6:60–69

Truths of Our Catholic Faith

What if we saw the Son of Man ascending to where he was before? We would have witnessed the Ascension of Jesus just as His disciples did. Jesus, the Holy One of God, is somehow with the Father physically with a glorified body. Bodily, Christ will come again.

> *Christ's ascension marks the definitive entrance of Jesus' humanity into God's heavenly domain, whence he will come again (cf.* Acts 1:11*); this humanity in the*

> *meantime hides him from the eyes of men (cf.* Col *3:3). (CCC 665)*

Faith is not always easy to acquire or receive. Thankfully, we are not alone on our journey of faith. As the Twelve had each other in coming to believe Jesus' divinity, so we have our Church to accompany us as we strive to deepen and strengthen our belief.

> *"Believing" is a human act, conscious and free, corresponding to the dignity of the human person. (CCC 180)*

A Question for Me

Where is Jesus right now?

For a Child in My Life

What does the word ascend mean? What is the Ascension of Jesus?

My Role in the Community

Who in my community finds the teaching of Jesus to be a hard concept; how might I support them so that, in faith, they can accept it?

For Depth and Further Life Application

Joshua 24:1–2a, 15–17, 18b
Psalm 34
Ephesians 5:2a, 25–32

📖 United States Catholic Catechism for Adults, pages 44–47

REFLECTION

Your words, Lord, are Spirit and life; you have the words of everlasting life.

—John 6:63c, 68c

B Twenty-second Sunday of Ordinary Time

The Gospel

When the Pharisees with some scribes who had come from Jerusalem
gathered around Jesus,
they observed that some of his disciples ate their meals
with unclean, that is, unwashed, hands.
—For the Pharisees and, in fact, all Jews,
do not eat without carefully washing their hands,
keeping the tradition of the elders.
And on coming from the marketplace
they do not eat without purifying themselves.
And there are many other things that they have traditionally observed,
the purification of cups and jugs and kettles and beds. —
So the Pharisees and scribes questioned him,
"Why do your disciples not follow the tradition of the elders
but instead eat a meal with unclean hands?"
He responded,
"Well did Isaiah prophesy about you hypocrites, as it is written:
This people honors me with their lips,
but their hearts are far from me;
in vain do they worship me,
teaching as doctrines human precepts.
You disregard God's commandment but cling to human tradition."

He summoned the crowd again and said to them,
"Hear me, all of you, and understand.
Nothing that enters one from outside can defile that person;
but the things that come out from within are what defile.

"From within people, from their hearts,
come evil thoughts, unchastity, theft, murder,
adultery, greed, malice, deceit,
licentiousness, envy, blasphemy, arrogance, folly.
All these evils come from within and they defile."

—Mark 7:1–8, 14–15, 21–23

Truths of Our Catholic Faith

The word unchastity appears in this gospel passage. Jesus modeled all virtue, including that of chastity. In answering our call to live chastely, surrendering our hearts to the Lord of life and love will help keep our hearts filled with peace from deep within.

> *Christ is the model of chastity. Every baptized person is called to lead a chaste life, each according to his particular state of life.* (CCC 2394)

What Jesus is describing is something called concupiscence. The ninth commandment reminds us that along with avoiding sinful behavior—perhaps as a helpful way of avoiding it—we should be mindful of our thoughts and feelings, always confidently asking God to cleanse our hearts with His grace.

> *The ninth commandment warns against lust or carnal concupiscence.* (CCC 2529)

A Question for Me

What are the similarities and differences between Tradition with a capital T and tradition with a small t?

For a Child in My Life

Why did Jesus not get married? (Answers will vary, of course.) How is Jesus an example for everyone whether they are married or single?

My Role in the Community

How does anything mentioned in verses 21–23 affect those around me? What can I do to help minimize these effects?

For Depth and Further Life Application

Deuteronomy 4:1–2, 6–8
Psalm 15
James 1:17–18, 21b–22, 27

📖 United States Catholic Catechism for Adults, pages 441–443

REFLECTION

The Father willed to give us birth by the word of truth that we may be a kind of firstfruits of his creatures.

—James 1:18

B Twenty-third Sunday of Ordinary Time

The Gospel

Again Jesus left the district of Tyre
and went by way of Sidon to the Sea of Galilee,
into the district of the Decapolis.
And people brought to him a deaf man who had
a speech impediment
and begged him to lay his hand on him.
He took him off by himself away from the crowd.
He put his finger into the man's ears
and, spitting, touched his tongue;
then he looked up to heaven and groaned, and said to him,
"*Ephphatha*!"— that is, "Be opened!" —
And immediately the man's ears were opened,
his speech impediment was removed,
and he spoke plainly.
He ordered them not to tell anyone.
But the more he ordered them not to,
the more they proclaimed it.
They were exceedingly astonished and they said,
"He has done all things well.
He makes the deaf hear and the mute speak."

—Mark 7:31–37

Truths of Our Catholic Faith

Ordinary objects can sometimes point us toward God in a concrete way. Holy water in the font, touched lightly to our forehead, heart and shoulders. The crucifix on our blessed rosary reminding us of Jesus' love. A blessed palm displayed in our home, calling to mind how quickly fame can turn to persecution in a world where human hearts can shift positions all too easily.

These objects are called sacramentals. Jesus knows that engaging our senses helps us encounter Him at deeper levels; He made use of this man's senses in curing him. Sacramentals can fill everyday life with sensory reminders of God's grace, readying us to receive this grace quite abundantly in one or more of the seven sacraments.

> *Sacramentals are sacred signs instituted by the Church. They prepare men to receive the fruit of the sacraments and sanctify different circumstances of life. (CCC 1677)*

As Jesus embodies His Father's goodness by doing all things well, so the Church He founded concretizes God's presence in our world and makes communion with Him accessible to all people. Astonishingly, salvation can actually be ours.

> *The Church in this world is the sacrament of salvation, the sign and the instrument of the communion of God and men. (CCC 780)*

A Question for Me

Why did Jesus bother touching this man? Why did he not just will him to be healed and get it over with?

For a Child in My Life

What did the astonished people say about Jesus?

My Role in the Community

What are some different circumstances of life I see that might need to be sanctified and how might I help bring this about?

For Depth and Further Life Application

Isaiah 35:4–7a
Psalm 146
James 2:1–5

United States Catholic Catechism for Adults, pages 111–112

REFLECTION

Jesus proclaimed the Gospel of the kingdom and cured every disease among the people.

—cf. Matthew 4:23

B Twenty-fourth Sunday of Ordinary Time

The Gospel

Jesus and his disciples set out
for the villages of Caesarea Philippi.
Along the way he asked his disciples,
"Who do people say that I am?"
They said in reply,
"John the Baptist, others Elijah,
still others one of the prophets."
And he asked them,
"But who do you say that I am?"
Peter said to him in reply,
"You are the Christ."
Then he warned them not to tell anyone about him.

He began to teach them
that the Son of Man must suffer greatly
and be rejected by the elders, the chief priests, and the scribes,
and be killed, and rise after three days.
He spoke this openly.
Then Peter took him aside and began to rebuke him.
At this he turned around and, looking at his disciples,
rebuked Peter and said, "Get behind me, Satan.
You are thinking not as God does, but as human beings do."

He summoned the crowd with his disciples and said to them,
"Whoever wishes to come after me must deny himself,
take up his cross, and follow me.
For whoever wishes to save his life will lose it,
but whoever loses his life for my sake
and that of the gospel will save it."

—Mark 8:27–35

Truths of Our Catholic Faith

Apparently human beings, sometimes at least, think differently from God. This makes sense because, although we are made in God's image, we are certainly different from God. One significant example is the fact that God is Love, and God is Truth.

The God of our faith has revealed himself as He who is; and he has made himself known as "abounding in steadfast love and faithfulness" (Ex *34:6). God's very being is Truth and Love. (CCC 231)*

Denying ourselves might mean turning toward God and toward others. One way we can serve others is by working in the framework of our governmental bodies. When we help embody the Gospel of Life by working concretely to build a civilization of love, we move toward thinking and acting more like God.

It is the duty of citizens to work with civil authority for building up society in a spirit of truth, justice, solidarity, and freedom. (CCC 2255)

A Question for Me

What in my life might I need to get behind me?

For a Child in My Life

What does it mean to say that God is Love and that God is Truth?

My Role in the Community

In what ways can I work with civil authority to build society in truth, justice, solidarity and freedom?

For Depth and Further Life Application

Isaiah 50:5–9a
Psalm 116
James 2:14–18

📖 United States Catholic Catechism for Adults, pages 50–57

REFLECTION

May I never boast except in the cross of our Lord through which the world has been crucified to me and I to the world.

—Galatians 6:14

B Twenty-fifth Sunday of Ordinary Time

The Gospel

Jesus and his disciples left from there and began a journey
through Galilee,
but he did not wish anyone to know about it.
He was teaching his disciples and telling them,
"The Son of Man is to be handed over to men
and they will kill him,
and three days after his death the Son of Man will rise."
But they did not understand the saying,
and they were afraid to question him.

They came to Capernaum and, once inside the house,
he began to ask them,
"What were you arguing about on the way?"
But they remained silent.
They had been discussing among themselves on the way
who was the greatest.
Then he sat down, called the Twelve, and said to them,
"If anyone wishes to be first,
he shall be the last of all and the servant of all."
Taking a child, he placed it in their midst,
and putting his arms around it, he said to them,
"Whoever receives one child such as this in my name, receives me;
and whoever receives me,
receives not me but the One who sent me."

—Mark 9:30–37

Truths of Our Catholic Faith

Children are the supreme gifts of married life. Jesus in this gospel passage allows a child to help Him make a point. His affection for the child seems obvious. (He did not have to put His arms around the child.) Jesus knows that children are gifts from the One who sent Him.

> *Unity, indissolubility, and openness to fertility are essential to marriage. Polygamy is incompatible with the unity of marriage; divorce separates what God has joined*

> *together; the refusal of fertility turns married life away from its "supreme gift," the child* (GS 50 §1). *(CCC 1664)*

The idea of receiving a child can of course be taken several different, complementary ways. Parents are not required in all cases to seek large quantities of children for their families; the number of children that God calls a married couple to accept varies from family-to-family. What does not vary is the moral acceptability of methods for spacing children in a marriage. Some methods, for legitimate intentions, are appropriate—most specifically Natural Family Planning.

NFP is to be distinguished from the old rhythm method for which some mistake it even today. Please contact your diocesan offices for accurate, up-to-date information on Natural Family Planning.

> *The regulation of births represents one of the aspects of responsible fatherhood and motherhood. Legitimate intentions on the part of the spouses do not justify recourse to morally unacceptable means (for example, direct sterilization or contraception). (CCC 2399)*

A Question for Me

How responsible of a parent am I—either literally (my own children) or figuratively (young people in general) or both?

For a Child in My Life

Jesus loves children; how do we know this is true?

My Role in the Community

How child-friendly and family-friendly is my community? How are families with an above-average number of children (in America, the average is three) treated? What might I do to help make all of my communities more family- and child-friendly?

For Depth and Further Life Application

Wisdom 2:12, 17–20
Psalm 54
James 3:16–4:3

📖 United States Catholic Catechism for Adults, pages 404–411

REFLECTION

God has called us through the Gospel to possess the glory of our Lord Jesus Christ.

—cf. 2 Thessalonians 2:14

B Twenty-sixth Sunday of Ordinary Time

The Gospel

At that time, John said to Jesus,
"Teacher, we saw someone driving out demons in your name,
and we tried to prevent him because he does not follow us."
Jesus replied, "Do not prevent him.
There is no one who performs a mighty deed in my name
who can at the same time speak ill of me.
For whoever is not against us is for us.
Anyone who gives you a cup of water to drink
because you belong to Christ,
amen, I say to you, will surely not lose his reward.

"Whoever causes one of these little ones who believe in me to sin,
it would be better for him if a great millstone
were put around his neck
and he were thrown into the sea.
If your hand causes you to sin, cut it off.
It is better for you to enter into life maimed
than with two hands to go into Gehenna,
into the unquenchable fire.
And if your foot causes you to sin, cut if off.
It is better for you to enter into life crippled
than with two feet to be thrown into Gehenna.
And if your eye causes you to sin, pluck it out.
Better for you to enter into the kingdom of God with one eye
than with two eyes to be thrown into Gehenna,
where 'their worm does not die, and the fire is not quenched.'"

—Mark 9:38–43, 45, 47–48

Truths of Our Catholic Faith

Whoever is not against us is for us. Many Christians, through no fault of their own, do not live in full communion with the fullness of Christ's Body on earth, the faithful of our Catholic Church. Yet these Christians share many beliefs and life-giving practices with us; they should be considered sisters and brothers in Jesus, moving ever closer to the full unity willed by our Father.

Those "who believe in Christ and have been properly baptized are put in a certain, although imperfect, communion with the Catholic Church."[19] *(CCC 838)*

Modesty is a much misunderstood virtue. Noticing an attractive body brashly displayed in immodest clothing may be a stimulation for many people. Therefore, dressing modestly is a good moral course of action.

Purity of heart requires the modesty which is patience, decency, and discretion. Modesty protects the intimate center of the person. (CCC 2533)

A Question for Me

Who in my life, if anyone, may lead me toward sin? How might I alter this relationship toward good?

For a Child in My Life

What would be a nice outfit for a boy to wear to some place really special? How about a girl? (The goal here is to touch upon the topic of modesty.)

My Role in the Community

How might I move toward praying in a more focused way for real, honest unity between all who believe in Christ and have been properly baptized?

For Depth and Further Life Application

Numbers 11:25–29
Psalm 19
James 5:1–6

📖 United States Catholic Catechism for Adults, pages 443–446

REFLECTION

Your word, O Lord, is truth; consecrate us in the truth.

—cf. John 17:17b, 17a

B Twenty-seventh Sunday of Ordinary Time

The Gospel

The Pharisees approached Jesus and asked,
"Is it lawful for a husband to divorce his wife?"
They were testing him.
He said to them in reply, "What did Moses command you?"
They replied,
"Moses permitted a husband to write a bill of divorce
and dismiss her."
But Jesus told them,
"Because of the hardness of your hearts
he wrote you this commandment.
But from the beginning of creation, *God made them male and female.*
For this reason a man shall leave his father and mother
and be joined to his wife,
and the two shall become one flesh.
So they are no longer two but one flesh.
Therefore what God has joined together,
no human being must separate."
In the house the disciples again questioned Jesus about this.
He said to them,
"Whoever divorces his wife and marries another
commits adultery against her;
and if she divorces her husband and marries another,
she commits adultery."

—Mark 10:2–12

Truths of Our Catholic Faith

The partnership of woman and man in marriage is so essential to healthy human communities and society that our Church takes it very, very seriously. From the communion of persons in marriage flows all other levels of unity.

> *"God did not create man a solitary being. From the beginning, 'male and female he created them'* (Gen 1:27). *This partnership of man and woman constitutes the first form of communion between persons"* (GS 12 §4). *(CCC 383)*

Divorce is one of those actions that is legal but not necessarily moral. When a woman and man freely choose to enter what they truly understand to be lifelong, a God-authored marriage covenant, they are simply not free to dissolve that covenant at will.

Volumes of research document divorce's harm to children as well as adults. (A good resource that summarizes many of these studies is Why Marriage Matters from americanvalues.org.) While each case is different and competent advice should be sought, the bottom line is that reconciliation rather than divorce is the strong preference revealed by the God who loves us, wishes for our best and makes the amazing possible with His grace.

> *The covenant which spouses have freely entered into entails faithful love. It imposes on them the obligation to keep their marriage indissoluble. (CCC 2397)*

A Question for Me

How hard is my heart when it comes to accepting specific moral teachings? (For example, Jesus' teaching against divorce.)

For a Child in My Life

How can we tell that God does not want anyone to be lonely?

My Role in the Community

The Church encourages troubled couples to pursue reconciliation rather than divorce (except in life-threatening or similarly grave situations—and even then what occurs is essentially a separation rather than immediate pursuit of a divorce per se). If I know any troubled couples, how might I help guide them up the path of reconciliation rather than down divorce's dark road?

For Depth and Further Life Application

Genesis 2:18–24
Psalm 128
Hebrews 2:9–11

United States Catholic Catechism for Adults, pages 412–414

REFLECTION

If we love one another, God remains in us and his love is brought to perfection in us.

—1 John 4:12

B Twenty-eighth Sunday of Ordinary Time

The Gospel

As Jesus was setting out on a journey, a man ran up,
knelt down before him, and asked him,
"Good teacher, what must I do to inherit eternal life?"
Jesus answered him, "Why do you call me good?
No one is good but God alone.
You know the commandments: *You shall not kill;*
you shall not commit adultery;
you shall not steal;
you shall not bear false witness;
you shall not defraud;
honor your father and your mother."
He replied and said to him,
"Teacher, all of these I have observed from my youth."
Jesus, looking at him, loved him and said to him,
"You are lacking in one thing.
Go, sell what you have, and give to the poor
and you will have treasure in heaven; then come, follow me."
At that statement his face fell,
and he went away sad, for he had many possessions.

Jesus looked around and said to his disciples,
"How hard it is for those who have wealth
to enter the kingdom of God!"
The disciples were amazed at his words.
So Jesus again said to them in reply,
"Children, how hard it is to enter the kingdom of God!
It is easier for a camel to pass through the eye of a needle
than for one who is rich to enter the kingdom of God."
They were exceedingly astonished and said among themselves,
"Then who can be saved?"
Jesus looked at them and said,
"For human beings it is impossible, but not for God.
All things are possible for God."

—Mark 10:17–27

Truths of Our Catholic Faith

"You know the commandments." Essentially this statement applies to just about everyone. The Ten Commandments are not a shrouded-in-mystery cryptic code. They are, for the most part, the logical conclusions of God-given human reason left to function unencumbered by self-serving excuses to behave badly. We know the Commandments because God has planted them in our heart and shed further light on them by His revealed truth.

> *The Decalogue contains a privileged expression of the natural law. It is made known to us by divine revelation and by human reason. (CCC 2080)*

Having many possessions is not bad in and of itself. Getting our priorities mixed up regarding our possessions, though, is an age-old pitfall. Relying on God and focusing on His kingdom over and above acquiring material possessions will help us use wisely whatever wealth we have, thereby keeping ourselves healthy spiritually as well as physically.

> *The goods of creation are destined for the entire human race. The right to private property does not abolish the universal destination of goods. (CCC 2452)*

A Question for Me

When I consider that all things are possible for God, what challenge in my life might I feel more confident about overcoming?

For a Child in My Life

Why is it important to know that all things are possible for God?

My Role in the Community

How well do I make use of my private property in light of the truth that the goods of creation are destined for the entire human race?

For Depth and Further Life Application

Wisdom 7:7–11
Psalm 90
Hebrews 4:12–13

📖 United States Catholic Catechism for Adults, pages 606–613

REFLECTION

Blessed are the poor in spirit, for theirs is the kingdom of heaven.

—Matthew 5:3

B Twenty-ninth Sunday of Ordinary Time

The Gospel

Jesus summoned the twelve and said to them,
"You know that those who are recognized as rulers over the Gentiles lord it over them,
and their great ones make their authority over them felt.
But it shall not be so among you.
Rather, whoever wishes to be great among you will be your servant;
whoever wishes to be first among you will be the slave of all.
For the Son of Man did not come to be served
but to serve and to give his life as a ransom for many."

—Mark 10:42–45

Truths of Our Catholic Faith

How the Twelve understand power is very important to Jesus. He intends to give them authority unparalleled in human history. How will they use it? To serve even if this requires tough love? Or to lord it over those entrusted to their care? Thankfully, in the successors of the Twelve, our bishops, we see for the most part power being used in loving service.

> *To proclaim the faith and to plant his reign, Christ sends his apostles and their successors. He gives them a share in his own mission. From him they receive the power to act in his person. (CCC 935)*

God's preferred way of making authority felt is to help as many people as feasible develop their God-given human potentials—physical, mental, spiritual, emotional, etc. When the goals of those in authority are truly good, pursuing these ends will consist exclusively of using morally suitable means or methods.

> *Authority is exercised legitimately if it is committed to the common good of society. To attain this it must employ morally acceptable means. (CCC 1921)*

A Question for Me
Power is for service. To what degree do I live up to this teaching?

For a Child in My Life
In whose name do our bishops often act?

My Role in the Community
Do I enjoy having or wish to have a place of honor at social gatherings? Or am I content not to be the center of attention, to serve as well as being served?

For Depth and Further Life Application

Isaiah 53:10–11
Psalm 33
Hebrews 4:14–16

📖 United States Catholic Catechism for Adults, pages 518–520

REFLECTION

The Son of Man came to serve and to give his life as a ransom for many.

—Mark 10:45

B Thirtieth Sunday of Ordinary Time

The Gospel

As Jesus was leaving Jericho with his disciples and a sizable crowd,
 Bartimaeus, a blind man, the son of Timaeus,
 sat by the roadside begging.
On hearing that it was Jesus of Nazareth,
 he began to cry out and say,
 "Jesus, son of David, have pity on me."
And many rebuked him, telling him to be silent.
But he kept calling out all the more,
 "Son of David, have pity on me."
Jesus stopped and said, "Call him."
So they called the blind man, saying to him,
 "Take courage; get up, Jesus is calling you."
He threw aside his cloak, sprang up, and came to Jesus.
Jesus said to him in reply, "What do you want me to do for you?"
The blind man replied to him, "Master, I want to see."
Jesus told him, "Go your way; your faith has saved you."
Immediately he received his sight
and followed him on the way.

—Mark 10:46–52

Truths of Our Catholic Faith

Why was Bartimaeus blind? Maybe it was an accident. Maybe someone's sinful, violent act caused his blindness. This would be easy to understand.

But what if he was born blind for no apparent reason? Why does God permit physical evil like illness and earthquakes?

The vast majority of evil in our world traces itself back to at least one person's poor choice or decision. As for physical evil, we really do not know why certain things occur. Yet we know that ultimately all evil, moral and physical, will be defeated because of Jesus' passion, death and resurrection.

> *The fact that God permits physical and even moral evil is a mystery that God illuminates by his Son Jesus Christ who died and rose to vanquish evil.* (CCC 324)

Why did Bartimaeus ask for his sight back? Would not a truly admirable person have asked for something less self-centered?

This blind man knew that he had not earned any favors from Jesus. He needed pity. He sensed, amidst all his needs, that being able to see is a good thing, and asking the Lord of Life to restore his sight was okay to do.

Jesus, who gives eternal life, freely gave the blind beggar the ability to see. Bartimaeus had faith. He was given a physical good. And he was saved.

> *No one can merit the initial grace which is at the origin of conversion. Moved by the Holy Spirit, we can merit for ourselves and for others all the graces needed to attain eternal life, as well as necessary temporal goods. (CCC 2027)*

A Question for Me

When physical evil occurs, how do I react? How does my reaction reflect a faith in Jesus Christ?

For a Child in My Life

For what do you usually pray? Besides physical things, for what should we ask God?

My Role in the Community

Do I rebuke people who make their needs known? Do I provide encouragement? How might I help others have their spiritual and material needs satisfied?

For Depth and Further Life Application

Jeremiah 31:7–9
Psalm 126
Hebrews 5:1–6

📖 United States Catholic Catechism for Adults, pages 57–61

REFLECTION

Our Savior Jesus Christ destroyed death and brought life to light through the Gospel.

—cf. 2 Timothy 1:10

B Thirty-first Sunday of Ordinary Time

The Gospel

One of the scribes came to Jesus and asked him,
"Which is the first of all the commandments?"
Jesus replied, "The first is this:
Hear, O Israel!
The Lord our God is Lord alone!
You shall love the Lord your God with all your heart,
with all your soul,
with all your mind,
and with all your strength.
The second is this:
You shall love your neighbor as yourself.
There is no other commandment greater than these."
The scribe said to him, "Well said, teacher.
You are right in saying,
'He is One and there is no other than he.'
And 'to love him with all your heart,
with all your understanding,
with all your strength,
and to love your neighbor as yourself'
is worth more than all burnt offerings and sacrifices."
And when Jesus saw that he answered with understanding,
he said to him,
"You are not far from the kingdom of God."
And no one dared to ask him any more questions.

—Mark 12:28b–34

Truths of Our Catholic Faith

This scribe, we might presume, heard Jesus proclaim the Good News of salvation from sin and death. Already, though, he seems on the way to forming his conscience excellently, allowing God's grace to penetrate his heart. While God has revealed to us the ordinary way to salvation (and we should pursue it!), God Himself is not limited to this way. God knows a sincere heart when He sees one.

> *This affirmation is not aimed at those who, through no fault of their own, do not know Christ and his Church:*
>
> > *Those who, through no fault of their own, do not know the Gospel of Christ or his Church, but who nevertheless seek God with a sincere heart, and, moved by grace, try in their actions to do his will as they know it through the dictates of their conscience—those too may achieve eternal salvation.*[20] *(CCC 847)*

To love God as described in this passage sounds like a lot of work. Showing love for neighbor is, of course, one way to show this love. Another is participating in liturgical worship. At liturgy we join Jesus, the Head of the Body of Christ, in offering love to our Father with heart, soul, mind and strength.

> *The liturgy is the work of the whole Christ, head and body. Our high priest celebrates it unceasingly in the heavenly liturgy, with the holy Mother of God, the apostles, all the saints, and the multitude of those who have already entered the kingdom. (CCC 1187)*

A Question for Me

A person can, through no fault of her or his own, not know the Gospel of Jesus or His Church. How can I be at fault in such cases? How might I avoid being guilty of contributing to ignorance of the Good News?

For a Child in My Life

What is liturgy?

My Role in the Community

Jesus gives a compliment to the scribe in this passage. Compliments are important. Who in my community needs to hear a compliment from me this very week?

For Depth and Further Life Application

Deuteronomy 6:2–6
Psalm 18
Hebrews 7L23–28

📖 United States Catholic Catechism for Adults, pages 177–179

REFLECTION

Whoever loves me will keep my word, says the Lord; and my Father will love him and we will come to him.

—John 14:23

B Thirty-second Sunday of Ordinary Time

The Gospel

Jesus sat down opposite the treasury
and observed how the crowd put money into the treasury.
Many rich people put in large sums.
A poor widow also came and put in two small coins
worth a few cents.
Calling his disciples to himself, he said to them,
"Amen, I say to you, this poor widow put in more
than all the other contributors to the treasury.
For they have all contributed from their surplus wealth,
but she, from her poverty, has contributed all she had,
her whole livelihood."

—Mark 12:41–44

Truths of Our Catholic Faith

The poor widow probably never heard of the Church. She may not even have been baptized. Yet clearly she loves God and is trying sincerely to please Him.

God has revealed the ordinary way to salvation, because He loves us and wants all to be saved. In extraordinary situations, though, God may save by ways other than baptism.

> *Those who die for the faith, those who are catechumens, and all those who, without knowing of the Church but acting under the inspiration of grace, seek God sincerely and strive to fulfill his will, can be saved even if they have not been baptized (cf.* LG *16). (CCC 1281)*

This widow allows her natural orientation toward God to shine through. Every person is so oriented, from the womb, throughout life and right up to the tomb.

> *Endowed with a spiritual soul, with intellect and with free will, the human person is from his very conception ordered to God and destined for eternal beatitude. He pursues his perfection in "seeking and loving what is true and good"* (GS 15 § 2)*. (CCC 1711)*

A Question for Me

Would I die for the faith? If not literally, how might God be calling me to die for the faith even today?

For a Child in My Life

What does Jesus mean when He says the poor widow put in more than all the others? What is He trying to tell you by saying this?

My Role in the Community

When I pause to consider that each person in all of my communities is endowed with a spiritual soul, ordered to God and destined for eternal beatitude, what thoughts and/or feelings does this bring about?

For Depth and Further Life Application

1 Kings 17:10–16
Psalm 146
Hebrews 9:24–28

📖 United States Catholic Catechism for Adults, pages 195–197

REFLECTION

Blessed are the poor in spirit, for theirs is the kingdom of heaven.

—Matthew 5:3

B Thirty-third Sunday of Ordinary Time

The Gospel

Jesus said to his disciples:
"In those days after that tribulation
the sun will be darkened,
and the moon will not give its light,
and the stars will be falling from the sky,
and the powers in the heavens will be shaken.

"And then they will see 'the Son of Man coming in the clouds'
with great power and glory,
and then he will send out the angels
and gather his elect from the four winds,
from the end of the earth to the end of the sky.

"Learn a lesson from the fig tree.
When its branch becomes tender and sprouts leaves,
you know that summer is near.
In the same way, when you see these things happening,
know that he is near, at the gates.
Amen, I say to you,
this generation will not pass away
until all these things have taken place.
Heaven and earth will pass away,
but my words will not pass away.

"But of that day or hour, no one knows,
neither the angels in heaven, nor the Son, but only the Father."

—Mark 13:24–32

Truths of Our Catholic Faith

Jesus said many things to His disciples. Not all of what He said was written down. How did the Gospel writers know what to record and what to let pass? Simply put, God helped them decide. This is called inspiration, and because God was involved in the writing process, we can say that He is the author.

God is the author of Sacred Scripture because he inspired its human authors; he acts in them and by means of

> *them. He thus gives assurance that their writings teach without error his saving truth (cf.* DV *11). (CCC 136)*

By saying "The Gospel of the Lord" we acknowledge that the Good News is to be held in very high esteem. Why? Because the Lord is holy. All that is associated with His name is holy. The name of the Lord, the Lord Himself, and His Good News of salvation from sin and death all deserve our most profound appreciation and respect.

> *The second commandment enjoins respect for the Lord's name. The name of the Lord is holy. (CCC 2161)*

A Question for Me

In what ways do I use the Lord's name? How do these uses reflect a belief that my Lord's name is sacred?

For a Child in My Life

Why is it good to show respect for God's name?

My Role in the Community

How might I help instill a greater respect for the name of God in my communities?

For Depth and Further Life Application

Daniel 12:1–3
Psalm 16
Hebrews 10:11–14, 18

United States Catholic Catechism for Adults, pages 351–356

REFLECTION

Be vigilant at all times and pray that you may have the strength to stand before the Son of Man.

—Luke 21:36

B Christ the King

The Gospel

Pilate said to Jesus,
"Are you the King of the Jews?"
Jesus answered, "Do you say this on your own
or have others told you about me?"
Pilate answered, "I am not a Jew, am I?
Your own nation and the chief priests handed you over to me.
What have you done?"
Jesus answered, "My kingdom does not belong to this world.
If my kingdom did belong to this world,
my attendants would be fighting
to keep me from being handed over to the Jews.
But as it is, my kingdom is not here."
So Pilate said to him, "Then you are a king?"
Jesus answered, "You say I am a king.
For this I was born and for this I came into the world,
to testify to the truth.
Everyone who belongs to the truth listens to my voice."

—John 18:33b–37

Truths of Our Catholic Faith

Truth is so important that Jesus associates it with the basic reason for His Incarnation. Because of truth's importance, we must take it very seriously. We must belong to the truth, listening for the voice of our Lord.

> *False oaths call on God to be witness to a lie. Perjury is a grave offence against the Lord who is always faithful to his promises. (CCC 2163)*

"Thy kingdom come." Each time we pray the Our Father we acknowledge God's lordship and pledge our allegiance to the one kingdom that is truly under Him. This truth sets us free to pursue the priorities of God's kingdom and in the process have a profoundly positive impact on the world around us.

In the Our Father, the object of the first three petitions is the glory of the Father: the sanctification of his name, the coming of the kingdom, and the fulfillment of his will. The four others present our wants to him: they ask that our lives be nourished, healed of sin, and made victorious in the struggle of good over evil. (CCC 2857)

A Question for Me

Do I pray the Lord's Prayer daily? Do I pray it slowly enough to focus on its words?

For a Child in My Life

What kind of king is Jesus?

My Role in the Community

In the Lord's Prayer we refer to Our Father, not just My Father. How does this affect my perception of the various communities around me?

For Depth and Further Life Application

Daniel 7:13–14
Psalm 93
Revelation 1:5–8

United States Catholic Catechism for Adults, pages 493–495

REFLECTION

Blessed is he who comes in the name of the Lord! Blessed is the kingdom of our father David that is to come!

—Mark 11:9, 10

C First Sunday of Advent

The Gospel

Jesus said to his disciples:
"There will be signs in the sun, the moon, and the stars,
and on earth nations will be in dismay,
perplexed by the roaring of the sea and the waves.
People will die of fright
in anticipation of what is coming upon the world,
for the powers of the heavens will be shaken.
And then they will see the Son of Man
coming in a cloud with power and great glory.
But when these signs begin to happen,
stand erect and raise your heads
because your redemption is at hand.

"Beware that your hearts do not become drowsy
from carousing and drunkenness
and the anxieties of daily life,
and that day catch you by surprise like a trap.
For that day will assault everyone
who lives on the face of the earth.
Be vigilant at all times
and pray that you have the strength
to escape the tribulations that are imminent
and to stand before the Son of Man."

—Luke 21:25–28, 34–36

Truths of Our Catholic Faith

The stars, the sun, the earth, the moon: God almighty created them out of nothing. When He chooses, He who through His Son—the Word—made and sustains everything with His Holy Spirit's power, will draw history as we know it to a conclusion. This will mark a transition that we do not yet grasp. For now, we remind ourselves just who God is and the role of our triune Godhead—Father, Son and Spirit.

> *God created the universe and keeps it in existence by his Word, the Son "upholding the universe by his word of power"* (Heb *1:3) and by his Creator Spirit, the giver of life. (CCC 320)*

In order not to die of fright or succumb to drunkenness, we need the virtues of fortitude and temperance. Virtues are good habits of thought and action that we can work to acquire. Through prayer and effort we can grow in virtue, better fulfill our God-given potential for goodness and be in reasonably good shape (by God's grace) when we stand before the Son of Man.

> *The human virtues are stable dispositions of the intellect and the will that govern our acts, order our passions, and guide our conduct in accordance with reason and faith. They can be grouped around the four cardinal virtues: prudence, justice, fortitude, and temperance. (CCC 1834)*

A Question for Me

How do the anxieties of daily life affect my heart? What might I do to help lessen their impact?

For a Child in My Life

Have you ever heard of P.J. Fortem? He will help you recall the four cardinal virtues: (P)rudence, (J)ustice, (For)titude and (Tem)perance. What is an example showing each of these virtues?

My Role in the Community

How might I help community members better understand virtues, which go beyond values because they are objectively good? (Everyone has values. A crack dealer values money gained from selling drugs. Virtue is a word we should use more.)

For Depth and Further Life Application

Jeremiah 33:14–16
Psalm 25
1 Thessalonians 3:12–4:2

📖 United States Catholic Catechism for Adults, pages 61–63

REFLECTION

Show us, Lord, your love; and grant us your salvation.

—Psalm 85:8

C Second Sunday of Advent

The Gospel

In the fifteenth year of the reign of Tiberius Caesar,
when Pontius Pilate was governor of Judea,
and Herod was tetrarch of Galilee,
and his brother Philip tetrarch of the region
of Ituraea and Trachonitis,
and Lysanias was tetrarch of Abilene,
during the high priesthood of Annas and Caiaphas,
the word of God came to John the son of Zechariah in the desert.
John went throughout the whole region of the Jordan,
proclaiming a baptism of repentance for the forgiveness of sins,
as it is written in the book of the words of the prophet Isaiah:
A voice of one crying out in the desert:
"Prepare the way of the Lord,
make straight his paths.
Every valley shall be filled
and every mountain and hill shall be made low.
The winding roads shall be made straight,
and the rough ways made smooth,
and all flesh shall see the salvation of God."

—Luke 3:1–6

Truths of Our Catholic Faith

John baptized quite a few people. The Church established Christian baptism's essential action (immersing in water or pouring water on the head) and words ("I baptize you in the name of the Father, the Son and the Holy Spirit"). What John previewed, Jesus and His Church brought to fruition and the Sacrament of Baptism continues to this very day.

> *The essential rite of Baptism consists in immersing the candidate in water or pouring water on his head, while pronouncing the invocation of the Most Holy Trinity: the Father, the Son, and the Holy Spirit. (CCC 1278)*

By mentioning Caesar as well as the two high priests, Luke calls to mind two systems that affect virtually everyone: civil law and religious rules. Governments and moral codes stand or fall on how faithfully they extend the natural law. Natural law precedes other types of law. All that our Church teaches about civil government and moral life in general is based on natural law enlightened by truth revealed, out of love, by our God.

> *The natural law is immutable, permanent throughout history. The rules that express it remain substantially valid. It is a necessary foundation for the erection of moral rules and civil law.* (CCC 1979)

A Question for Me

How would I baptize someone if in an emergency I were called upon to do so?

For a Child in My Life

What action is performed and what words are said when someone is baptized?

My Role in the Community

What evidence do I see in my community that the natural law is being upheld? In what ways might the natural law be violated during my community's daily life?

For Depth and Further Life Application

Baruch 5:1–9
Psalm 126
Philippians 1:4–6, 8–11

📖 United States Catholic Catechism for Adults, pages 197–198

REFLECTION

Prepare the way of the Lord, make straight his paths: all flesh shall see the salvation of God.

—Luke 3:4, 6

C Third Sunday of Advent

The Gospel

The crowds asked John the Baptist,
"What should we do?"
He said to them in reply,
"Whoever has two cloaks
should share with the person who has none.
And whoever has food should do likewise."
Even tax collectors came to be baptized and they said to him,
"Teacher, what should we do?"
He answered them,
"Stop collecting more than what is prescribed."
Soldiers also asked him,
"And what is it that we should do?"
He told them,
"Do not practice extortion,
do not falsely accuse anyone,
and be satisfied with your wages."

Now the people were filled with expectation,
and all were asking in their hearts
whether John might be the Christ.
John answered them all, saying,
"I am baptizing you with water,
but one mightier than I is coming.
I am not worthy to loosen the thongs of his sandals.
He will baptize you with the Holy Spirit and fire.
His winnowing fan is in his hand to clear his threshing floor
and to gather the wheat into his barn,
but the chaff he will burn with unquenchable fire."
Exhorting them in many other ways,
he preached good news to the people.

—Luke 3:10–18

Truths of Our Catholic Faith

John is revealing something very important to the people. He is helping them understand who the Holy Spirit is. While not fully revealing the threefold or triune nature of God, John gives them a preview of sorts by naming the third Person of the Most Holy Trinity.

> *The mystery of the Most Holy Trinity is the central mystery of the Christian faith and of Christian life. God alone can make it known to us by revealing himself as Father, Son, and Holy Spirit. (CCC 261)*

John does not tell the soldiers to stop being soldiers. Rather, he reminds them that soldiering must be done within appropriate boundaries of human behavior. To collect taxes honestly, to serve in the military with integrity, to share the fruits of labor with those needing clothing and food, are all ways of living the Good News.

> *The Church and human reason assert the permanent validity of the moral law during armed conflicts. Practices deliberately contrary to the law of nations and to its universal principles are crimes. (CCC 2328)*

A Question for Me

How might I show appreciation to God this week for revealing His triune nature to me: Father, Son and Holy Spirit?

For a Child in My Life

How do we know that God is three Persons in one God—Father, Son and Holy Spirit?

My Role in the Community

In my parish community, how might I see to it that the Most Holy Trinity—Father, Son and Holy Spirit—receives appropriate honor? How about in my own household?

For Depth and Further Life Application

Zephaniah 3:14–18a
Isaiah 12:2–6
Philippians 4:4–7

United States Catholic Catechism for Adults, pages 400–402

REFLECTION

The Spirit of the Lord is upon me, because he has anointed me to bring glad tidings to the poor.

—Isaiah 61:1 (cited in Luke 4:18)

C Fourth Sunday of Advent

The Gospel

Mary set out
and traveled to the hill country in haste
to a town of Judah,
where she entered the house of Zechariah
and greeted Elizabeth.
When Elizabeth heard Mary's greeting,
the infant leaped in her womb,
and Elizabeth, filled with the Holy Spirit,
cried out in a loud voice and said,
"Blessed are you among women,
and blessed is the fruit of your womb.
And how does this happen to me,
that the mother of my Lord should come to me?
For at the moment the sound of your greeting reached my ears,
the infant in my womb leaped for joy.
Blessed are you who believed
that what was spoken to you by the Lord
would be fulfilled."

—Luke 1:39–45

Truths of Our Catholic Faith

The Holy Spirit is very busy in Elizabeth's and Mary's lives. It is by the Holy Spirit that Mary's womb bears the fruit of life, Jesus. The Holy Spirit helps fulfill what was spoken to Mary by the Lord. And we are filled with joy.

> *In the fullness of time the Holy Spirit completes in Mary all the preparations for Christ's coming among the People of God. By the action of the Holy Spirit in her, the Father gives the world Emmanuel, "God-with-us"* (Mt *1:23). (CCC 744)*

Elizabeth does not say "the blob of tissue in my womb seemed to leap for joy." Filled with the Holy Spirit, Elizabeth knows that she carries within her a human person, a divinely-created being with integrity and priceless dignity. And Mary is not referred to as "the woman who may become the mother of my Lord if and when the bundle of cells in her womb becomes a person at some debatable point." To Elizabeth, both the mother of her Lord as well as the unborn Lord Himself, have come.

> *Because it should be treated as a person from conception, the embryo must be defended in its integrity, cared for, and healed like every other human being. (CCC 2323)*

A Question for Me
What role does prayer for unborn children—that they be granted their God-given right to life—play in my daily prayer commitments? How might I enhance this role if need be?

For a Child in My Life
What is the first sentence Elizabeth says to Mary?

My Role in the Community
What concrete steps might I take to defend the life of preborn babies in my communities?

For Depth and Further Life Application

Micah 5:1–4a
Psalm 80
Hebrews 10:5–10

United States Catholic Catechism for Adults, pages 106–108

REFLECTION

Behold, I am the handmaid of the Lord. May it be done to me according to your word.

—Luke 1:38

C The Holy Family

The Gospel

Each year Jesus' parents went to Jerusalem for the feast
of Passover,
and when he was twelve years old,
they went up according to festival custom.
After they had completed its days, as they were returning,
the boy Jesus remained behind in Jerusalem,
but his parents did not know it.
Thinking that he was in the caravan,
they journeyed for a day
and looked for him among their relatives and acquaintances,
but not finding him,
they returned to Jerusalem to look for him.
After three days they found him in the temple,
sitting in the midst of the teachers,
listening to them and asking them questions,
and all who heard him were astounded
at his understanding and his answers.
When his parents saw him,
they were astonished,
and his mother said to him,
"Son, why have you done this to us?
Your father and I have been looking for you with great anxiety."
And he said to them,
"Why were you looking for me?
Did you not know that I must be in my Father's house?"
But they did not understand what he said to them.
He went down with them and came to Nazareth,
and was obedient to them;
and his mother kept all these things in her heart.
And Jesus advanced in wisdom and age and favor
before God and man.

—Luke 2:41–52

Truths of Our Catholic Faith

Jesus was obedient to Mary and Joseph. He obeyed because His heavenly Father, and ours, wills it so. God gives people authority and, provided that it is used well, we have an obligation to honor, to cooperate, to obey.

> *According to the fourth commandment, God has willed that, after him, we should honor our parents and those whom he has vested with authority for our good. (CCC 2248)*

Mary is referred to twice in this passage as Jesus' mother. In the early days of Christianity there was some debate as to whether Mary should only be thought of as the mother of Jesus' human nature and not His divine nature. Because Jesus is one Person, though, such distinctions end up contradicting the fact that Jesus is true God and true Man. Mary, then, literally is the Mother of God; we honor her with this title each time we pray a Hail Mary or various other Marian prayers.

> *Called in the Gospels "the mother of Jesus," Mary is acclaimed by Elizabeth, at the prompting of the Spirit and even before the birth of her son, as "the mother of my Lord."*[21] *In fact, the One whom she conceived as man by the Holy Spirit, who truly became her Son according to the flesh, was none other than the Father's eternal Son, the second person of the Holy Trinity. Hence the Church confesses that Mary is truly "Mother of God"* (Theotokos*).*[22] *(CCC 495)*

A Question for Me

What role do I play in helping form the faith habits of the children in my life?

For a Child in My Life

Why do we call Mary the "Mother of God?"

My Role in the Community

How am I at honoring those whom God has vested with authority for my good?

For Depth and Further Life Application

1 Samuel 1:20–22, 24–28
Psalm 84
1 John 3:1–2, 21–24

📖 United States Catholic Catechism for Adults, pages 141–149

REFLECTION

Open our hearts, O Lord, to listen to the words of your Son.

—cf. Acts 16:14b

C The Baptism of the Lord

The Gospel

The people were filled with expectation,
  and all were asking in their hearts
  whether John might be the Christ.
John answered them all, saying,
  "I am baptizing you with water,
  but one mightier than I is coming.
I am not worthy to loosen the thongs of his sandals.
He will baptize you with the Holy Spirit and fire."

After all the people had been baptized
  and Jesus also had been baptized and was praying,
  heaven was opened and the Holy Spirit descended upon him
  in bodily form like a dove.
And a voice came from heaven,
  "You are my beloved Son;
with you I am well pleased."

—Luke 3:15–16, 21–22

Truths of Our Catholic Faith

Many have speculated as to why Jesus was baptized. The possibilities are beyond the scope of a catechism. Definitively we do know that baptism is the ordinary means revealed by God to obtain salvation and, as such, can be said to be necessary. Baptized into the Church, we receive new life in Jesus and are saved from sin and death.

> *Baptism is birth into the new life in Christ. In accordance with the Lord's will, it is necessary for salvation, as is the Church herself, which we enter by Baptism. (CCC 1277)*

Prayer and the Holy Spirit seem to go hand-in-hand. It is He, the Holy Spirit, who animates our prayer life and gives us everything we need to pray faithfully and effectively, pleasing God.

> *By a living transmission—Tradition—the Holy Spirit in the Church teaches the children of God to pray. (CCC 2661)*

A Question for Me
To what extent am I allowing myself to be taught to pray?

For a Child in My Life
What was Jesus doing after being baptized?

My Role in the Community
How might I gently encourage a person toward baptism for herself or himself, or a child?

For Depth and Further Life Application

Isaiah 40:1–5, 9–11
Psalm 104
Titus 2:11–14; 3:4–7

📖 United States Catholic Catechism for Adults, page 536

REFLECTION

John said: One mightier than I is coming; he will baptize you with the Holy Spirit and with fire.

—cf. Luke 3:16

C First Sunday of Lent

The Gospel

Filled with the Holy Spirit, Jesus returned from the Jordan
and was led by the Spirit into the desert for forty days,
to be tempted by the devil.
He ate nothing during those days,
and when they were over he was hungry.
The devil said to him,
"If you are the Son of God,
command this stone to become bread."
Jesus answered him,
"It is written, *One does not live on bread alone*."
Then he took him up and showed him
all the kingdoms of the world in a single instant.
The devil said to him,
"I shall give to you all this power and glory;
for it has been handed over to me,
and I may give it to whomever I wish.
All this will be yours, if you worship me."
Jesus said to him in reply,
"It is written:
You shall worship the Lord, your God,
and him alone shall you serve."
Then he led him to Jerusalem,
made him stand on the parapet of the temple, and said to him,
"If you are the Son of God,
throw yourself down from here, for it is written:
He will command his angels concerning you, to guard you,
and:
With their hands they will support you,
lest you dash your foot against a stone."
Jesus said to him in reply,
"It also says,
You shall not put the Lord, your God, to the test."
When the devil had finished every temptation,
he departed from him for a time.

—Luke 4:1–13

Truths of Our Catholic Faith

Ironically, the devil believes in God. He even has the Scriptures at his disposal. Those who have reasonable access to the Good News may have a hard time justifying unbelief if and when the time comes to do so. Even those with no substantial resources other than the natural light of human reason, though, can come to know God—largely by observing His Creation.

> *The Church teaches that the one true God, our Creator and Lord, can be known with certainty from his works, by the natural light of human reason (cf. Vatican Council I, can. 2, § 1: DS 3026). (CCC 47)*

Jesus' Jewish upbringing sensitizes him in a specific way to this second temptation. Above all else, God is the One to be worshiped. More so than kingdoms. More so than all principalities and powers. We are to worship the Lord, our God, and Him alone are we to serve.

> *The first commandment summons man to believe in God, to hope in him, and to love him above all else. (CCC 2134)*

A Question for Me

How do I usually handle temptation? What might enhance my ability to handle it?

For a Child in My Life

What does Jesus say when the devil tempts Jesus to worship him? Where have you heard this before? (What commandment?)

My Role in the Community

In my own way, do I seek kingdoms, power and glory? What is my response to the second temptation?

For Depth and Further Life Application

Deuteronomy 26:4–10
Psalm 91
Romans 10:8–13

United States Catholic Catechism for Adults, pages 7–9

REFLECTION

One does not live on bread alone, but on every word that comes forth from the mouth of God.

—Matthew 4:4b

C Second Sunday of Lent

The Gospel

Jesus took Peter, John, and James
 and went up the mountain to pray.
While he was praying his face changed in appearance
 and his clothing became dazzling white.
And behold, two men were conversing with him, Moses and Elijah,
 who appeared in glory and spoke of his exodus
 that he was going to accomplish in Jerusalem.
Peter and his companions had been overcome by sleep,
 but becoming fully awake,
 they saw his glory and the two men standing with him.
As they were about to part from him, Peter said to Jesus,
 "Master, it is good that we are here;
 let us make three tents,
 one for you, one for Moses, and one for Elijah."
But he did not know what he was saying.
While he was still speaking,
 a cloud came and cast a shadow over them,
 and they became frightened when they entered the cloud.
Then from the cloud came a voice that said,
 "This is my chosen Son; listen to him."
After the voice had spoken, Jesus was found alone.
They fell silent and did not at that time
tell anyone what they had seen.

—Luke 9:28b–36

Truths of Our Catholic Faith

Special things seem to happen on mountains. On this mountain Peter, James and John have an experience bound to deepen their faith so that, listening to Jesus, they may receive the New Law and eventually live it by God's grace.

Jesus prays on mountains. Jesus teaches on a mountain. Special things seem to happen on mountains.

The New Law is the grace of the Holy Spirit received by faith in Christ, operating through charity. It finds

> *expression above all in the Lord's Sermon on the Mount and uses the sacraments to communicate grace to us. (CCC 1983)*

Jesus has His own way of praying. While He taught His friends quite a bit about prayer, He did not mandate that they all pray exactly the same way at all times.

Several different ways of approaching prayer, of perceiving what it means that life has a spiritual dimension, have arisen in the course of history. United on the key doctrinal points, several great spiritual masters from Moses and Elijah to Francis and Faustina have taught us much about the many facets of being a child of God.

> *The different schools of Christian spirituality share in the living tradition of prayer and are precious guides for the spiritual life. (CCC 2693)*

A Question for Me

How might I describe my spirituality?

For a Child in My Life

What did the voice from a cloud say?

My Role in the Community

What different spiritualities are present in my faith community? How does each show itself united to the entire Body of Christ in the living tradition of prayer?

For Depth and Further Life Application

Genesis 15:5–12, 17–18
Psalm 27
Philippians 3:20–4:1

United States Catholic Catechism for Adults, pages 318–319

REFLECTION

From the shining cloud the Father's voice is heard: This is my beloved Son, hear him.

—cf. Matthew 17:5

C Third Sunday of Lent

The Gospel

Some people told Jesus about the Galileans
 whose blood Pilate had mingled with the blood of their sacrifices.
Jesus said to them in reply,
 "Do you think that because these Galileans suffered in this way
 they were greater sinners than all other Galileans?
By no means!
But I tell you, if you do not repent,
 you will all perish as they did!
Or those eighteen people who were killed
 when the tower at Siloam fell on them—
 do you think they were more guilty
 than everyone else who lived in Jerusalem?
By no means!
But I tell you, if you do not repent,
 you will all perish as they did!"

And he told them this parable:
 "There once was a person who had a fig tree planted in his orchard,
 and when he came in search of fruit on it but found none,
 he said to the gardener,
 'For three years now I have come in search of fruit on this fig tree
 but have found none.
So cut it down.
Why should it exhaust the soil?'
He said to him in reply,
 'Sir, leave it for this year also,
 and I shall cultivate the ground around it and fertilize it;
 it may bear fruit in the future.
If not you can cut it down.'"

—Luke 13:1–9

Truths of Our Catholic Faith

Again we see that Jesus is not exactly subtle at times. Repentance is, as they say, hugely important to Him. After baptism we must continually repent for our misdeeds and other sins. God confers forgiveness on us through a specific sacrament that is known by several names. We show repentance by celebrating the Sacrament of Penance.

> *The forgiveness of sins committed after Baptism is conferred by a particular sacrament called the sacrament of conversion, confession, penance, or reconciliation. (CCC 1486)*

God wants all of creation to experience His glory. Far from taking pleasure at any person's moral downfall, our Lord cheers us on and seems willing to give us chance, after chance, after chance (up to a point). The Master Gardener tills and nourishes the ground around us, for our good, that we may one day enter into glory.

> *God willed the diversity of his creatures and their own particular goodness, their interdependence, and their order. He destined all material creatures for the good of the human race. Man, and through him all creation, is destined for the glory of God. (CCC 353)*

A Question for Me

Do I ever take pleasure in the misfortune of others? What is Jesus saying to me in this gospel passage?

For a Child in My Life

What are some other names for the Sacrament of Penance? What do these different names mean? Why do we call this sacrament by each of these names?

My Role in the Community

How might I encourage members of my community to repent? (The Son of God says they will perish if they do not repent.)

For Depth and Further Life Application

Exodus 3:1–8a, 13–15
Psalm 103
1 Corinthians 10:1–6, 10–12

📖 United States Catholic Catechism for Adults, pages 242–244

REFLECTION

Repent, says the Lord; the kingdom of heaven is at hand.

—Matthew 4:17

C Fourth Sunday of Lent

The Gospel

Tax collectors and sinners were all drawing near to listen to Jesus,
but the Pharisees and scribes began to complain, saying,
"This man welcomes sinners and eats with them."
So to them Jesus addressed this parable:
"A man had two sons, and the younger son said to his father,
'Father give me the share of your estate that should come to me.'
So the father divided the property between them.
After a few days, the younger son collected all his belongings
and set off to a distant country
where he squandered his inheritance on a life of dissipation.
When he had freely spent everything,
a severe famine struck that country,
and he found himself in dire need.
So he hired himself out to one of the local citizens
who sent him to his farm to tend the swine.
And he longed to eat his fill of the pods on which the swine fed,
but nobody gave him any.
Coming to his senses he thought,
'How many of my father's hired workers
have more than enough food to eat,
but here am I, dying from hunger.
I shall get up and go to my father and I shall say to him,
"Father, I have sinned against heaven and against you.
I no longer deserve to be called your son;
treat me as you would treat one of your hired workers."'
So he got up and went back to his father.
While he was still a long way off,
his father caught sight of him, and was filled with compassion.
He ran to his son, embraced him and kissed him.
His son said to him,
'Father, I have sinned against heaven and against you;
I no longer deserve to be called your son.'
But his father ordered his servants,
'Quickly bring the finest robe and put it on him;
put a ring on his finger and sandals on his feet.
Take the fattened calf and slaughter it.

Then let us celebrate with a feast,
  because this son of mine was dead, and has come to life again;
  he was lost, and has been found.'
Then the celebration began.
Now the older son had been out in the field
  and, on his way back, as he neared the house,
  he heard the sound of music and dancing.
He called one of the servants and asked what this might mean.
The servant said to him,
  'Your brother has returned
  and your father has slaughtered the fattened calf
  because he has him back safe and sound.'
He became angry,
  and when he refused to enter the house,
  his father came out and pleaded with him.
He said to his father in reply,
'Look, all these years I served you
  and not once did I disobey your orders;
  yet you never gave me even a young goat to feast on
    with my friends.
But when your son returns
  who swallowed up your property with prostitutes,
  for him you slaughter the fattened calf.'
He said to him,
  'My son, you are here with me always;
  everything I have is yours.
But now we must celebrate and rejoice,
  because your brother was dead and has come to life again;
he was lost and has been found.'"

—Luke 15:1–3, 11–32

Truths of Our Catholic Faith

The young son in this gospel passage intends to repair his damage by serving like a hired worker. He undergoes a process roughly paralleling a penitent's three acts in the Sacrament of Penance: he repents, feeling sorrow for his sinful actions; he confesses that he has sinned; then, he states an intention to make amends.

The sacrament of Penance is a whole consisting in three actions of the penitent and the priest's absolution. The penitent's acts are repentance, confession or disclosure of sins to the priest, and the intention to make reparation and do works of reparation. (CCC 1491)

It was unreasonable for the young son to leave the way he did. He found himself sinking below the dignity of his human nature, believing he would be better off living like a swine. His solidarity with various people, especially father and brother, was wounded by his sin.

Sin is an act contrary to reason. It wounds man's nature and injures human solidarity. (CCC 1872)

A Question for Me

In what ways may I occasionally be like the older son? What might I do to help improve my behavior in this regard?

For a Child in My Life

What does the son say to the father after being hugged by him?

My Role in the Community

What, if any, works of reparation might I need to do toward fellow community members?

For Depth and Further Life Application

Joshua 5:9a, 10–12
Psalm 34
2 Corinthians 5:17–21

📖 United States Catholic Catechism for Adults, pages 244–247

REFLECTION

I will get up and go to my Father and shall say to him: Father, I have sinned against heaven and against you.

—Luke 15:18

C Fifth Sunday of Lent

The Gospel

Jesus went to the Mount of Olives.
But early in the morning he arrived again in the temple area,
and all the people started coming to him,
and he sat down and taught them.
Then the scribes and the Pharisees brought a woman
who had been caught in adultery
and made her stand in the middle.
They said to him,
"Teacher, this woman was caught
in the very act of committing adultery.
Now in the law, Moses commanded us to stone such women.
So what do you say?"
They said this to test him,
so that they could have some charge to bring against him.
Jesus bent down and began to write on the ground with his finger.
But when they continued asking him,
he straightened up and said to them,
"Let the one among you who is without sin
be the first to throw a stone at her."
Again he bent down and wrote on the ground.
And in response, they went away one by one,
beginning with the elders.
So he was left alone with the woman before him.
Then Jesus straightened up and said to her,
"Woman, where are they?
Has no one condemned you?"
She replied, "No one, sir."
Then Jesus said, "Neither do I condemn you.
Go, and from now on do not sin any more."

—John 8:1–11

Truths of Our Catholic Faith

Jesus gestures in this encounter, writing on the ground with His finger. He remains silent while doing so. The Pharisees call Him teacher, and rightfully so as He is in the act of teaching when they approach Him. Little did they know that it was they who would be taught a lesson, by His silence, by His gestures, by His love.

> *"The whole of Christ's life was a continual teaching: his silences, his miracles, his gestures, his prayer, his love for people, his special affection for the little and the poor, his acceptance of the total sacrifice on the Cross for the redemption of the world, and his Resurrection are the actualization of his word and the fulfillment of Revelation" (John Paul II,* CT *9). (CCC 561)*

The woman caught in adultery needs to be healed of sin; Jesus certainly does not deny this truth. He helps to make her holy, freely giving her new life and giving us a preview of what would come to be known as sanctifying grace.

> *Sanctifying grace is the gratuitous gift of his life that God makes to us; it is infused by the Holy Spirit into the soul to heal it of sin and to sanctify it. (CCC 2023)*

A Question for Me

What do my gestures—my actions—teach others about my beliefs and priorities?

For a Child in My Life

When God freely gives us the gift of His life, what is that gift called?

My Role in the Community

How quick am I to condemn, or at least accuse, others in my community? What might I do to tone down this negative impulse?

For Depth and Further Life Application

Isaiah 43:16–21
Psalm 126
Philippians 3:8–14

📖 United States Catholic Catechism for Adults, pages 84–85

REFLECTION

Even now, says the Lord, return to me with your whole heart; for I am gracious and merciful.

—Joel 2:12–13

C Palm Sunday

The Gospel

The elders of the people, chief priests and scribes,
arose and brought Jesus before Pilate.
They brought charges against him, saying,
"We found this man misleading our people;
he opposes the payment of taxes to Caesar
and maintains that he is the Christ, a king."
Pilate asked him, "Are you the king of the Jews?"
He said to him in reply, "You say so."
Pilate then addressed the chief priests and the crowds,
"I find this man not guilty."
But they were adamant and said,
"He is inciting the people with his teaching throughout all Judea,
from Galilee where he began even to here."

On hearing this Pilate asked if the man was a Galilean;
and upon learning that he was under Herod's jurisdiction,
he sent him to Herod who was in Jerusalem at that time.
Herod was very glad to see Jesus;
he had been wanting to see him for a long time,
for he had heard about him
and had been hoping to see him perform some sign.
He questioned him at length,
but he gave him no answer.
The chief priests and scribes, meanwhile,
stood by accusing him harshly.
Herod and his soldiers treated him contemptuously and mocked him,
and after clothing him in resplendent garb,
he sent him back to Pilate.
Herod and Pilate became friends that very day,
even though they had been enemies formerly.
Pilate then summoned the chief priests, the rulers, and the people
and said to them, "You brought this man to me
and accused him of inciting the people to revolt.
I have conducted my investigation in your presence
and have not found this man guilty
of the charges you have brought against him,
nor did Herod, for he sent him back to us.

So no capital crime has been committed by him.
Therefore I shall have him flogged and then release him."

But all together they shouted out,
"Away with this man!
Release Barabbas to us."
—Now Barabbas had been imprisoned for a rebellion
that had taken place in the city and for murder. —
Again Pilate addressed them, still wishing to release Jesus,
but they continued their shouting,
"Crucify him! Crucify him!"
Pilate addressed them a third time,
"What evil has this man done?
I found him guilty of no capital crime.
Therefore I shall have him flogged and then release him."
With loud shouts, however,
they persisted in calling for his crucifixion,
and their voices prevailed.
The verdict of Pilate was that their demand should be granted.
So he released the man who had been imprisoned
for rebellion and murder, for whom they asked,
and he handed Jesus over to them to deal with as they wished.

As they led him away
they took hold of a certain Simon, a Cyrenian,
who was coming in from the country;
and after laying the cross on him,
they made him carry it behind Jesus.
A large crowd of people followed Jesus,
including many women who mourned and lamented him.
Jesus turned to them and said,
"Daughters of Jerusalem, do not weep for me;
weep instead for yourselves and for your children
for indeed, the days are coming when people will say,
'Blessed are the barren,
the wombs that never bore
and the breasts that never nursed.'
At that time people will say to the mountains,
'Fall upon us!'
and to the hills, 'Cover us!'
for if these things are done when the wood is green
what will happen when it is dry?"

Now two others, both criminals,
were led away with him to be executed.

When they came to the place called the Skull,
they crucified him and the criminals there,
one on his right, the other on his left.
Then Jesus said,
"Father, forgive them, they know not what they do."
They divided his garments by casting lots.
The people stood by and watched;
the rulers, meanwhile, sneered at him and said,
"He saved others, let him save himself
if he is the chosen one, the Christ of God."
Even the soldiers jeered at him.
As they approached to offer him wine they called out,
"If you are King of the Jews, save yourself."
Above him there was an inscription that read,
"This is the King of the Jews."

Now one of the criminals hanging there reviled Jesus, saying,
"Are you not the Christ?
Save yourself and us."
The other, however, rebuking him, said in reply,
"Have you no fear of God,
for you are subject to the same condemnation?
And indeed, we have been condemned justly,
for the sentence we received corresponds to our crimes,
but this man has done nothing criminal."
Then he said,
"Jesus, remember me when you come into your kingdom."
He replied to him,
"Amen, I say to you,
today you will be with me in Paradise."

It was now about noon and darkness came over the whole land
until three in the afternoon
because of an eclipse of the sun.
Then the veil of the temple was torn down the middle.
Jesus cried out in a loud voice,
"Father, into your hands I commend my spirit";
and when he had said this he breathed his last.

Here all kneel and pause for a short time.

The centurion who witnessed what had happened
glorified God and said,
"This man was innocent beyond doubt."
When all the people who had gathered for this spectacle
saw what had happened,
they returned home beating their breasts;
but all his acquaintances stood at a distance,
including the women who had followed him from Galilee
and saw these events.

—Luke 23:1–49

Truths of Our Catholic Faith

What happened to Jesus' soul after He breathed His last; where did it go? According to our creed, He descended to the dead. Surely it would have been unfair of God to condemn everyone who lived before Jesus—even those who knew God and lived as they should—just because of the timing of their birth. Jesus proclaims the Gospel to the souls of the just, leading them into Paradise.

> *In his human soul united to his divine person, the dead Christ went down to the realm of the dead. He opened heaven's gates for the just who had gone before him. (CCC 637)*

Public authority figures do not behave well during Jesus' trial and crucifixion. This, however, should not turn us against all political leaders. When leaders lead well, they truly collaborate with God. It is good to remind ourselves occasionally that, even though authority can be abused, it is part of God's plan and is meant to be very helpful.

> *"The political community and public authority are based on human nature and therefore . . . belong to an order established by God"* (GS 74 § 3). *(CCC 1920)*

A Question for Me

How might I grow toward being as forgiving as Jesus, or at least closer to His example of forgiveness?

For a Child in My Life

What is the first thing Jesus says in this Gospel after He is placed on the cross?

My Role in the Community

Jesus is mocked—made fun of. In some ways, we may never outgrow the temptation to make fun of people. If I make fun of anyone in my community, how can I stop and make amends for this hurtful behavior?

For Depth and Further Life Application

Isaiah 50:4–7
Psalm 22
Philippians 2:6–11

📖 United States Catholic Catechism for Adults, pages 97–98

REFLECTION

Christ became obedient to the point of death, even death on a cross. Because of this, God greatly exulted him and bestowed on him the name which is above every name.

—Philippians 2:8–9

C Second Sunday of Easter

The Gospel

On the evening of that first day of the week,
when the doors were locked, where the disciples were,
for fear of the Jews,
Jesus came and stood in their midst
and said to them, "Peace be with you."
When he had said this, he showed them his hands and his side.
The disciples rejoiced when they saw the Lord.
Jesus said to them again, "Peace be with you.
As the Father has sent me, so I send you."
And when he had said this, he breathed on them and said to them,
"Receive the Holy Spirit.
Whose sins you forgive are forgiven them,
and whose sins you retain are retained."

Thomas, called Didymus, one of the Twelve,
was not with them when Jesus came.
So the other disciples said to him, "We have seen the Lord."
But he said to them,
"Unless I see the mark of the nails in his hands
and put my finger into the nailmarks
and put my hand into his side, I will not believe."

Now a week later his disciples were again inside
and Thomas was with them.
Jesus came, although the doors were locked,
and stood in their midst and said, "Peace be with you."
Then he said to Thomas, "Put your finger here and see my hands,
and bring your hand and put it into my side,
and do not be unbelieving, but believe."
Thomas answered and said to him, "My Lord and my God!"
Jesus said to him, "Have you come to believe because
you have seen me?
Blessed are those who have not seen and have believed."

Now Jesus did many other signs in the presence of his disciples
that are not written in this book.

> But these are written that you may come to believe
> that Jesus is the Christ, the Son of God,
> and that through this belief you may have life in his name.
>
> —John 20:19–31

Truths of Our Catholic Faith

If all of the signs that Jesus did were recorded in writing, your Bible would be too huge to carry. That, of course, would not be helpful.

God the Father wants all to have life in the name of His only Son, Jesus the Christ; therefore, the Holy Spirit was sent, inspiring writers to record all we need in order to arrive at the basic faith that Jesus does indeed grant us peace by saving us from sin and death, offering us eternal life. The Holy Spirit guided our Church in assembling the Bible, and inspires Her today to interpret Scripture authoritatively as we apply God's Word to daily living.

> *The Church accepts and venerates as inspired the 46 books of the Old Testament and the 27 books of the New. (CCC 138)*

Sin's harm must be repaired satisfactorily. Acts of penance can help do this, renewing practices that are appropriate for Jesus' followers and friends. In the Sacrament of Penance, a priest, the confessor, assigns a penance to you, the penitent, in order to help your relationships with both God and neighbor.

> *The confessor proposes the performance of certain acts of "satisfaction" or "penance" to be performed by the penitent in order to repair the harm caused by sin and to re-establish habits befitting a disciple of Christ. (CCC 1494)*

A Question for Me

What habits are befitting a disciple of Christ? Which ones are firmly established in me? How can I best help maintain them? If any poor habits have crept into my life, what must I do to repair their harm?

For a Child in My Life

Why does the priest give you a penance when you celebrate the Sacrament of Penance?

My Role in the Community

Which of my habits are especially helpful to my community? Do any habits of mine cause noticeable harm to the community, and again, how can I help to repair that harm? (Note: all virtues and vices affect the community—the Body of Christ. This question concerns those whose impact is particularly evident.)

For Depth and Further Life Application

Acts of the Apostles 5:12–16
Psalm 118
Revelation 1:9–11a, 12–13, 17–19

📖 United States Catholic Catechism for Adults, pages 21–28

REFLECTION

You believe in me, Thomas, because you have seen me, says the Lord; blessed are they who have not seen me, but still believe!

—John 20:29

C Third Sunday of Easter

The Gospel

At that time, Jesus revealed himself to his disciples
at the Sea of Tiberias.
He revealed himself in this way.
Together were Simon Peter, Thomas called Didymus,
Nathanael from Cana in Galilee,
Zebedee's sons, and two others of his disciples.
Simon Peter said to them, "I am going fishing."
They said to him, "We also will come with you."
So they went out and got into the boat,
but that night they caught nothing.
When it was already dawn, Jesus was standing on the shore;
but the disciples did not realize that it was Jesus.
Jesus said to them, "Children, have you caught anything to eat?"
They answered him, "No."
So he said to them, "Cast the net over the right side of the boat
and you will find something."
So they cast it, and were not able to pull it in
because of the number of fish.
So the disciple whom Jesus loved said to Peter, "Alt is the Lord."
When Simon Peter heard that it was the Lord,
he tucked in his garment, for he was lightly clad,
and jumped into the sea.
The other disciples came in the boat,
for they were not far from shore, only about a hundred yards,
dragging the net with the fish.
When they climbed out on shore,
they saw a charcoal fire with fish on it and bread.
Jesus said to them, "Bring some of the fish you just caught."
So Simon Peter went over and dragged the net ashore
full of one hundred fifty-three large fish.
Even though there were so many, the net was not torn.
Jesus said to them, "Come, have breakfast."
And none of the disciples dared to ask him, "Who are you?"
because they realized it was the Lord.
Jesus came over and took the bread and gave it to them,
and in like manner the fish.

> This was now the third time Jesus was revealed to his disciples after being raised from the dead.
>
> —John 21:1–14

Truths of Our Catholic Faith

Jesus gathers His friends and nourishes them. Similarly, our Church is gathered by Jesus, the living Word. He calls us together, nourishing us for our good and the good of all His world.

> *The word "Church" means "convocation." It designates the assembly of those whom God's Word "convokes," i.e., gathers together to form the People of God, and who themselves, nourished with the Body of Christ, become the Body of Christ. (CCC 777)*

The disciples responded to Jesus' call. Jesus offered them not only teaching for their minds, but also food for their bodies, grace for their souls and love for their hearts. Our Lord desires genuine growth of the whole person. Strengthened by God almighty, we can do all that He asks of us.

> *True development concerns the whole man. It is concerned with increasing each person's ability to respond to his vocation and hence to God's call (cf.* CA 29*). (CCC 2461)*

A Question for Me

What is God calling me to do so that I may continue truly developing as a whole person?

For a Child in My Life

What do you think God might be calling you to do in life?

My Role in the Community

In what ways can I help increase others' ability to respond to their vocation and hence to God's call?

For Depth and Further Life Application

Acts of the Apostles 5:27–32, 40b–41
Psalm 30
Revelation 5:11–14

📖 United States Catholic Catechism for Adults, pages 112–119

REFLECTION

Christ is risen, creator of all; he has shown pity on all people.

C Fourth Sunday of Easter

The Gospel

Jesus said:
"My sheep hear my voice;
I know them, and they follow me.
I give them eternal life, and they shall never perish.
No one can take them out of my hand.
My Father, who has given them to me, is greater than all,
and no one can take them out of the Father's hand.
The Father and I are one."

—John 10:27–30

Truths of Our Catholic Faith

The ordinary means to eternal life is baptism. This occasionally causes people to worry about children who die without being baptized. Jesus knows all of His sheep, though, and assures us that they will never perish. Regarding children who remain unbaptized, then, the Church encourages us to take comfort in our Father's boundless mercy.

> *With respect to children who have died without Baptism, the liturgy of the Church invites us to trust in God's mercy and to pray for their salvation. (CCC 1283)*

Many voices compete for our attention and obedience. The voice of law at times can chart a course that is foreign to the way of Jesus. (I.e., just because something is legal, it is not necessarily moral.)

In circumstances when human law contradicts God's law, we have an obligation to uphold the way of righteousness. We follow the voice of Jesus, the Good Shepherd.

> *Citizens are obliged in conscience not to follow the directives of civil authorities when they are contrary to the demands of the moral order. "We must obey God rather than men"* (Acts *5:29). (CCC 2256)*

A Question for Me

When Jesus says to me "No one can take (you) out of my hand," what is my reaction?

For a Child in My Life

Does anyone have the power to take you away from Jesus? In other words, is anyone more powerful than God?

My Role in the Community

Does anyone in my community seem to be trying to take people away from Jesus, away from God? If so, what might I do about it?

For Depth and Further Life Application

Acts of the Apostles 13:14, 43–52
Psalm 100
Revelation 7:9, 14b–17

📖 United States Catholic Catechism for Adults, pages 541–542

REFLECTION

I am the good shepherd, says the Lord; I know my sheep, and mine know me.

—John 10:14

C Fifth Sunday of Easter

The Gospel

> When Judas had left them, Jesus said,
> "Now is the Son of Man glorified, and God is glorified in him.
> If God is glorified in him,
> God will also glorify him in himself,
> and God will glorify him at once.
> My children, I will be with you only a little while longer.
> I give you a new commandment: love one another.
> As I have loved you, so you also should love one another.
> This is how all will know that you are my disciples,
> if you have love for one another."
>
> —John 13:31–33a, 34–35

Truths of Our Catholic Faith

Judas apparently succumbed to the effects of original sin. Originally, our human nature was fair-minded and holy. Mysteriously, the sin of the first human persons has a lasting impact on our inclination to love as we should.

Jesus does not command the impossible. Still, it would be naïve not to be mindful of our woundedness as we strive to live, with God's help, a life of holiness, justice and Christ-like love.

> *Adam and Eve transmitted to their descendants human nature wounded by their own first sin and hence deprived of original holiness and justice; this deprivation is called "original sin."* (CCC 417)

Some have said, "I have no problem with love. It is all those one-anothers that trouble me!" Getting along perfectly with everyone at all times is a tall order. Surely, though, there is a sisterly and brotherly love that can permeate our interactions with each other, even if we occasionally get on one another's nerves.

The Holy Trinity is our example: three individual Persons, yet united ultimately by love. A tall order? Yes. But again, our Lord does not command what is impossible. If we set our sights on glorifying God, allowing Him to work in us, we will be drawn to one another by a love that knows no limits—the love with which Jesus has loved us.

> *There is a certain resemblance between the unity of the divine persons and the fraternity that men ought to establish among themselves.* (CCC 1890)

A Question for Me

How has Jesus loved me? How is He currently loving me? In what ways is He likely to love me in the future? What does all this say about how I ought to treat my fellow women and men?

For a Child in My Life

How does Jesus say people will know that you are His disciple—His follower and friend?

My Role in the Community

Sisterly and brotherly affection and unity are to be the community goals of those believing God is a communion of Persons—Father, Son and Holy Spirit. How might I do an even better job of establishing these sorts of relations in my various communities?

For Depth and Further Life Application

Acts of the Apostles 14:21–27
Psalm 145
Revelation 21:1–5a

📖 United States Catholic Catechism for Adults, pages 73–75

REFLECTION

I give you a new commandment, says the Lord: love one another as I have loved you.

—John 13:34

C Sixth Sunday of Easter

The Gospel

Jesus said to his disciples:
"Whoever loves me will keep my word,
and my Father will love him,
and we will come to him and make our dwelling with him.
Whoever does not love me does not keep my words;
yet the word you hear is not mine
but that of the Father who sent me.

"I have told you this while I am with you.
The Advocate, the Holy Spirit,
whom the Father will send in my name,
will teach you everything
and remind you of all that I told you.
Peace I leave with you; my peace I give to you.
Not as the world gives do I give it to you.
Do not let your hearts be troubled or afraid.
You heard me tell you,
'I am going away and I will come back to you.'
If you loved me,
you would rejoice that I am going to the Father;
for the Father is greater than I.
And now I have told you this before it happens,
so that when it happens you may believe."

—John 14:23–29

Truths of Our Catholic Faith

The Holy Spirit has a major role to play in each Christian's life, as well as the life of the Church. It is the Holy Spirit who animates the Body of Christ, our Church, giving all the gifts that are needed for Christ's Body to thrive in our world today.

> *The Church is the Temple of the Holy Spirit. The Spirit is the soul, as it were, of the Mystical Body, the source of its life, of its unity in diversity, and of the riches of its gifts and charisms. (CCC 809)*

At confirmation, the Holy Spirit is poured out in a powerful way. Following are the requirements to be confirmed in God's Church.

Confirmation candidates who are at least seven or eight years old must

- † profess our Catholic faith.
- † be in a state of grace.
- † intend to receive this sacrament.
- † be ready to live a life of following Jesus' way and testifying to the transforming beauty of a life lived in communion with Him. This life includes both Church-related activities and daily interaction with various worldly matters, seeking to alter their course for the better.

Strengthened by the Holy Spirit, our hearts move beyond fear and trouble. We experience peace beyond all worldly definition.

> *A candidate for Confirmation who has attained the age of reason must profess the faith, be in the state of grace, have the intention of receiving the sacrament, and be prepared to assume the role of disciple and witness to Christ, both within the ecclesial community and in temporal affairs. (CCC 1319)*

A Question for Me

What seem to be my gifts and charisms?

For a Child in My Life

What is the relationship between the Holy Spirit and the Mystical Body of Christ, the Church?

My Role in the Community

What charisms and gifts do I see in my community? How might I encourage others to develop these traits, applying them for the common good?

For Depth and Further Life Application

Acts of the Apostles 15:1–2, 22–29
Psalm 67
Revelation 21:10–14, 22–23

📖 United States Catholic Catechism for Adults, pages 210–211

REFLECTION

Whoever loves me will keep my word, says the Lord, and my Father will love him and we will come to him.

—John 14:23

C Seventh Sunday of Easter

The Gospel

Lifting up his eyes to heaven, Jesus prayed saying:
"Holy Father, I pray not only for them,
but also for those who will believe in me through their word,
so that they may all be one,
as you, Father, are in me and I in you,
that they also may be in us,
that the world may believe that you sent me.
And I have given them the glory you gave me,
so that they may be one, as we are one,
I in them and you in me,
that they may be brought to perfection as one,
that the world may know that you sent me,
and that you loved them even as you loved me.
Father, they are your gift to me.
I wish that where I am they also may be with me,
that they may see my glory that you gave me,
because you loved me before the foundation of the world.
Righteous Father, the world also does not know you,
but I know you, and they know that you sent me.
I made known to them your name and I will make it known,
that the love with which you loved me
may be in them and I in them."

—John 17:20–26

Truths of Our Catholic Faith

Jesus prayed that we may all be one. Sometimes people mistake unity for uniformity, as if we should all be cookie-cutter images of each other. All too often, the opposite mistake occurs: people mistaking diversity for an anything-goes concept of Church.

Our Lord knows that when love is allowed to guide our relationships, we are truly united as His Body. Within a legitimate diversity, a variety of functions serves to build up the Church and glorify God—our Righteous, Holy Father.

> *In the unity of this Body, there is a diversity of members and functions. All members are linked to one another, especially to those who are suffering, to the poor and persecuted. (CCC 806)*

Make no mistake about it: God's name is to be considered as very special. It is not to be used improperly.

This would seem to be an overly harsh way of stating God's wishes if not for the fact that so often we hear the opposite treatment of His name filling everyday conversation and entertainment. Names of close relation to God (e.g., Jesus, Christ, Mary, etc.) are also to be treated with suitable respect. Using these names respectfully usually indicates an appropriate internal attitude toward the Almighty.

> *The second commandment forbids every improper use of God's name. Blasphemy is the use of the name of God, of Jesus Christ, of the Virgin Mary, and of the saints in an offensive way. (CCC 2162)*

A Question for Me

What functions(s) do I fulfill in the Body of Christ? How do I collaborate with other members of His Body—members with whom I am truly united, yet who fulfill a legitimate diversity of functions?

For a Child in My Life

What are some ways that different members of the Body of Christ work together in unity for the good of the Body?

My Role in the Community

What evidence in my community shows that in some ways the world does not know God our righteous and Holy Father? How might I work, with love, so that His name will be made known?

For Depth and Further Life Application

Acts of the Apostles 7:55–60
Psalm 97
Revelation 22:12–14, 16–17, 20

📖 United States Catholic Catechism for Adults, pages 356–359

REFLECTION

I will not leave you orphans, says the Lord. I will come back to you, and your hearts will rejoice.

—cf. John 14:18

C Pentcost Sunday

The Gospel

Jesus said to his disciples:
"If you love me, you will keep my commandments.
And I will ask the Father,
and he will give you another Advocate to be with you always.

"Whoever loves me will keep my word,
and my Father will love him,
and we will come to him and make our dwelling with him.
Those who do not love me do not keep my words;
yet the word you hear is not mine
but that of the Father who sent me.

"I have told you this while I am with you.
The Advocate, the Holy Spirit whom the Father will send in my name,
will teach you everything
and remind you of all that I told you."

—John 14:15–16, 23b–26

Truths of Our Catholic Faith

Violating God's commandments displeases Him. Sometimes we are both sorry for having offended God, and we detest our sins because we fear the loss of heaven and the pains of hell. This is perfectly understandable; when this predominates the motives behind our contrition, though, we are imperfectly (albeit legitimately) contrite.

When we are whole-heartedly sorry for having offended God, and we detest all our sins primarily because they displease Him, who is all good and who we should love above all things, we are perfectly contrite. We then firmly resolve, with the help of God's grace, to confess our sins, do penance and amend our life.

> *Repentance (also called contrition) must be inspired by motives that arise from faith. If repentance arises from love of charity for God, it is called "perfect" contrition; if it is founded on other motives, it is called "imperfect." (CCC 1492)*

Every commandment, every word of God, is to be obeyed. God loves us and always looks out for our good.

When we fail to keep God's word in relatively minor (yet serious, because all sin is serious) ways, God's loving reminders to us bear fruit with relative ease when we remain open to His grace. We can reorder our life, repairing sin's damage, thanks to the mercy of God.

> *Venial sin constitutes a moral disorder that is reparable by charity, which it allows to subsist in us. (CCC 1875)*

A Question for Me
In what ways am I taught by God? What ways, specifically, does the Holy Spirit remind me of all that Jesus said?

For a Child in My Life
What is the difference between perfect contrition and imperfect contrition?

My Role in the Community
What venial sins have I committed against community members? By what specific actions might I help repair the effects of this venial sin?

For Depth and Further Life Application

Acts of the Apostles 2:1–11
Psalm 104
1 Corinthians 12:3b–7, 12–13

📖 United States Catholic Catechism for Adults, pages 614–620

REFLECTION

Come, Holy Spirit, fill the hearts of your faithful and kindle in them the fire of your love.

C Trinity Sunday

The Gospel

Jesus said to his disciples:
"I have much more to tell you, but you cannot bear it now.
But when he comes, the Spirit of truth,
he will guide you to all truth.
He will not speak on his own,
but he will speak what he hears,
and will declare to you the things that are coming.
He will glorify me,
because he will take from what is mine and declare it to you.
Everything that the Father has is mine;
for this reason I told you that he will take from what is mine
and declare it to you."

—John 16:12–15

Truths of Our Catholic Faith

The Holy Spirit is the Spirit of truth. Each Person of the Blessed Trinity contributes to the holiness of our Church. Our Triune God declares this truth among many others: that the Church is holy.

> *The Church is holy: the Most Holy God is her author; Christ, her bridegroom, gave himself up to make her holy; the Spirit of holiness gives her life. Since she still includes sinners, she is "the sinless one made up of sinners." Her holiness shines in the saints; in Mary she is already all-holy. (CCC 867)*

Sometimes, circumstances that seem unbearable enter our life in dramatic ways. It is conceivable that a situation could arise whereby an emergency baptism would be in order. Medical emergencies involving infants can be good examples of this. When appropriate, due to unusual circumstances, any person can baptize, invoking the Most Holy Trinity.

> *In case of necessity, any person can baptize provided that he have the intention of doing that which the Church does and provided that he pours water on the candidate's*

head while saying: "I baptize you in the name of the Father, and of the Son, and of the Holy Spirit." (CCC 1284)

A Question for Me

What circumstances might make it necessary for me to conduct a baptism? How exactly would I go about doing this?

For a Child in My Life

In what ways is our Church holy?

My Role in the Community

Who in my community has not been baptized? How might I help bring this person closer to the sacrament that is our ordinary means of salvation?

For Depth and Further Life Application

Proverbs 8:22–31
Psalm 8
Romans 5:1–5

United States Catholic Catechism for Adults, pages 521–522

REFLECTION

Glory to the Father, the Son, and the Holy Spirit; to God who is, who was, and who is to come.

—cf. Revelation 1:8

C Corpus Christi

The Gospel

Jesus spoke to the crowds about the kingdom of God,
 and he healed those who needed to be cured.
As the day was drawing to a close,
 the Twelve approached him and said,
 "Dismiss the crowd
 so that they can go to the surrounding villages and farms
 and find lodging and provisions;
 for we are in a deserted place here."
He said to them, "Give them some food yourselves."
They replied, "Five loaves and two fish are all we have,
 unless we ourselves go and buy food for all these people."
Now the men there numbered about five thousand.
Then he said to his disciples,
 "Have them sit down in groups of about fifty."
They did so and made them all sit down.
Then taking the five loaves and the two fish,
 and looking up to heaven,
 he said the blessing over them, broke them,
 and gave them to the disciples to set before the crowd.
They all ate and were satisfied.
And when the leftover fragments were picked up,
they filled twelve wicker baskets.

—Luke 9:11b–17

Truths of Our Catholic Faith

Jesus said the blessing over the loaves and fish similarly, in a sense, to how He had just blessed the crowds with His teaching and His healing power. In this regard, the food can be said to represent the people. And certainly the meal provided by Jesus united these people in breaking bread together.

In the Eucharist, the unity that is fitting for the Body of Christ is brought about as well as being represented. The Holy Eucharist is a sign and a cause of unity.

> *The Church is a "communion of saints": this expression refers first to the "holy things"* (sancta), *above all the Eucharist, by which "the unity of believers, who form one body in Christ, is both represented and brought about"* (LG 3). *(CCC 960)*

The Lord could have made the people work harder for their meal. Instead He helped to serve them. In order to observe the Lord's Day, it is helpful when others refrain from making demands that might cause such observation to be unnecessarily difficult.

> *Every Christian should avoid making unnecessary demands on others that would hinder them from observing the Lord's Day. (CCC 2195)*

A Question for Me

How is the Eucharist both a sign and a cause of unity in the Church?

For a Child in My Life

What is the communion of saints?

My Role in the Community

What might I do to help bring about more unity—unity in holiness—within my community?

For Depth and Further Life Application

Genesis 14:18–20
Psalm 110
1 Corinthians 11:23–26

📖 United States Catholic Catechism for Adults, pages 367–369

REFLECTION

I am the living bread that came down from heaven, says the Lord; whoever eats this bread will live forever.

—John 6:51

C Sacred Heart

The Gospel

Jesus addressed this parable to the Pharisees and scribes:
"What man among you having a hundred sheep and
losing one of them
would not leave the ninety-nine in the desert
and go after the lost one until he finds it?
And when he does find it,
he sets it on his shoulders with great joy
and, upon his arrival home,
he calls together his friends and neighbors and says to them,
'Rejoice with me because I have found my lost sheep.'
I tell you, in just the same way
there will be more joy in heaven over one sinner who repents
than over ninety-nine righteous people
who have no need of repentance."

—Luke 15:3–7

Truths of Our Catholic Faith

When the first human persons fell from God's grace by rejecting His will, God desired that they repent. Even after the fall, He continued revealing truth to them so they could be saved from sin and death. God continually speaks to us, also—through His creation and with truth revealed in Scripture and Tradition—so that we might turn away from sin and find the joy of heaven.

> *Beyond the witness to himself that God gives in created things, he manifested himself to our first parents, spoke to them and, after the fall, promised them salvation (cf.* Gen *3:15) and offered them his covenant. (CCC 70)*

There is joy in heaven each time a person accepts and achieves, by God's grace, eternal salvation. The Church must be about the business of helping to save souls; for this reason she has much to say about many aspects of daily human life, because little things can mean a lot, and small goods can go a long way toward helping to unite us with the ultimate Good: our loving, saving God.

The Church makes a judgment about economic and social matters when the fundamental rights of the person or the salvation of souls requires it. She is concerned with the temporal common good of men because they are ordered to the sovereign Good, their ultimate end. (CCC 2458)

A Question for Me

When does the Church make judgments about social and economic matters? Why is she concerned with our common good in the temporal realm?

For a Child in My Life

Who were the first human persons, the first couple who became our first parents?

My Role in the Community

How joyful am I over a sinner or sinners who repent(s)?

For Depth and Further Life Application

Ezekiel 34:11–16
Psalm 23
Romans 5:5b–11

United States Catholic Catechism for Adults, pages 15–19

REFLECTION

Take my yoke upon you, says the Lord, and learn from me, for I am meek and humble of heart.

—Matthew 11:29ab

OR

REFLECTION

I am the good shepherd, says the Lord, I know my sheep, and mine know me.

—John 10:14

C Second Sunday of Ordinary Time

The Gospel

There was a wedding at Cana in Galilee,
  and the mother of Jesus was there.
Jesus and his disciples were also invited to the wedding.
When the wine ran short,
  the mother of Jesus said to him,
  "They have no wine."
And Jesus said to her,
  "Woman, how does your concern affect me?
My hour has not yet come."
His mother said to the servers,
  "Do whatever he tells you."
Now there were six stone water jars there for
    Jewish ceremonial washings,
  each holding twenty to thirty gallons.
Jesus told the them,
  "Fill the jars with water."
So they filled them to the brim.
Then he told them,
  "Draw some out now and take it to the headwaiter."
So they took it.
And when the headwaiter tasted the water that had become wine,
  without knowing where it came from
  —although the servers who had drawn the water knew—,
  the headwaiter called the bridegroom and said to him,
  "Everyone serves good wine first,
  and then when people have drunk freely, an inferior one;
  but you have kept the good wine until now."
Jesus did this as the beginning of his signs at Cana in Galilee
  and so revealed his glory,
and his disciples began to believe in him.

—John 2:1–11

Truths of Our Catholic Faith

Mary shared in the revelation of her Son's glory. Similarly, she shares in the glory of Jesus' Resurrection. Mary was assumed bodily into heaven at her earthly life's end—a preview of what we can expect. When Jesus' hour came, He suffered, died and rose for us, so we may drink the good wine of eternal life.

> *The Most Blessed Virgin Mary, when the course of her earthly life was completed, was taken up body and soul into the glory of heaven, where she already shares in the glory of her Son's Resurrection, anticipating the resurrection of all members of his Body.* (CCC 974)

Weddings, properly understood, are in a sense public affairs. Although the couple's relationship with each other is entirely unique, they remain disciples among disciples and as such have an important role in the life of the community. The beginning of a marriage, then, generally includes guests of various sorts.

> *Since marriage establishes the couple in a public state of life in the Church, it is fitting that its celebration be public, in the framework of a liturgical celebration, before the priest (or a witness authorized by the Church), the witnesses, and the assembly of the faithful.* (CCC 1663)

A Question for Me

When I imagine myself as a server at this wedding feast, what is my reaction to what Mary says to me?

For a Child in My Life

What did Jesus' mom, Mary, say to the servers?

My Role in the Community

The next time I attend a wedding, how might I continue being of help to the couple, particularly in the realm of prayer?

For Depth and Further Life Application

Isaiah 62:1–5

Psalm 96

1 Corinthians 12:4–11

📖 United States Catholic Catechism for Adults, pages 279–288

REFLECTION

God has called us through the Gospel to possess the glory of our Lord Jesus Christ.

—cf. 2 Thessalonians 2:14

C Third Sunday of Ordinary Time

The Gospel

Since many have undertaken to compile a narrative of the events
that have been fulfilled among us,
just as those who were eyewitnesses from the beginning
and ministers of the word have handed them down to us,
I too have decided,
after investigating everything accurately anew,
to write it down in an orderly sequence for you,
most excellent Theophilus,
so that you may realize the certainty of the teachings
you have received.

Jesus returned to Galilee in the power of the Spirit,
and news of him spread throughout the whole region.
He taught in their synagogues and was praised by all.

He came to Nazareth, where he had grown up,
and went according to his custom
into the synagogue on the sabbath day.
He stood up to read and was handed a scroll of the prophet Isaiah.
He unrolled the scroll and found the passage where it was written:

> The Spirit of the Lord is upon me,
> because he has anointed me
> to bring glad tidings to the poor.
> He has sent me to proclaim liberty to captives
> and recovery of sight to the blind,
> to let the oppressed go free,
> and to proclaim a year acceptable to the Lord.

Rolling up the scroll, he handed it back to the attendant and
sat down,
and the eyes of all in the synagogue looked intently at him.
He said to them,
"Today this Scripture passage is fulfilled in your hearing."

—Luke 1:1–4, 4:14–21

Truths of Our Catholic Faith

Jesus observes the Sabbath according to His custom. He is in the habit of taking time to cultivate life in a truly well-rounded sense.

*The institution of Sunday helps all "to be allowed sufficient rest and leisure to cultivate their familial, cultural, social, and religious lives" (*GS *67 § 3). (CCC 2194)*

Liberty to captives, and freedom for those oppressed are major components of the Jesus, Good News, of His Gospel. Human persons can be oppressed in many ways, some of them new (such as unborn persons being bought and sold in embryonic form). Where there is real oppression, captivity and enslavement, the Good News must be proclaimed in ever-new, authentically-liberating ways.

The moral law forbids acts which, for commercial or totalitarian purposes, lead to the enslavement of human beings, or to their being bought, sold or exchanged like merchandise. (CCC 2455)

A Question for Me

According to tradition, Saint Luke was a physician—a man of science; what might this imply about the reliability of his narrative?

For a Child in My Life

Why does Saint Luke say he is writing this Gospel?

My Role in the Community

How are people sold and bought—exchanged like merchandise? What might I do to help relieve these sorts of situations?

For Depth and Further Life Application

Nehemiah 8:2–4a, 5–6, 8–10
Psalm 19
1 Corinthians 12:12–30

📖 United States Catholic Catechism for Adults, pages 369–371

REFLECTION

The Lord sent me to bring glad tidings to the poor, and to proclaim liberty to captives.

—cf. Luke 4:18

C Fourth Sunday of Ordinary Time

The Gospel

Jesus began speaking in the synagogue, saying:
"Today this Scripture passage is fulfilled in your hearing."
And all spoke highly of him
and were amazed at the gracious words that came from his mouth.
They also asked, "Isn't this the son of Joseph?"
He said to them, "Surely you will quote me this proverb,
'Physician, cure yourself,' and say,
'Do here in your native place
the things that we heard were done in Capernaum.'"
And he said, "Amen, I say to you,
no prophet is accepted in his own native place.
Indeed, I tell you,
there were many widows in Israel in the days of Elijah
when the sky was closed for three and a half years
and a severe famine spread over the entire land.
It was to none of these that Elijah was sent,
but only to a widow in Zarephath in the land of Sidon.
Again, there were many lepers in Israel
during the time of Elisha the prophet;
yet not one of them was cleansed, but only Naaman the Syrian."
When the people in the synagogue heard this,
they were all filled with fury.
They rose up, drove him out of the town,
and led him to the brow of the hill
on which their town had been built,
to hurl him down headlong.
But Jesus passed through the midst of them and went away.

—Luke 4:21–30

Truths of Our Catholic Faith

When Jesus mentions Scripture passages being fulfilled, He doesn't necessarily mean that all guidance contained in them is abolished. This is a source of misunderstanding with the people. Jesus usually tends to teach quite clearly. What people hear when He speaks, though, is often another story.

> *Jesus did not abolish the Law of Sinai, but rather fulfilled it (cf.* Mt *5:17–19) with such perfection (cf.* Jn *8:46) that he revealed its ultimate meaning (cf.* Mt *5:33) and redeemed the transgressions against it (cf.* Heb *9:15). (CCC 592)*

Jesus has the luxury of passing through the midst of those who would harm Him. We at times, though, may have a legitimate need to defend ourselves and others.

Building solid defenses does not mean that the sky is the limit financially speaking. Always we must balance the legitimate needs of others with our desire to outdo our would-be opponents in the realm of weaponry.

> *"The arms race is one of the greatest curses on the human race and the harm it inflicts on the poor is more than can be endured"* (GS *81 § 3). (CCC 2329)*

A Question for Me

What might I communicate to my elected officials regarding the arms race?

For a Child in My Life

What is God's opinion about countries spending massive amounts of money to outdo each other in highly sophisticated, hugely expensive weaponry while their poor go without the help they deserve?

My Role in the Community

If a negative fury ever fills my community (as opposed to a righteous anger) what might I do to help calm the situation?

For Depth and Further Life Application

Jeremiah 1:4–5, 17–19
Psalm 71
1 Corinthians 12:31–13:13

📖 United States Catholic Catechism for Adults, pages 98–100

REFLECTION

The Lord sent me to bring glad tidings to the poor, to proclaim liberty to captives.

—Luke 4:18

C Fifth Sunday of Ordinary Time

The Gospel

While the crowd was pressing in on Jesus and listening
to the word of God,
he was standing by the Lake of Gennesaret.
He saw two boats there alongside the lake;
the fishermen had disembarked and were washing their nets.
Getting into one of the boats, the one belonging to Simon,
he asked him to put out a short distance from the shore.
Then he sat down and taught the crowds from the boat.
After he had finished speaking, he said to Simon,
"Put out into deep water and lower your nets for a catch."
Simon said in reply,
"Master, we have worked hard all night and have caught nothing,
but at your command I will lower the nets."
When they had done this, they caught a great number of fish
and their nets were tearing.
They signaled to their partners in the other boat
to come to help them.
They came and filled both boats
so that the boats were in danger of sinking.
When Simon Peter saw this, he fell at the knees of Jesus and said,
"Depart from me, Lord, for I am a sinful man."
For astonishment at the catch of fish they had made seized him
and all those with him,
and likewise James and John, the sons of Zebedee,
who were partners of Simon.
Jesus said to Simon, "Do not be afraid;
from now on you will be catching men."
When they brought their boats to the shore,
they left everything and followed him.

—Luke 5:1–11

Truths of Our Catholic Faith

Peter blurts out that he is a sinful man. Regardless of any sinful decisions on his part, Peter, like all of us, is wounded by original sin. This is a mystery not so much to understand, but to be aware of and to address by allowing ourselves to be caught up in the saving love of Jesus.

> *"We therefore hold, with the Council of Trent, that original sin is transmitted with human nature, 'by propagation, not by imitation' and that it is . . . 'proper to each'" (Paul VI,* CPG *§ 16). (CCC 419)*

Today's fishers of men are our loyal corps of priests. United with his bishop, a priest leaves much to follow Jesus in a unique way. Bishops and priests together—partners in ministry—form a team of ordained coworkers who bring us, in many ways, God's astonishing goodness.

> *Priests are united with the bishops in sacerdotal dignity and at the same time depend on them in the exercise of their pastoral functions; they are called to be the bishops' prudent co-workers. They form around their bishop the presbyterium which bears responsibility with him for the particular Church. They receive from the bishop the charge of a parish community or a determinate ecclesial office. (CCC 1595)*

A Question for Me

What might Jesus be saying to me by the words "Put out into deep water"?

For a Child in My Life

What is the relationship between bishops and priests?

My Role in the Community

Like Peter's partners, how can I be of help to my coworkers?

For Depth and Further Life Application

Isaiah 6:1–2a, 3–8
Psalm 138
1 Corinthians 15:1–11

United States Catholic Catechism for Adults, pages 271–273

REFLECTION

Come after me and I will make you fishers of men.

—Matthew 4:19

C Sixth Sunday of Ordinary Time

The Gospel

Jesus came down with the twelve
 and stood on a stretch of level ground
 with a great crowd of his disciples
 and a large number of the people
 from all Judea and Jerusalem
 and the coastal region of Tyre and Sidon.
And raising his eyes toward his disciples he said:
 "Blessed are you who are poor,
  for the kingdom of God is yours.
 Blessed are you who are now hungry,
  for you will be satisfied.
 Blessed are you who are now weeping,
  for you will laugh.
 Blessed are you when people hate you,
  and when they exclude and insult you,
  and denounce your name as evil
  on account of the Son of Man.
Rejoice and leap for joy on that day!
Behold, your reward will be great in heaven.
For their ancestors treated the prophets in the same way.
 But woe to you who are rich,
  for you have received your consolation.
 Woe to you who are filled now,
  for you will be hungry.
 Woe to you who laugh now,
  for you will grieve and weep.
 Woe to you when all speak well of you,
  for their ancestors treated the false
prophets in this way."

—Luke 6:17, 20–26

Truths of Our Catholic Faith

It is okay to desire blessings from God. It is acceptable to look forward with some degree of eagerness toward our heavenly reward. The Beatitudes tell us how to live on earth so we might one day join God's holy prophets of old in the true and eternal paradise.

> *The Beatitudes teach us the final end to which God calls us: the Kingdom, the vision of God, participation in the divine nature, eternal life, filiation, rest in God. (CCC 1726)*

The Beatitudes in Luke's Gospel are accompanied by their corresponding woes. These woes are, in a sense, the opposite of envy. Rather than jealousy over another's possessions, people living the Beatitudes abandon themselves to God's providence, regardless of what earthly experiences He has in store.

> *The baptized person combats envy through good-will, humility, and abandonment to the providence of God. (CCC 2554)*

A Question for Me

For God's sake, who denounces my name as evil, insults me, excludes and hates me—on account of Jesus?

For a Child in My Life

How do we work against the sin of envy?

My Role in the Community

Who do I envy, and what are some examples of how to fight this sinful attitude?

For Depth and Further Life Application

Jeremiah 17:5–8
Psalm 1
1 Corinthians 15:12, 16–20

📖 United States Catholic Catechism for Adults, pages 455–457

REFLECTION

Rejoice and be glad; your reward will be great in heaven.

—Luke 6:23ab

C Seventh Sunday of Ordinary Time

The Gospel

Jesus said to his disciples:
"To you who hear I say,
love your enemies, do good to those who hate you,
bless those who curse you, pray for those who mistreat you.
To the person who strikes you on one cheek,
offer the other one as well,
and from the person who takes your cloak,
do not withhold even your tunic.
Give to everyone who asks of you,
and from the one who takes what is yours do not demand it back.
Do to others as you would have them do to you.
For if you love those who love you,
what credit is that to you?
Even sinners love those who love them.
And if you do good to those who do good to you,
what credit is that to you?
Even sinners do the same.
If you lend money to those from whom you expect repayment,
what credit is that to you?
Even sinners lend to sinners,
and get back the same amount.
But rather, love your enemies and do good to them,
and lend expecting nothing back;
then your reward will be great
and you will be children of the Most High,
for he himself is kind to the ungrateful and the wicked.
Be merciful, just as your Father is merciful.

"Stop judging and you will not be judged.
Stop condemning and you will not be condemned.
Forgive and you will be forgiven.
Give, and gifts will be given to you;
a good measure, packed together, shaken down, and overflowing,
will be poured into your lap.
For the measure with which you measure
will in return be measured out to you."

—Luke 6:27–38

Truths of Our Catholic Faith

Jesus has practical and specific teaching to offer those who would be His disciples. Even when circumstances are not ideal, we are called to be Christ-like. When things get messy as they sometimes do in the course of our human relationships, it is then that Jesus challenges all people—especially the laity because we permeate every facet of society—to teach by example, to display His merciful heart through our actions along with our speech.

> *By virtue of their prophetic mission, lay people "are called . . . to be witnesses to Christ in all circumstances and at the very heart of the community of mankind"* (GS *43 § 4). (CCC 942)*

Regarding the availability of His mercy, God does not distinguish between the grateful and ungrateful, the wicked and the good. So in turn each person has a right not to be judged with finality by another—not to be, literally, condemned. In their basic dignity and authentic human rights, all persons are truly equal.

> *The equality of men concerns their dignity as persons and the rights that flow from it. (CCC 1945)*

A Question for Me

In what ways is my Father in heaven merciful? How might I show mercy as He does? (You might consider acquiring information about devotion to the Divine Mercy.)

For a Child in My Life

What does it mean to say that everyone is equal in dignity?

My Role in the Community

By way of practical examples, how can I answer my call to be a witness to Christ in all circumstances and at the very heart of the community?

For Depth and Further Life Application

Samuel 26:2, 7–9, 12–13, 22–23
Psalm 103
1 Corinthians 15:45–49

📖 United States Catholic Catechism for Adults, pages 621–628

REFLECTION

I give you a new commandment, says the Lord: love one another as I have loved you.

—John 13:34

C Eighth Sunday of Ordinary Time

The Gospel

Jesus told his disciples a parable,
"Can a blind person guide a blind person?
Will not both fall into a pit?
No disciple is superior to the teacher;
but when fully trained,
every disciple will be like his teacher.
Why do you notice the splinter in your brother's eye,
but do not perceive the wooden beam in your own?
How can you say to your brother,
'Brother, let me remove that splinter in your eye,'
when you do not even notice the wooden beam in your own eye?
You hypocrite! Remove the wooden beam from your eye first;
then you will see clearly
to remove the splinter in your brother's eye.

"A good tree does not bear rotten fruit,
nor does a rotten tree bear good fruit.
For every tree is known by its own fruit.
For people do not pick figs from thornbushes,
nor do they gather grapes from brambles.
A good person out of the store of goodness in his heart
produces good,
but an evil person out of a store of evil produces evil;
for from the fullness of the heart the mouth speaks."

—Luke 6:39–45

Truths of Our Catholic Faith

Notice that Jesus does not forbid the removal of splinters. He does insist that our hearts be in the right places.

As a Church, we are called to be in all places, to speak goodness and help all peoples to live well. In terms of comprehensiveness in her efforts—even if occasional splinter-removing is warranted—our Church then is recognized as catholic.

> *The Church is catholic: she proclaims the fullness of the faith. She bears in herself and administers the totality of*

> *the means of salvation. She is sent out to all peoples. She speaks to all men. She encompasses all times. She is "missionary of her very nature"* (AG 2). *(CCC 868)*

Some fruit is rotten. Some plants yield only thorns. Some trees produce evil.

Homosexual acts, pornography, masturbation and inappropriate sexual behavior of any sort are wooden beams that obstruct moral vision. If we notice such obstructions in our eyes, we would do well, with God's help, to remove them. Thus our hearts will be full, our lives will be chaste, and we will by God's grace produce good.

> *Among the sins gravely contrary to chastity are masturbation, fornication, pornography, and homosexual practices. (CCC 2396)*

A Question for Me

How might I do the merciful work of instructing the ignorant without seeming to be an overly hasty splinter-remover?

For a Child in My Life

What does it mean to say that the Church is catholic?

My Role in the Community

How prominent in my community are sins gravely contrary to chastity? What might I do to help lessen their occurrence or impact?

For Depth and Further Life Application

Sirach 27:4–7
Psalm 92
1 Corinthians 15:54–58

United States Catholic Catechism for Adults, pages 414–416

REFLECTION

Shine like lights in the world as you hold on to the word of life.

—Philippians 2:15d, 16a

C Ninth Sunday of Ordinary Time

The Gospel

When Jesus had finished all his words to the people,
he entered Capernaum.
A centurion there had a slave who was ill and about to die,
and he was valuable to him.
When he heard about Jesus, he sent elders of the Jews to him,
asking him to come and save the life of his slave.
They approached Jesus and strongly urged him to come, saying,
"He deserves to have you do this for him,
for he loves our nation and built the synagogue for us."
And Jesus went with them,
but when he was only a short distance from the house,
the centurion sent friends to tell him,
"Lord, do not trouble yourself,
for I am not worthy to have you enter under my roof.
Therefore, I did not consider myself worthy to come to you;
but say the word and let my servant be healed.
For I too am a person subject to authority,
with soldiers subject to me.
And I say to one, 'Go,'and he goes;
and to another, 'Come here,'and he comes;
and to my slave, 'Do this,'and he does it."
When Jesus heard this he was amazed at him
and, turning, said to the crowd following him,
"I tell you, not even in Israel have I found such faith."
When the messengers returned to the house,
they found the slave in good health.

—Luke 7:1–10

Truths of Our Catholic Faith

"Lord, I am not worthy to receive you. But only say the word and I shall be healed."

In one sense, none of us is ever worthy to receive Jesus; yet He out of His unfathomable love apparently considers us quite worthy to experience Him in many ways. In order to balance despair about our unworthiness with presumption regarding our readiness to meet the Son of God, Jesus wisely counsels us, through His Church, that we should at the very least be in a state of grace to receive Holy Communion; if we are not, this Doctor of Souls provides the remedy in the Sacrament of Penance.

> *Anyone who desires to receive Christ in Eucharistic communion must be in the state of grace. Anyone aware of having sinned mortally must not receive communion without having received absolution in the sacrament of penance. (CCC 1415)*

The centurion is under authority, and possesses authority over others as well. Jesus does not strip him of this authority; rather, our Lord holds the centurion up as having an exemplary grasp of how authority can be a good thing, used well in service to bring about good results. Authority must be used well, coexisting with certain freedoms among the governed.

> *Political authority must be exercised within the limits of the moral order and must guarantee the conditions for the exercise of freedom. (CCC 1923)*

A Question for Me

On a scale between completely unworthy and totally worthy to receive Christ, where do I see myself? How might I go about making any needed adjustments?

For a Child in My Life

What are the first two sentences spoken to Jesus by the centurion's friends? Where have you heard a statement similar to this before?

My Role in the Community

If I were to receive Holy Communion while not in a state of grace, what effect would that have on my community of faith?

For Depth and Further Life Application

1 Kings 8:41–43
Psalm 117
Galatians 1:1–2, 6–10

📖 United States Catholic Catechism for Adults, pages 523–524

REFLECTION

God so loved the world that he gave his only Son, so that everyone who believes in him might have eternal life.

—John 3:16

C Tenth Sunday of Ordinary Time

The Gospel

Jesus journeyed to a city called Nain,
and his disciples and a large crowd accompanied him.
As he drew near to the gate of the city,
a man who had died was being carried out,
the only son of his mother, and she was a widow.
A large crowd from the city was with her.
When the Lord saw her,
he was moved with pity for her and said to her,
"Do not weep."
He stepped forward and touched the coffin;
at this the bearers halted,
and he said, "Young man, I tell you, arise!"
The dead man sat up and began to speak,
and Jesus gave him to his mother.
Fear seized them all, and they glorified God, exclaiming,
"A great prophet has arisen in our midst, "
and "God has visited his people."
This report about him spread through the whole of Judea
and in all the surrounding region.

—Luke 7:11–17

Truths of Our Catholic Faith

One day, each soul that is undergoing final purification in what is known as purgatory will hear the voice of Jesus say "I tell you, arise!" Like our young man in this Gospel, they will experience God's joy in a direct and personal way.

> *Those who die in God's grace and friendship imperfectly purified, although they are assured of their eternal salvation, undergo a purification after death, so as to achieve the holiness necessary to enter the joy of God. (CCC 1054)*

Jesus did not give up on the young man because he was dead. Similarly, we can be of help to those who have gone before us by praying that God will remove at least some of the temporal punishment they deserve for having sinned. Special prayers and actions oriented toward this desire have been termed indulgences.

We can seek and be granted indulgences for ourselves. Capitalizing on this manifestation of God's mercy is an excellent habit to acquire.

> *Through indulgences the faithful can obtain the remission of temporal punishment resulting from sin for themselves and also for the souls in Purgatory.* (CCC 1498)

A Question for Me

What is my understanding of indulgences? How might I make prayer for the souls in purgatory a more regular part of my spiritual routine?

For a Child in My Life

What happens in purgatory?

My Role in the Community

Widows and orphans seem to hold a special place in God's heart. Who are the orphans and widows in my community, and how might I best assist them?

For Depth and Further Life Application

1 Kings 17:17–24
Psalm 30
Galatians 1:11–19

📖 United States Catholic Catechism for Adults, pages 158–160

REFLECTION

A great prophet has arisen in our midst, God has visited his people.

—Luke 7:16

C Eleventh Sunday of Ordinary Time

The Gospel

A Pharisee invited Jesus to dine with him,
and he entered the Pharisee's house and reclined at table.
Now there was a sinful woman in the city
who learned that he was at table in the house of the Pharisee.
Bringing an alabaster flask of ointment,
she stood behind him at his feet weeping
and began to bathe his feet with her tears.
Then she wiped them with her hair,
kissed them, and anointed them with the ointment.
When the Pharisee who had invited him saw this he said to himself,
"If this man were a prophet,
he would know who and what sort of woman this is
who is touching him,
that she is a sinner."
Jesus said to him in reply,
"Simon, I have something to say to you."
"Tell me, teacher, " he said.
"Two people were in debt to a certain creditor;
one owed five hundred day's wages and the other owed fifty.
Since they were unable to repay the debt, he forgave it for both.
Which of them will love him more?"
Simon said in reply,
"The one, I suppose, whose larger debt was forgiven."
He said to him, "You have judged rightly."

Then he turned to the woman and said to Simon,
"Do you see this woman?
When I entered your house, you did not give me water for my feet,
but she has bathed them with her tears
and wiped them with her hair.
You did not give me a kiss,
but she has not ceased kissing my feet since the time I entered.
You did not anoint my head with oil,
but she anointed my feet with ointment.
So I tell you, her many sins have been forgiven
because she has shown great love.
But the one to whom little is forgiven, loves little."

He said to her, "Your sins are forgiven."
The others at table said to themselves,
"Who is this who even forgives sins?"
But he said to the woman,
"Your faith has saved you; go in peace."

—Luke 7:36–50

Truths of Our Catholic Faith

Sin is, in a sense, prominent in this passage. Jesus desires that the woman of this Gospel experience peace. He does not grant her peace by ignoring her sins; rather Jesus, who knows of the inborn weaknesses of human nature wounded by original sin, grants her salvation from sin and death. Wounded by original sin, we all need a Savior.

> *As a result of original sin, human nature is weakened in its powers; subject to ignorance, suffering, and the domination of death; and inclined to sin (This inclination is called "concupiscence."). (CCC 418)*

This Gospel's woman shows great love by the profound and intimate act of washing and anointing Jesus' feet. A holy, wholesome intimacy is healthy for us in many ways. The Holy Trinity models an intimacy for us. Grace can help us experience intimacy in ways that make us truly happy, in ways that help us live in God's peace.

> *Grace is the help God gives us to respond to our vocation of becoming his adopted sons. It introduces us into the intimacy of the Trinitarian life. (CCC 2021)*

A Question for Me

How has an inclination toward sin—original sin—been noticeable in my life? Why is acknowledging original sin important as a step toward overcoming it?

For a Child in My Life

What did Jesus tell the woman in this Gospel to do?

My Role in the Community

With whom in my community am I intimate (in an appropriate sense)? What words describe healthy intimacy, including that of the Trinitarian life?

For Depth and Further Life Application

2 Samuel 12:7–10, 13
Psalm 32
Galatians 2:16, 19–21

United States Catholic Catechism for Adults, pages 319–321

REFLECTION

God loved us and sent his Son as expiation for our sins.

—1 John 4:10b

C Twelfth Sunday of Ordinary Time

The Gospel

Once when Jesus was praying in solitude,
and the disciples were with him,
he asked them, "Who do the crowds say that I am?"
They said in reply, "John the Baptist;
others, Elijah;
still others, 'One of the ancient prophets has arisen.'"
Then he said to them, "But who do you say that I am?"
Peter said in reply, "The Christ of God."
He rebuked them
and directed them not to tell this to anyone.

He said, "The Son of Man must suffer greatly
and be rejected by the elders, the chief priests, and the scribes,
and be killed and on the third day be raised."

Then he said to all,
"If anyone wishes to come after me, he must deny himself
and take up his cross daily and follow me.
For whoever wishes to save his life will lose it,
but whoever loses his life for my sake will save it."

—Luke 9:18–24

Truths of Our Catholic Faith

When Peter correctly identifies Jesus as the Christ of God, he does not use phrases like second Person of the Trinity; these would come in time as the Church penetrates the magnitude of just who Jesus is. Eventually we came to articulate that Jesus is fully God and fully man simultaneously. This is a mystery in every positive sense of the word, a mystery leading to our salvation from sin and death.

> *The Incarnation is therefore the mystery of the wonderful union of the divine and human natures in the one person of the Word. (CCC 483)*

Christ is God's. Jesus is our Father's Son, and Jesus helps us to be united with both of them. By following the Lord Jesus we share in eternal life. Praying the Our Father helps to keep us close to God—Father, Son and Holy Spirit.

> *The Lord's Prayer brings us into communion with the Father and with his Son, Jesus Christ. At the same time it reveals us to ourselves (cf.* GS 22 § 1*). (CCC 2799)*

A Question for Me

What is my cross today? How might I best follow Jesus while carrying this cross?

For a Child in My Life

Jesus is one Person with two natures; what are those natures?

My Role in the Community

When I am in communion with God the Father and Jesus His only Son, how does this communion influence my actions within my communities?

For Depth and Further Life Application

Zechariah 12:10–11; 13:1
Psalm 63
Galatians 3:26–29

📖 United States Catholic Catechism for Adults, pages 85–87

REFLECTION

My sheep hear my voice, says the Lord; I know them, and they follow me.

—John 10:27

C Thirteenth Sunday of Ordinary Time

The Gospel

When the days for Jesus' being taken up were fulfilled,
he resolutely determined to journey to Jerusalem,
and he sent messengers ahead of him.
On the way they entered a Samaritan village
to prepare for his reception there,
but they would not welcome him
because the destination of his journey was Jerusalem.
When the disciples James and John saw this they asked,
"Lord, do you want us to call down fire from heaven
to consume them?"
Jesus turned and rebuked them, and they journeyed
to another village.

As they were proceeding on their journey someone said to him,
"I will follow you wherever you go."
Jesus answered him,
"Foxes have dens and birds of the sky have nests,
but the Son of Man has nowhere to rest his head."

And to another he said, "Follow me."
But he replied, "Lord, let me go first and bury my father."
But he answered him, "Let the dead bury their dead.
But you, go and proclaim the kingdom of God."
And another said, "I will follow you, Lord,
but first let me say farewell to my family at home."
To him Jesus said, "No one who sets a hand to the plow
and looks to what was left behind is fit for the kingdom of God."

—Luke 9:51–62

Truths of Our Catholic Faith

Fitness for God's kingdom is easier said than done. Our loving Father sends special graces upon those He assigns specific tasks. Ordination to the ministerial priesthood is one such example.

> *The sacrament of Holy Orders is conferred by the laying on of hands followed by a solemn prayer of consecration asking God to grant the ordinand the graces of the Holy*

> *Spirit required for his ministry. Ordination imprints an indelible sacramental character.* (CCC 1597)

Moral virtues keep us about the work of God's kingdom. Grace helps bring about growth in virtue, allowing our good habits of thought, word and deed to bring about good effects.

> *The moral virtues grow through education, deliberate acts, and perseverance in struggle. Divine grace purifies and elevates them.* (CCC 1839)

A Question for Me

How much of my time, treasure and talent are devoted to making sure my nest or den is just so? Could I make due with a more modest home if it meant freeing up resources—like time spent with family, for example?

For a Child in My Life

What are three ways you can grow in moral virtue?

My Role in the Community

The high cost of housing contributes significantly to poverty in America. What are some ways I can work, directly and indirectly, for more affordable housing in my community?

For Depth and Further Life Application

1 Kings 19:16b, 19–21
Psalm 16
Galatians 5:1, 13–18

📖 United States Catholic Catechism for Adults, pages 273–275

REFLECTION

Speak, Lord, your servant is listening; you have the words of everlasting life.

—1 Samuel 3:9; John 6:68c

C Fourteenth Sunday of Ordinary Time

The Gospel

At that time the Lord appointed seventy-two others
whom he sent ahead of him in pairs
to every town and place he intended to visit.
He said to them,
"The harvest is abundant but the laborers are few;
so ask the master of the harvest
to send out laborers for his harvest.
Go on your way;
behold, I am sending you like lambs among wolves.
Carry no money bag, no sack, no sandals;
and greet no one along the way.
Into whatever house you enter, first say,
'Peace to this household.'
If a peaceful person lives there,
your peace will rest on him;
but if not, it will return to you.
Stay in the same house and eat and drink what is offered to you,
for the laborer deserves his payment.
Do not move about from one house to another.
Whatever town you enter and they welcome you,
eat what is set before you,
cure the sick in it and say to them,
'The kingdom of God is at hand for you.'"

—Luke 10:1–9

Truths of Our Catholic Faith

The seventy-two are not the Twelve. Yet clearly they have an appointed role intended by Jesus Himself.

Similarly, permanent deacons are assigned specific tasks in the Church while they are not ordained for priestly ministry. They are sent out like laborers for our Lord's harvest.

> *Deacons are ministers ordained for tasks of service of the Church; they do not receive the ministerial priesthood, but ordination confers on them important functions in*

> *the ministry of the word, divine worship, pastoral governance, and the service of charity, tasks which they must carry out under the pastoral authority of their bishop. (CCC 1596)*

In God's kingdom, His goods reach everyone fairly. Sometimes this requires direct acts of charity. Other times it may mean working to correct an unjust law. Essentially, then, social and economic life are made for man; man is not made solely to further economic and social matters.

> *Man is himself the author, center, and goal of all economic and social life. The decisive point of the social question is that goods created by God for everyone should in fact reach everyone in accordance with justice and with the help of charity. (CCC 2459)*

A Question for Me

How do I see to it that full-time laborers for the kingdom (clergy, religious, lay ministers, etc.) receive their payment? In other words, to what extent do I financially support authentically Catholic ministries of various sorts?

For a Child in My Life

What is a deacon?

My Role in the Community

What are the root causes of long-term poverty in my communities? How am I helping by, in addition to charitable deeds, advocating for longer-term changes in areas like laws, policies, etc.?

For Depth and Further Life Application

Isaiah 66:10–14c
Psalm 66
Galatians 6:14–18

United States Catholic Catechism for Adults, pages 525–526

REFLECTION

Let the peace of Christ control your hearts; let the word of Christ dwell in you richly.

—Colossians 3:15a, 16a

C Fifteenth Sunday of Ordinary Time

The Gospel

There was a scholar of the law who stood up to test him and said,
"Teacher, what must I do to inherit eternal life?"
Jesus said to him, "What is written in the law?
How do you read it?"
He said in reply,
You shall love the Lord, your God,
with all your heart,
with all your being,
with all your strength,
and with all your mind,
and your neighbor as yourself."
He replied to him, "You have answered correctly;
do this and you will live."

But because he wished to justify himself, he said to Jesus,
"And who is my neighbor?"
Jesus replied,
"A man fell victim to robbers
as he went down from Jerusalem to Jericho.
They stripped and beat him and went off leaving him half-dead.
A priest happened to be going down that road,
but when he saw him, he passed by on the opposite side.
Likewise a Levite came to the place,
and when he saw him, he passed by on the opposite side.
But a Samaritan traveler who came upon him
was moved with compassion at the sight.
He approached the victim,
poured oil and wine over his wounds and bandaged them.
Then he lifted him up on his own animal,
took him to an inn, and cared for him.
The next day he took out two silver coins
and gave them to the innkeeper with the instruction,
'Take care of him.
If you spend more than what I have given you,
I shall repay you on my way back.'
Which of these three, in your opinion,
was neighbor to the robbers' victim?"

He answered, "The one who treated him with mercy."
Jesus said to him, "Go and do likewise."

—Luke 10:25–37

Truths of Our Catholic Faith

Loving the Lord our God as described here implies a remarkable closeness. This is one way of understanding the Church as Jesus' very own Body. And when we treat others with mercy, it is in a sense Jesus Himself who we serve.

> *The Church is this Body of which Christ is the head: she lives from him, in him, and for him; he lives with her and in her. (CCC 807)*

The Samaritan gets it. He understands that human life is sacred. Also, to those among His hearers who may have regarded Samaritans unkindly, Jesus makes clear that all human persons are made to image God.

> *Every human life, from the moment of conception until death, is sacred because the human person has been willed for its own sake in the image and likeness of the living and holy God. (CCC 2319)*

A Question for Me

I am made in the likeness and image of the holy and living God; what does that mean?

For a Child in My Life

The Church is the Body of Christ. Who is the Head of this Body?

My Role in the Community

What are some ways I can treat community members with mercy?

For Depth and Further Life Application

Deuteronomy 30:10–14
Psalm 69 and Psalm 19
Colossians 1:15–20

📖 United States Catholic Catechism for Adults, pages 119–121

REFLECTION

Your words, Lord, are Spirit and life; you have the words of everlasting life.

—cf. John 6:63c, 68c

C Sixteenth Sunday of Ordinary Time

The Gospel

Jesus entered a village
where a woman whose name was Martha welcomed him.
She had a sister named Mary
who sat beside the Lord at his feet listening to him speak.
Martha, burdened with much serving, came to him and said,
"Lord, do you not care
that my sister has left me by myself to do the serving?
Tell her to help me."
The Lord said to her in reply,
"Martha, Martha, you are anxious and worried about many things.
There is need of only one thing.
Mary has chosen the better part
and it will not be taken from her."

—Luke 10:38–42

Truths of Our Catholic Faith

Mary sat at Jesus' feet and listened to Him speak. To her, this was an integral part of having Jesus visit. Similarly, we have an opportunity to hear the Word of God proclaimed each time we celebrate Mass. The Liturgy of the Word is very significant.

> *The Liturgy of the Word is an integral part of the celebration. The meaning of the celebration is expressed by the Word of God which is proclaimed and by the response of faith to it. (CCC 1190)*

Martha and her sister sensed who Jesus is. Each in their own way they showed Jesus homage. Once we come to know God, He becomes our top priority. While not neglecting any other legitimate responsibility, we always choose the better.

> *"You shall worship the Lord your God"* (Mt 4:10). *Adoring God, praying to him, offering him the worship that belongs to him, fulfilling the promises and vows made to him are acts of the virtue of religion which fall under obedience to the first commandment. (CCC 2135)*

A Question for Me

When have I been Martha? When have I been Mary? When have I spoken like Jesus in this Gospel passage?

For a Child in My Life

What is the Liturgy of the Word?

My Role in the Community

Is God calling me to serve my parish community as a lector?

For Depth and Further Life Application

Genesis 18:1–10a
Psalm 15
Colossians 1:24–28

📖 United States Catholic Catechism for Adults, pages 346–349

REFLECTION

Blessed are they who have kept the word with a generous heart and yield a harvest through perseverance.

—cf. Luke 8:15

C Seventeenth Sunday of Ordinary Time

The Gospel

Jesus was praying in a certain place, and when he had finished,
one of his disciples said to him,
"Lord, teach us to pray just as John taught his disciples."
He said to them, "When you pray, say:
Father, hallowed be your name,
your kingdom come.
Give us each day our daily bread
and forgive us our sins
for we ourselves forgive everyone in debt to us,
and do not subject us to the final test."

And he said to them, "Suppose one of you has a friend
to whom he goes at midnight and says,
'Friend, lend me three loaves of bread,
for a friend of mine has arrived at my house from a journey
and I have nothing to offer him,'
and he says in reply from within,
'Do not bother me; the door has already been locked
and my children and I are already in bed.
I cannot get up to give you anything.'
I tell you,
if he does not get up to give the visitor the loaves
because of their friendship,
he will get up to give him whatever he needs
because of his persistence.

"And I tell you, ask and you will receive;
seek and you will find;
knock and the door will be opened to you.
For everyone who asks, receives;
and the one who seeks, finds;
and to the one who knocks, the door will be opened.
What father among you would hand his son a snake
when he asks for a fish?
Or hand him a scorpion when he asks for an egg?

If you then, who are wicked,
know how to give good gifts to your children,
how much more will the Father in heaven
give the Holy Spirit to those who ask him?"

—Luke 11:1–13

Truths of Our Catholic Faith

Our Father gives us the Holy Spirit. The Holy Spirit Himself offers us seven gifts. These gifts are available to all who seek the Holy Spirit's help.

> *The seven gifts of the Holy Spirit bestowed upon Christians are wisdom, understanding, counsel, fortitude, knowledge, piety, and fear of the Lord.* (CCC 1845)

Jesus chooses His words very carefully. He who proclaims the Good News summarizes it in the form of a prayer—the Lord's Prayer.

> *"The Lord's Prayer is truly the summary of the whole gospel,"*[23] *the "most perfect of prayers."*[24] *It is at the center of the Scriptures.* (CCC 2774)

A Question for Me

What is the difference between wisdom and knowledge?

For a Child in My Life

What are the Holy Spirit's gifts?

My Role in the Community

From whom in my community should I seek counsel? To whom might I offer counsel?

For Depth and Further Life Application

Genesis 18:20–32
Psalm 138
Colossians 2:12–14

📖 United States Catholic Catechism for Adults, page 537

REFLECTION

You have received a Spirit of adoption, through which we cry, Abba, Father.

—Romans 8:15bc

C Eighteenth Sunday of Ordinary Time

The Gospel

Someone in the crowd said to Jesus,
"Teacher, tell my brother to share the inheritance with me."
He replied to him,
"Friend, who appointed me as your judge and arbitrator?"
Then he said to the crowd,
"Take care to guard against all greed,
for though one may be rich,
one's life does not consist of possessions."

Then he told them a parable.
"There was a rich man whose land produced a bountiful harvest.
He asked himself, 'What shall I do,
for I do not have space to store my harvest?'
And he said, 'This is what I shall do:
I shall tear down my barns and build larger ones.
There I shall store all my grain and other goods
and I shall say to myself, "Now as for you,
you have so many good things stored up for many years,
rest, eat, drink, be merry!"'
But God said to him,
'You fool, this night your life will be demanded of you;
and the things you have prepared, to whom will they belong?'
Thus will it be for all who store up treasure for themselves
but are not rich in what matters to God."

—Luke 12:13–21

Truths of Our Catholic Faith

It seems unlikely that this rich man feels obligated to obey anyone in particular. To be obedient to another for the sake of furthering God's kingdom would probably be a strange concept to the man; professing a vow of poverty would definitely be.

Yet obedience and poverty, as well as chastity, are firmly based on a Gospel vision of life. Some are called by God to live according to these vows, all for the sake of advancing His will for our world.

> *The life consecrated to God is characterized by the public profession of the evangelical counsels of poverty, chastity, and obedience, in a stable state of life recognized by the Church. (CCC 944)*

Treasure can help one acquire vast quantities of rich foods, choice beverages and merriment of many sorts. Possessions can purchase a lot of pleasure.

Yet pleasure and happiness are not the same. Feeling and being at one with God—united with Him—is ultimately what helps us to be happy.

Money itself is not evil, and pleasure of a wholesome sort is good up to a point. Ultimately, though, doing God's will is what matters and brings happiness, and God reveals His will in many ways. How much does God matter to you? How rich are you, really?

> *Man is made to live in communion with God in whom he finds happiness: "When I am completely united to you, there will be no more sorrow or trials; entirely full of you, my life will be complete" (St. Augustine,* Conf. *10, 28, 39: PL 32, 795). (CCC 45)*

A Question for Me

How does the time I spend storing up treasure for myself compare to that which I spend growing rich in what matters to God?

For a Child in My Life

What are poverty, chastity and obedience; who promises to live according to these vows? Why?

My Role in the Community

Is God calling a daughter or son of mine to consecrated life? How would I know? What are some ways that I can help support vocations to religious life?

For Depth and Further Life Application

Ecclesiastes 1:2; 2:21–23
Psalm 90
Colossians 3:1–5, 9–11

📖 United States Catholic Catechism for Adults, pages 1–2

REFLECTION

Blessed are the poor in spirit, for theirs is the kingdom of heaven.

—Matthew 5:3

C Nineteenth Sunday of Ordinary Time

The Gospel

Jesus said to his disciples:
"Gird your loins and light your lamps
and be like servants who await their master's return from a wedding,
ready to open immediately when he comes and knocks.
Blessed are those servants
whom the master finds vigilant on his arrival.
Amen, I say to you, he will gird himself,
have the servants recline at table, and proceed to wait on them.
And should he come in the second or third watch
and find them prepared in this way,
blessed are those servants.
Be sure of this:
if the master of the house had known the hour
when the thief was coming,
he would not have let his house be broken into.
You also must be prepared, for at an hour you do not expect,
the Son of Man will come."

—Luke 12:35–40

Truths of Our Catholic Faith

For so many servants of the Lord, the Master has already arrived. We hope that they were found vigilant. We pray that God will show mercy to all the departed as we continually strive to prepare ourselves for that hour when the Son of Man arrives.

> *By virtue of the "communion of saints," the Church commends the dead to God's mercy and offers her prayers, especially the holy sacrifice of the Eucharist, on their behalf. (CCC 1055)*

No superstitious practice will keep us in good graces with God. Only true worship, reliance on His mercy and an honest attempt to live a Godly life will prepare us for our meeting with the Creator of the universe, with our loving, merciful, true God.

Superstition is a departure from the worship that we give to the true God. It is manifested in idolatry, as well as in various forms of divination and magic. (CCC 2138)

A Question for Me

In what superstitious practices might I engage? How harmless are they, really?

For a Child in My Life

What is superstition? Why is it not appropriate?

My Role in the Community

In my community, who has passed away and will be remembered prayerfully by me the next time that I celebrate the holy sacrifice of the Eucharist?

For Depth and Further Life Application

Wisdom 18:6–9
Psalm 33
Hebrews 11:1–2, 8–19

📖 United States Catholic Catechism for Adults, pages 160–162

REFLECTION

Stay awake and be ready! For you do not know on what day the Son of Man will come.

—Matthew 24:42a, 44

C Twentieth Sunday of Ordinary Time

The Gospel

Jesus said to his disciples:
"I have come to set the earth on fire,
and how I wish it were already blazing!
There is a baptism with which I must be baptized,
and how great is my anguish until it is accomplished!
Do you think that I have come to establish peace on the earth?
No, I tell you, but rather division.
From now on a household of five will be divided,
three against two and two against three;
a father will be divided against his son
and a son against his father,
a mother against her daughter
and a daughter against her mother,
a mother-in-law against her daughter-in-law
and a daughter-in-law against her mother-in-law."

—Luke 12:49–53

Truths of Our Catholic Faith

Sometimes households become divided. People pursue divorce and then, without securing a decree of nullity, enter another marriage in the eyes of civil authority.

Protecting the integrity and meaning of marriage requires that these persons not attempt to receive Holy Communion. They are in the fold of our Church, though, and can participate in her mission by various means.

> *The remarriage of persons divorced from a living, lawful spouse contravenes the plan and law of God as taught by Christ. They are not separated from the Church, but they cannot receive Eucharistic communion. They will lead Christian lives especially by educating their children in the faith. (CCC 1665)*

Like baptism, the Sacrament of Confirmation is celebrated once in a person's life. One who is confirmed receives strength to face the inevitable challenges and occasional controversies involved with life as a friend and follower of Jesus.

> *Confirmation, like Baptism, imprints a spiritual mark or indelible character on the Christian's soul; for this reason one can receive this sacrament only once in one's life. (CCC 1317)*

A Question for Me

What support might I offer those who are remarried while divorced from a lawful, living spouse? How might I be of help to their children as well?

For a Child in My Life

Why is a person only confirmed once?

My Role in the Community

What part can I play, tangibly or spiritually, in the journey of young people at my parish who are preparing to celebrate the Sacrament of Confirmation?

For Depth and Further Life Application

Jeremiah 38:4–6, 8–10
Psalm 40
Hebrews 12:1–4

📖 United States Catholic Catechism for Adults, pages 289–290

REFLECTION

My sheep hear my voice, says the Lord; I know them, and they follow me.

—John 10:27

C Twenty-first Sunday of Ordinary Time

The Gospel

Jesus passed through towns and villages,
 teaching as he went and making his way to Jerusalem.
Someone asked him,
 "Lord, will only a few people be saved?"
He answered them,
 "Strive to enter through the narrow gate,
 for many, I tell you, will attempt to enter
 but will not be strong enough.
After the master of the house has arisen and locked the door,
 then will you stand outside knocking and saying,
 'Lord, open the door for us.'
He will say to you in reply,
 'I do not know where you are from.
And you will say,
 'We ate and drank in your company and you taught in our streets.'
Then he will say to you,
 'I do not know where you are from.
Depart from me, all you evildoers!'
And there will be wailing and grinding of teeth
 when you see Abraham, Isaac, and Jacob
 and all the prophets in the kingdom of God
 and you yourselves cast out.
And people will come from the east and the west
 and from the north and the south
 and will recline at table in the kingdom of God.
For behold, some are last who will be first,
and some are first who will be last."

—Luke 13:22–30

Truths of Our Catholic Faith

Striving to enter God's kingdom, we need a way in. The Church, properly understood, is that way. Our Church is also the closest thing to God's kingdom this side of heaven. Full membership and participation in the Church, then, should be our goal.

> *The Church is both the means and the goal of God's plan: prefigured in creation, prepared for in the Old Covenant, founded by the words and actions of Jesus Christ, fulfilled by his redeeming cross and his Resurrection, the Church has been manifested as the mystery of salvation by the outpouring of the Holy Spirit. She will be perfected in the glory of heaven as the assembly of all the redeemed of the earth (cf.* Rev *14:4). (CCC 778)*

Heaven is a feast in progress—a great liturgical feast. When we observe certain holy days and other Church-related practices, we are not engaging in arbitrary behavior. We are showing our unity with the communion of saints already enjoying the beautiful vision we hope to experience personally.

> *By keeping the memorials of the saints—first of all the holy Mother of God, then the apostles, the martyrs, and other saints—on fixed days of the liturgical year, the Church on earth shows that she is united with the liturgy of heaven. She gives glory to Christ for having accomplished his salvation in his glorified members; their example encourages her on her way to the Father. (CCC 1195)*

A Question for Me

How hard do I try being first? How hard do I try being last? What does Jesus' statement about the last and the first mean?

For a Child in My Life

What is the liturgy of heaven? How can you be a part of it?

My Role in the Community

Who in my community is first? Who is last? How does Jesus' statement about the last and the first apply to my community and my role in it?

For Depth and Further Life Application

Isaiah 66:18–21
Psalm 117
Hebrews 12:5–7, 11–13

📖 United States Catholic Catechism for Adults, pages 629–637

REFLECTION

I am the way, the truth and the life, says the Lord; no one comes to the Father, except through me.

—John 14:6

C Twenty-second Sunday of Ordinary Time

The Gospel

On a sabbath Jesus went to dine
at the home of one of the leading Pharisees,
and the people there were observing him carefully.

He told a parable to those who had been invited,
noticing how they were choosing the places of honor at the table.
"When you are invited by someone to a wedding banquet,
do not recline at table in the place of honor.
A more distinguished guest than you may have been invited by him,
and the host who invited both of you may approach you and say,
'Give your place to this man,'
and then you would proceed with embarrassment
to take the lowest place.
Rather, when you are invited,
go and take the lowest place
so that when the host comes to you he may say,
'My friend, move up to a higher position.'
Then you will enjoy the esteem of your companions at the table.
For every one who exalts himself will be humbled,
but the one who humbles himself will be exalted."
Then he said to the host who invited him,
"When you hold a lunch or a dinner,
do not invite your friends or your brothers
or your relatives or your wealthy neighbors,
in case they may invite you back and you have repayment.
Rather, when you hold a banquet,
invite the poor, the crippled, the lame, the blind;
blessed indeed will you be because of their inability to repay you.
For you will be repaid at the resurrection of the righteous."

—Luke 14:1, 7–14

Truths of Our Catholic Faith

Humbling oneself is fine; tearing down another person by using words is quite a different matter. We are not morally free to injure another's honor—her or his reputation. Knowing that actions sometimes speak louder than words, we also should be on guard about our nonverbal communication.

> *Respect for the reputation and honor of persons forbids all detraction and calumny in word or attitude.* (CCC 2507)

Exalting God sometimes can mean blessing Him. The idea of us blessing God may seem strange; still, the God who blesses us also empowers us to bless others, including Him.

> *Because God blesses the human heart, it can in return bless him who is the source of every blessing.* (CCC 2645)

A Question for Me

The next time someone starts gossiping to me, what might I say to steer the conversation in a positive direction?

For a Child in My Life

Why do people say "If you do not have something good to say about a person, do not say anything at all"?

My Role in the Community

What are some ways I can be of help to those in my community who have no way to pay me back?

For Depth and Further Life Application

Sirach 3:17–18, 20, 28–29
Psalm 68
Hebrews 12:18–19, 22–24a

📖 United States Catholic Catechism for Adults, pages 434–436

REFLECTION

Take my yoke upon you, says the Lord, and learn from me, for I am meek and humble of heart.

—Matthew 11:29ab

C Twenty-third Sunday of Ordinary Time

The Gospel

Great crowds were traveling with Jesus,
and he turned and addressed them,
"If anyone comes to me without hating his father and mother,
wife and children, brothers and sisters,
and even his own life,
he cannot be my disciple.
Whoever does not carry his own cross and come after me
cannot be my disciple.
Which of you wishing to construct a tower
does not first sit down and calculate the cost
to see if there is enough for its completion?
Otherwise, after laying the foundation
and finding himself unable to finish the work
the onlookers should laugh at him and say,
'This one began to build but did not have the resources to finish.'
Or what king marching into battle would not first sit down
and decide whether with ten thousand troops
he can successfully oppose another king
advancing upon him with twenty thousand troops?
But if not, while he is still far away,
he will send a delegation to ask for peace terms.
In the same way,
anyone of you who does not renounce all his possessions
cannot be my disciple."

—Luke 14:25–33

Truths of Our Catholic Faith

Authentically-educated children know that their eternal destiny lies beyond the scope of their immediate family. Christian spouses know that if their relationship with God is not in good shape, their marital relationship will only go so far.

This Gospel passage is about priorities. Family relationships—especially marriage—require very clear priorities. When marriage works as our Lord intends, both spouses benefit eternally.

> *The marriage covenant, by which a man and a woman form with each other an intimate communion of life and love, has been founded and endowed with its own special laws by the Creator. By its very nature it is ordered to the good of the couple, as well as to the generation and education of children. Christ the Lord raised marriage between the baptized to the dignity of a sacrament (cf. CIC, can. 1055 § 1; cf.* GS *48 § 1). (CCC 1660)*

The idea of hating one's parents is extreme, and Jesus uses it as a jolting example to make a strong, clear, serious point. In the course of everyday family life, certainly children do not hate their parents; quite the opposite. When the ideal of respecting, appreciating, appropriately obeying and generally helping parents is pursued by children (and presuming parents do not exploit these inclinations), life is apt to be essentially peaceful on the home front.

> *Children owe their parents respect, gratitude, just obedience, and assistance. Filial respect fosters harmony in all of family life. (CCC 2251)*

A Question for Me

"I would like to get married, but I do not know if I want to have children." How might you respond to someone who makes such a statement?

For a Child in My Life

What helps make family life peaceful?

My Role in the Community

In the community of my family, how can I encourage my children to give me respect, gratitude, just obedience and help?

For Depth and Further Life Application

Wisdom 9:13–18b
Psalm 90
Philemon 9–10, 12–17

United States Catholic Catechism for Adults, pages 290–292

REFLECTION

Let your face shine upon your servant; and teach me your laws.

—Psalm 119:135

C Twenty-fourth Sunday of Ordinary Time

The Gospel

Tax collectors and sinners were all drawing near to listen to Jesus,
but the Pharisees and scribes began to complain, saying,
"This man welcomes sinners and eats with them."
So to them he addressed this parable.
"What man among you having a hundred sheep and
losing one of them
would not leave the ninety-nine in the desert
and go after the lost one until he finds it?
And when he does find it,
he sets it on his shoulders with great joy
and, upon his arrival home,
he calls together his friends and neighbors and says to them,
'Rejoice with me because I have found my lost sheep.'
I tell you, in just the same way
there will be more joy in heaven over one sinner who repents
than over ninety-nine righteous people
who have no need of repentance.

"Or what woman having ten coins and losing one
would not light a lamp and sweep the house,
searching carefully until she finds it?
And when she does find it,
she calls together her friends and neighbors
and says to them,
'Rejoice with me because I have found the coin that I lost.'
In just the same way, I tell you,
there will be rejoicing among the angels of God
over one sinner who repents."

—Luke 15:1–10

Truths of Our Catholic Faith

God truly cares about what happens to us. The Most Holy Trinity—Father, Son and Holy Spirit—cares when sinners repent.

The embodiment of this caring relationship on earth is none other than our Church. A tangible sign, our Church is in a sense a sacrament.

> *The Holy Spirit, whom Christ the head pours out on his members, builds, animates, and sanctifies the Church. She is the sacrament of the Holy Trinity's communion with men.* (CCC 747)

The smallest of sheep is precious to our Good Shepherd. Babies who have not yet been born are the most vulnerable of persons, and God will not see them lost.

Regardless of all acrobatics of conscience that lead people to mouth the false words "Abortion is okay," it is not. It simply is not. It is better to know the truth even if it is challenging than to mistake an evil for a good.

Also, anyone who knowingly and willingly collaborates in an abortion chooses to place himself or herself outside of full communion with the flock united in the clear teaching of the Good Shepherd. Abortion procurers and providers literally excommunicate themselves unless and until they bring great joy to heaven by repenting.

> *From its conception, the child has the right to life. Direct abortion, that is, abortion willed as an end or as a means, is a "criminal" practice* (GS 27 § 3), *gravely contrary to the moral law. The Church imposes the canonical penalty of excommunication for this crime against human life.* (CCC 2322)

A Question for Me

What can I do to defend the life of preborn infants?

For a Child in My Life

What causes great joy in heaven—rejoicing among the angels?

My Role in the Community

Abortion affects people beyond the preborn infant involved. Who in my community may be hurting because of abortion, and what sort of efforts on my part might help? (An effort called Rachel's Vineyard is probably active in your diocese; maybe you could find out more about it.)

For Depth and Further Life Application

Exodus 32:7–11, 13–14
Psalm 51
1 Timothy 1:12–17

📖 United States Catholic Catechism for Adults, pages 108–110

REFLECTION

God was reconciling the world to himself in Christ and entrusting to us the message of reconciliation.

—2 Corinthians 5:19

C Twenty-fifth Sunday of Ordinary Time

The Gospel

Jesus said to his disciples:
"The person who is trustworthy in very small matters
is also trustworthy in great ones;
and the person who is dishonest in very small matters
is also dishonest in great ones.
If, therefore, you are not trustworthy with dishonest wealth,
who will trust you with true wealth?
If you are not trustworthy with what belongs to another,
who will give you what is yours?
No servant can serve two masters.
He will either hate one and love the other,
or be devoted to one and despise the other.
You cannot serve both God and mammon."

—Luke 16:10–13

Truths of Our Catholic Faith

Why choose to serve God? We choose to serve God because God is the Ultimate; He is greater than anyone or anything we could serve, consciously or otherwise. It is good to remind ourselves occasionally of God's awesomeness.

> *God alone created the universe freely, directly, and without any help. (CCC 317)*

A person who is not trustworthy with another's wealth uses it improperly. God has revealed that these misused resources must be repaid. It is not enough to apologize. A person who steals must make every reasonable effort to repair the damage that he or she has inflicted.

> *Every manner of taking and using another's property unjustly is contrary to the seventh commandment. The injustice committed requires reparation. Commutative justice requires the restitution of stolen goods. (CCC 2454)*

A Question for Me

How many masters am I trying to serve?

For a Child in My Life

Who created the whole universe without any help?

My Role in the Community

To whom might I owe reparation?

For Depth and Further Life Application

Amos 8:4–7
Psalm 113
1 Timothy 2:1–8

📖 United States Catholic Catechism for Adults, pages 527–528

REFLECTION

Though our Lord Jesus Christ was rich, he became poor, so that by his poverty you might become rich.

—cf. 2 Corinthians 8:9

C Twenty-sixth Sunday of Ordinary Time

The Gospel

Jesus said to the Pharisees:
"There was a rich man who dressed in purple garments and fine linen
and dined sumptuously each day.
And lying at his door was a poor man named Lazarus,
covered with sores,
who would gladly have eaten his fill of the scraps
that fell from the rich man's table.
Dogs even used to come and lick his sores.
When the poor man died,
he was carried away by angels to the bosom of Abraham.
The rich man also died and was buried,
and from the netherworld, where he was in torment,
he raised his eyes and saw Abraham far off
and Lazarus at his side.
And he cried out, 'Father Abraham, have pity on me.
Send Lazarus to dip the tip of his finger in water and cool my tongue,
for I am suffering torment in these flames.'
Abraham replied,
'My child, remember that you received
what was good during your lifetime
while Lazarus likewise received what was bad;
but now he is comforted here, whereas you are tormented.
Moreover, between us and you a great chasm is established
to prevent anyone from crossing who might wish to go
from our side to yours or from your side to ours.'
He said, 'Then I beg you, father,
send him to my father's house, for I have five brothers,
so that he may warn them,
lest they too come to this place of torment.'
But Abraham replied, 'They have Moses and the prophets.
Let them listen to them.'
He said, 'Oh no, father Abraham,
but if someone from the dead goes to them, they will repent.'
Then Abraham said, 'If they will not listen to Moses and the prophets,
neither will they be persuaded if someone should rise from the dead.'"

—Luke 16:19–31

Truths of Our Catholic Faith

The rich man in this gospel passage made choices throughout his earthly life, choices that were dead wrong. He neglected to use well his God-given gift of conscience.

> *Faced with a moral choice, conscience can make either a right judgment in accordance with reason and the divine law or, on the contrary, an erroneous judgment that departs from them.* (CCC 1799)

An example of poor choice, morally speaking, is a decision to lie. Sometimes, lies cause tangible damage; an example would be lying about a business competitor so she or he loses sales revenue. Always, if a lie is told, the person telling it must set the record straight, repairing the lie's damage as thoroughly as is feasible.

> *An offense committed against the truth requires reparation.* (CCC 2509)

A Question for Me

Jesus is risen from the dead. To what degree am I persuaded to repent, and why?

For a Child in My Life

Where is Lazarus in this gospel passage? Where is the rich man in the passage?

My Role in the Community

Many people are convinced of heaven's existence, but fewer acknowledge the reality of hell. How might I help educate my community about hell to give community members a greater likelihood of avoiding its eternal torment?

For Depth and Further Life Application

Amos 6:1a, 4–7
Psalm 146
1 Timothy 6:11–16

📖 United States Catholic Catechism for Adults, pages 436–438

REFLECTION

Though our Lord Jesus Christ was rich, he became poor, so that by his poverty you might become rich.

—cf. 2 Corinthians 8:9

C Twenty-seventh Sunday of Ordinary Time

The Gospel

The apostles said to the Lord, "Increase our faith."
The Lord replied,
"If you have faith the size of a mustard seed,
you would say to this mulberry tree,
'Be uprooted and planted in the sea,' and it would obey you.

"Who among you would say to your servant
who has just come in from plowing or tending sheep in the field,
'Come here immediately and take your place at table'?
Would he not rather say to him,
'Prepare something for me to eat.
Put on your apron and wait on me while I eat and drink.
You may eat and drink when I am finished'?
Is he grateful to that servant because he did what was commanded?
So should it be with you.
When you have done all you have been commanded,
say, 'We are unprofitable servants;
we have done what we were obliged to do.'"

—Luke 17:5–10

Truths of Our Catholic Faith

"Increase our faith." One way to grow in faith is to engage in ongoing faith formation. When we make it a point to study the Bible and collected wisdom of Catholic teaching (summarized, for example, in the Catechism of the Catholic Church), we interact with the living Word of God. We grow closer to the source of every blessing—our loving Father in heaven.

> *"Sacred Tradition and Sacred Scripture make up a single sacred deposit of the Word of God"* (DV 10), *in which, as in a mirror, the pilgrim Church contemplates God, the source of all her riches. (CCC 97)*

When a bishop celebrates Mass, during the Eucharistic prayer, he refers to himself as an unworthy (i.e., unprofitable) servant. In doing so, he offers a simple reminder that God ultimately is the source of all that is good. Even bishops, who have the power to ordain deacons, priests and even other bishops, stand humbly before the Father, Son and Holy Spirit—the giver and main actor of holy orders.

> *It is bishops who confer the sacrament of Holy Orders in the three degrees. (CCC 1600)*

A Question for Me

How might I explain the relationship between sacred Scripture and sacred Tradition?

For a Child in My Life

What do sacred Scripture and sacred Tradition have in common?

My Role in the Community

What are some ways I might join with members of my communities to learn more about sacred Tradition and sacred Scripture?

For Depth and Further Life Application

Habakkuk 1:2–3, 2:2–4
Psalm 95
2 Timothy 1:6–8, 13–14

📖 United States Catholic Catechism for Adults, pages 28–33

REFLECTION

The word of the Lord remains forever. This is the word that has been proclaimed to you.

—1 Peter 1:25

C Twenty-eighth Sunday of Ordinary Time

The Gospel

As Jesus continued his journey to Jerusalem,
he traveled through Samaria and Galilee.
As he was entering a village, ten lepers met him.
They stood at a distance from him and raised their voices, saying,
"Jesus, Master! Have pity on us!"
And when he saw them, he said,
"Go show yourselves to the priests."
As they were going they were cleansed.
And one of them, realizing he had been healed,
returned, glorifying God in a loud voice;
and he fell at the feet of Jesus and thanked him.
He was a Samaritan.
Jesus said in reply,
"Ten were cleansed, were they not?
Where are the other nine?
Has none but this foreigner returned to give thanks to God?"
Then he said to him, "Stand up and go;
your faith has saved you."

—Luke 17:11–19

Truths of Our Catholic Faith

Because God is responsible for creation and all the laws of nature, it stands to reason that He can adjust these laws as He sees fit even if it means occasionally healing a leper—or ten.

> *Though the work of creation is attributed to the Father in particular, it is equally a truth of faith that the Father, Son, and Holy Spirit together are the one, indivisible principle of creation.* (CCC 316)

Lepers were considered in many cases to be as good as dead. Some suffered significantly before surrendering their spirit. Maybe some others—those without leprosy—were tempted to help them on their way with a form of mercy killing.

Yet in the end there is no such thing as a mercy killing.

Directly taking the life of an ill or elderly person in the name of mercy is nonnegotiable in that it is a gravely sinful act.

> *Intentional euthanasia, whatever its forms or motives, is murder. It is gravely contrary to the dignity of the human person and to the respect due to the living God, his Creator. (CCC 2324)*

A Question for Me

What instructions might I leave to decrease the likelihood that anyone would be able to commit euthanasia against me?

For a Child in My Life

Why is euthanasia not really merciful at all?

My Role in the Community

What are the laws in my state regarding euthanasia? What might I do to help ensure that the law continually reflects the truth as it relates to this matter.

For Depth and Further Life Application

2 Kings 5:14–17
Psalm 98
2 Timothy 2:8–13

📖 United States Catholic Catechism for Adults, pages 398–400

REFLECTION

In all circumstances, give thanks, for this is the will of God for you in Christ Jesus.

—1 Thessalonians 5:18

C Twenty-ninth Sunday of Ordinary Time

The Gospel

Jesus told his disciples a parable
about the necessity for them to pray always
without becoming weary.
He said, "There was a judge in a certain town
who neither feared God nor respected any human being.
And a widow in that town used to come to him and say,
'Render a just decision for me against my adversary.'
For a long time the judge was unwilling, but eventually he thought,
'While it is true that I neither fear God nor respect any human being,
because this widow keeps bothering me
I shall deliver a just decision for her
lest she finally come and strike me.'"
The Lord said, "Pay attention to what the dishonest judge says.
Will not God then secure the rights of his chosen ones
who call out to him day and night?
Will he be slow to answer them?
I tell you, he will see to it that justice is done for them speedily.
But when the Son of Man comes, will he find faith on earth?"

—Luke 18:1–8

Truths of Our Catholic Faith

The faith that is found on our earth helps us see clearly, interpret accurately and penetrate life's mysteries. One such mystery is our Church: spiritual yet visible as well; divine as well as human.

> *The Church is both visible and spiritual, a hierarchical society and the Mystical Body of Christ. She is one, yet formed of two components, human and divine. That is her mystery, which only faith can accept.* (CCC 779)

Faith also joins the other theological virtues (hope and charity) as well as our Church's liturgy and God's Word as sources of what Jesus tells us is so very much needed: prayer. Such rich sources help keep us from growing weary as we answer Jesus' call to pray always.

The Word of God, the liturgy of the Church, and the virtues of faith, hope, and charity are sources of prayer. (CCC 2662)

A Question for Me

What role do faith, hope and charity currently play in my life? How might these virtues become more noticeable in me?

For a Child in My Life

What is the lesson for us in this parable of Jesus?

My Role in the Community

Some in my community might deny the validity of the visible, hierarchical Church—our Church's human component. How can I help these individuals or groups come to understand and appreciate the twofold mystery that is God's holy Church, the Mystical Body of Jesus?

For Depth and Further Life Application

Exodus 17:8–13
Psalm 121
2 Timothy 3:14–4:2

📖 United States Catholic Catechism for Adults, pages 538–539

REFLECTION

The word of God is living and effective, discerning reflections and thoughts of the heart.

—Hebrews 4:12

C Thirtieth Sunday of Ordinary Time

The Gospel

Jesus addressed this parable
to those who were convinced of their own righteousness
and despised everyone else.
"Two people went up to the temple area to pray;
one was a Pharisee and the other was a tax collector.
The Pharisee took up his position and spoke this prayer to himself,
'O God, I thank you that I am not like the rest of humanity —
greedy, dishonest, adulterous — or even like this tax collector.
I fast twice a week, and I pay tithes on my whole income.'
But the tax collector stood off at a distance
and would not even raise his eyes to heaven
but beat his breast and prayed,
'O God, be merciful to me a sinner.'
I tell you, the latter went home justified, not the former;
for whoever exalts himself will be humbled,
and the one who humbles himself will be exalted."

—Luke 18:9–14

Truths of Our Catholic Faith

The Pharisee is not incorrect in observing that adultery is a problem for our human community. An alternate vision of family life is the Sacrament of Matrimony, properly understood. This sacrament gives spouses real power—power they can choose to accept and incorporate into their entire married life.

> *The sacrament of Matrimony signifies the union of Christ and the Church. It gives spouses the grace to love each other with the love with which Christ has loved his Church; the grace of the sacrament thus perfects the human love of the spouses, strengthens their indissoluble unity, and sanctifies them on the way to eternal life (cf. Council of Trent: DS 1799). (CCC 1661)*

Whether married or single, it is important that we accept God's gift of sexuality and make it a part of our life in appropriate ways.

Always this requires a self control that, for many, grows over time. When we acknowledge that our sexuality is a part of who we are, and incorporate it within our life in ways proper to our vocational call from God, we live the virtue of chastity.

> *Chastity means the integration of sexuality within the person. It includes an apprenticeship in self-mastery. (CCC 2395)*

A Question for Me

How might the prayer "Lord Jesus Christ, Son of God, have mercy on me a sinner" become more prominent in my life?

For a Child in My Life

What does the Sacrament of Matrimony give spouses?

My Role in the Community

What might I do to strengthen and support the Sacrament of Matrimony in my community?

For Depth and Further Life Application

Sirach 35:12–14, 16–18
Psalm 34
2 Timothy 4:6–8, 16–18

📖 United States Catholic Catechism for Adults, pages 529–531

REFLECTION

God was reconciling the world to himself in Christ, and entrusting to us the message of salvation.

—2 Corinthians 5:19

C Thirty-first Sunday of Ordinary Time

The Gospel

At that time, Jesus came to Jericho and intended to pass
through the town.
Now a man there named Zacchaeus,
who was a chief tax collector and also a wealthy man,
was seeking to see who Jesus was;
but he could not see him because of the crowd,
for he was short in stature.
So he ran ahead and climbed a sycamore tree in order to see Jesus,
who was about to pass that way.
When he reached the place, Jesus looked up and said,
"Zacchaeus, come down quickly,
for today I must stay at your house."
And he came down quickly and received him with joy.
When they all saw this, they began to grumble, saying,
"He has gone to stay at the house of a sinner."
But Zacchaeus stood there and said to the Lord,
"Behold, half of my possessions, Lord, I shall give to the poor,
and if I have extorted anything from anyone
I shall repay it four times over."
And Jesus said to him,
"Today salvation has come to this house
because this man too is a descendant of Abraham.
For the Son of Man has come to seek
and to save what was lost."

—Luke 19:1–10

Truths of Our Catholic Faith

Zacchaeus has a strong inner desire to seek out Jesus about whom he has heard many good things. Jesus in turn calls him to act on these inner stirrings of religious inclination. Zacchaeus, like all of us, is created to be orientated toward God.

> *Man is by nature and vocation a religious being. Coming from God, going toward God, man lives a fully human life only if he freely lives by his bond with God.* (CCC 44)

Sadly, when people come down quickly from very high places, it is sometimes an act of doing away with oneself—a suicidal act. If knowingly and willingly committed, suicide, like all unjust killing, is a sinful action. The fifth commandment forbids suicide.

> *Suicide is seriously contrary to justice, hope, and charity. It is forbidden by the fifth commandment.* (CCC 2325)

A Question for Me

What are some examples showing me that people really are religious by nature?

For a Child in My Life

Why has Jesus, the Son of Man, come into our life?

My Role in the Community

What are the signs that someone may be suicidal, and what is the phone number of a local suicide prevention hotline?

For Depth and Further Life Application

Wisdom 11:22–12:2
Psalm 145
2 Thessalonians 1:11–2:2

📖 United States Catholic Catechism for Adults, pages 2–6

REFLECTION

God so loved the world that he gave his only Son, so that everyone who believes in him might have eternal life.

—John 3:16

C Thirty-second Sunday of Ordinary Time

The Gospel

Some Sadducees, those who deny that there is a resurrection,
came forward.

Jesus said to them,
"The children of this age marry and remarry;
but those who are deemed worthy to attain to the coming age
and to the resurrection of the dead
neither marry nor are given in marriage.
They can no longer die,
for they are like angels;
and they are the children of God
because they are the ones who will rise.
That the dead will rise
even Moses made known in the passage about the bush,
when he called out 'Lord, '
the God of Abraham, the God of Isaac, and the God of Jacob;
and he is not God of the dead, but of the living,
for to him all are alive."

—Luke 20:27, 34–38

Truths of Our Catholic Faith

Abraham, Isaac and Jacob are united in their relationship with God. Similarly, we are united with all who hold and teach the Catholic faith throughout our world. The Most Holy Trinity, united with one another, helps to further our union with all sisters and brothers in the living Lord.

> *"Hence the universal Church is seen to be 'a people brought into unity from the unity of the Father, the Son, and the Holy Spirit'" (*LG *4 citing St. Cyprian,* De Dom. orat. *23: PL 4, 553). (CCC 810)*

In saying that the children of this age marry, Jesus on the one hand points out the obvious; on the other hand it must be said that Jesus' understanding of what marriage is has very distinctive traits. From His teaching and through the continuing guidance of

His Church, we know that marriage must have certain features in order to be authentic, among them mutual consent, faithfulness and openness to the blessing of new life.

> *Marriage is based on the consent of the contracting parties, that is, on their will to give themselves, each to the other, mutually and definitively, in order to live a covenant of faithful and fruitful love.* (CCC 1662)

A Question for Me

How faithful is my marital love? How fruitful is it? (Note: there are many ways to be unfaithful, and many ways to be fruitful.)

For a Child in My Life

How does Jesus say that we know there is life after death?

My Role in the Community

How might I be an even greater force for unity in my family, neighborhood and parish?"

For Depth and Further Life Application

2 Maccabees 7:1–2, 9–14
Psalm 17
2 Thessalonians 2:16–3:5

United States Catholic Catechism for Adults, pages 122–123

REFLECTION

Jesus Christ is the firstborn of the dead; to him be glory and power, forever and ever.

—Revelation 1:5a, 6b

C Thirty-third Sunday of Ordinary Time

The Gospel

While some people were speaking about
how the temple was adorned with costly stones
and votive offerings,
Jesus said, "All that you see here—
the days will come when there will not be left
a stone upon another stone that will not be thrown down."

Then they asked him,
"Teacher, when will this happen?
And what sign will there be when all these things
are about to happen?"
He answered,
"See that you not be deceived,
for many will come in my name, saying,
'I am he,' and 'The time has come.'
Do not follow them!
When you hear of wars and insurrections,
do not be terrified; for such things must happen first,
but it will not immediately be the end."
Then he said to them,
"Nation will rise against nation, and kingdom against kingdom.
There will be powerful earthquakes, famines, and plagues
from place to place;
and awesome sights and mighty signs will come from the sky.

"Before all this happens, however,
they will seize and persecute you,
they will hand you over to the synagogues and to prisons,
and they will have you led before kings and governors
because of my name.
It will lead to your giving testimony.
Remember, you are not to prepare your defense beforehand,
for I myself shall give you a wisdom in speaking
that all your adversaries will be powerless to resist or refute.
You will even be handed over by parents, brothers,
relatives, and friends,
and they will put some of you to death.

> You will be hated by all because of my name,
> but not a hair on your head will be destroyed.
> By your perseverance you will secure your lives."
>
> —Luke 21:5–19

Truths of Our Catholic Faith

Jesus is the focus of this gospel passage, as He is throughout most of all four Gospels. This is why it is so important for us to make reading, reflecting on and applying the Gospels a central part of our life.

> *The four Gospels occupy a central place because Christ Jesus is their center. (CCC 139)*

Votive offerings of various sorts could be considered a part of what is known as popular piety. These religious practices, varying from culture-to-culture, can be of great help to a life of faith when they are properly understood and practiced.

> *In addition to the liturgy, Christian life is nourished by various forms of popular piety, rooted in the different cultures. While carefully clarifying them in the light of faith, the Church fosters the forms of popular piety that express an evangelical instinct and a human wisdom and that enrich Christian life. (CCC 1679)*

A Question for Me

In what ways might I be persecuted due to my friendship with Jesus? Who may hate me because of Him, and how can I best persevere in the Faith?

For a Child in My Life

What are the names of the four Gospels? Why is it so important that we are familiar with them?

My Role in the Community

What forms of popular piety are expressed in my community? How might I help them play an expanded role in providing enrichment for our life as Christians?

For Depth and Further Life Application

Malachi 3:19–20a
Psalm 98
2 Thessalonians 3:7–12

📖 United States Catholic Catechism for Adults, pages 293–303, 548–552

REFLECTION

Stand erect and raise your heads because your redemption is at hand.

—Luke 21:28

C Christ the King

The Gospel

The rulers sneered at Jesus and said,
"He saved others, let him save himself
if he is the chosen one, the Christ of God."
Even the soldiers jeered at him.
As they approached to offer him wine they called out,
"If you are King of the Jews, save yourself."
Above him there was an inscription that read,
"This is the King of the Jews."

Now one of the criminals hanging there reviled Jesus, saying,
"Are you not the Christ?
Save yourself and us."
The other, however, rebuking him, said in reply,
"Have you no fear of God,
for you are subject to the same condemnation?
And indeed, we have been condemned justly,
for the sentence we received corresponds to our crimes,
but this man has done nothing criminal."
Then he said,
"Jesus, remember me when you come into your kingdom."
He replied to him,
"Amen, I say to you,
today you will be with me in Paradise."

—Luke 23:35–43

Truths of Our Catholic Faith

Sneering, jeering and reviling are quite the opposite of blessing. Blessings have an important part in calling holiness upon various aspects of our life and the lives of others.

> *Among the sacramentals, blessings occupy an important place. They include both praise of God for his works and gifts, and the Church's intercession for men that they may be able to use God's gifts according to the spirit of the Gospel. (CCC 1678)*

A crucifix is one of the most sacred images that we venerate. We do not worship the crucifix; rather, we treat it with profound respect, because it calls to mind passages like today's Gospel and, of course, the most important Person ever to walk our earth—Jesus of Nazareth, Christ our King.

> *The veneration of sacred images is based on the mystery of the Incarnation of the Word of God. It is not contrary to the first commandment.* (CCC 2141)

A Question for Me

In what ways might I tend to make God prove Himself to me?

For a Child in My Life

When the second of two criminals crucified with Jesus said "Jesus, remember me when you come into your kingdom" what did Jesus say back to him?

My Role in the Community

If someone in my community were to say that Catholics violate the first commandment by worshiping sacred images, what might be my reply?

For Depth and Further Life Application

2 Samuel 5:1–3
Psalm 122
Colossians 1:12–20

📖 United States Catholic Catechism for Adults, pages 499–502

REFLECTION

Blessed is he who comes in the name of the Lord! Blessed is the kingdom of our father David that is to come!

—Mark 11:9, 10

Notes

[1] *Nostra aetate* 4.

[2] *Ad gentes* 1; cf. *Mt* 16:15.

[3] *Mt* 28:19–20.

[4] *2 Pet* 1:4.

[5] St. Irenaeus, *Adv. haeres.* 3, 19, 1: J. P. Migne, ed., Patrologia Graeca (Paris, 1857–1866) 7/1, 939.

[6] St. Athanasius, *De inc.*, 54, 3: J. P. Migne, ed., Patrologia Graeca (Paris, 1857–1866) 25, 192B.

[7] St. Thomas Aquinas, *Opusculum* 57: 1–4.

[8] *2 Cor* 5:14 ; cf. *Apostolicam actuositatem* 6; *Redemptoris Missio* 11.

[9] *1 Tim* 2:4.

[10] John Paul II, *Redemptoris Missio* 21.

[11] *Ad gentes* 5.

[12] Tertullian, *Apol.* 50, 13: J. P. Migne, ed., Patrologia Latina (Paris: 1841-1855) 1, 603.

[13] Cf. Codex Iuris Canonici, cann. 1246–1248; Corpus Canonum Ecclesiarum Orientalium, can. 880 § 3, 881 §§ 1, 2, 4.

[14] Cf. Codex Iuris Canonici, can. 989; Corpus Canonum Ecclesiarum Orientalium, can. 719.

[15] Cf. Codex Iuris Canonici, can. 920; Corpus Canonum Ecclesiarum Orientalium, cann. 708; 881 § 3.

[16] Cf. Codex Iuris Canonici, cann. 1249–1251: Corpus Canonum Ecclesiarum Orientalium can. 882.

[17] Cf. Codex Iuris Canonici, can. 222; Corpus Canonum Ecclesiarum Orientalium, can. 25; *Furthermore, episcopal conferences can establish other ecclesiastical precepts for their own territories* (Cf. Codex Iuris Canonici, can. 455).

[18] Cf. Codex Iuris Canonici, can. 222.

[19] *Unitatis redintegratio* 3.

[20] *Lumen gentium* 16; cf. Denzinger-Schönmetzer, *Enchiridion Symbolorum, definitionum et declarationum de rebus fidei et morum* (1965) 3866–3872.

[21] *Luke* 1:43; *John* 2:1; 19:25; cf. *Matthew* 13:55; et al.

[22] Council of Ephesus (431): Denzinger-Schönmetzer, *Enchiridion Symbolorum, definitionum et declarationum de rebus fidei et morum* (1965) 251.

[23] Tertullian, *De orat.* 1: J. P. Migne, ed., Patrologia Latina (Paris: 1841–1855) 1, 1251–1255.

[24] St. Thomas Aquinas, Summa Theologiae II–II, 83, 9.